The Deepening Sino-Nepal Relations: Should India Worry?

The Deepening Sino-Nepal Relations
Should India Worry?

Major (Retd.) S.K. Sharma

PRASHANT PUBLISHING HOUSE
DELHI-110094

Published by :
Prashant Publishing House
C-34, 28 Foota Road, Gali-3,
West Karwal Nagar, Delhi-110094
Phone : 011-22963970, Mob. : 9810396373
e-mail.: prashantpublishinghouse@gmail.com

The Deepening Sino-Nepal Relations: Should India Worry?

First Published 2013

ISBN 978-93-80565-43-9

PRINTED IN INDIA
Published by Mr. R.K. Jha M/s Prashant Publishing House and Published at H.S. Offset House Press, Delhi.

Preface

The bilateral relations between the Federal Democratic Republic of Nepal and the People's Republic of China have been friendly and defined by Nepal's policy of balancing the competing influence of China and Nepal's southern neighbour India, the only two neighbours of the Himalayan country.

The anticipated process of state restructuring in Nepal, ranging from an increasingly polarized populace for and against ethnicity-based federalization to the consistent ineptitude of political leaders failing to lead from the front to seek a meeting point between conflicting interests. But the increasingly prominent posturing of Nepal's two giant neighbours on these issues threatens to sabotage the whole process and push Nepal further into chaos.

Nepal, the only Hindu Kingdom in the world, underwent major transformation in its political landscape with the overthrow of monarchy ....years ago. The Maoists, backed, motivated and funded by China became a force to reckon with when they started a violent agitation. Ever since overthrow of the monarchy, the democratic process in the country has come under severe strain. Nepal's two immediate neighbours, India and China have apparently shown keen interest in the likely political outcome – an interest which has guided both the nations to protect their interests in the erstwhile Kingdom.

Certain scholars believe that India's China policy has undergone three major phases of adjustment since the end of the Cold War: the pre-1998 phase policy of reconciliation; the 1998–2000 phase policy of hostility; and the 2000 to present phase policy of engagement.

As the book addresses this crucial issue quite deftly, it is hoped that it would prove to be a source of great information for the reader.

—Editor

Preface

Contents

1

India's Disquiet at Deepening Sino-Nepal Relationship

Nepal is undergoing an unprecedented change. Things are in a flux. Dreams of the people are sky-high and have wings; albeit the leadership has been so far paid a lip service and are ambivalent in their deeds.

The historic election to the Constituent Assembly some how took place in April, 2008 after being deferred twice since April 2006 Jan Andolan and the 'government formation' has been made possible just now at the cost of four crucial months from the stipulated two years term within which the CA is suppose to draft a Constitution. This evokes to mind the days of 90s during which people were perplexed by the metamorphosing attitude of the political parties that brought about political instability in the Himalayan Country. The people today in a similar way are observing with caution and awe how their leaders (destiny makers) are deciding upon their future. Like Rousseau's citizens they are not free today and are in a state of servitude after the election is over. They have no options left other than following their leaders' way and are passive onlookers.

The inheritance of the King and Kingdom adorns the pages of history today after Nepal became a republic; the last 'Hindu State' has been converted into a secular one, Nepal is a federal state in the making and an inclusive democracy is taking shape in it through unceasing political squabbles among political parties who too lack consensus over national issues including the foreign policy of Nepal. In these moments of uncertainty and confusion Nepal's policy vis-à-vis China and India has witnessed a revolutionary change. This change in its attitude has aroused alarm in India and has shaken the security equation in South Asia.

Today a wedding of convenience has taken place in the Sino-Nepalese relationship. It is said that 'politics makes strange bed fellows' and it is true in case of the present Sino-Nepal relationship. Despite its change in its 'Peripheral Policy' China has been found to be pro-active in its dealing towards Nepal and vice versa.

From China's side say it the instances of sending congratulatory messages to the newly elected heads of Government and State; sending invitations to them to visit China during the 29th Olympics held in Beijing; holding of an hour long meeting between the PRC President and the just elected Nepalese Prime Minister and its agreeing to provide assistance amounting $300,000 to Nepal for the flood victims- are evidences of China's special attention given to Nepal. Nepal on the other hand has responded to Chinese gesturers in a similar manner. Even eight days after his election to the office of the Prime Minister in the 'Youngest Republic' Mr.Puspa Kamal Dahal (Prachanda) preferred China as his maiden international destination; his expression of his predilection for visiting Mao's village and lo! It is reported that both the heads(State and Government) have imported their official furniture from China paying a heavy amount that includes a very expensive cot for the Prime Minister and all the furniture, including sofa sets, for republic Nepal's first president Ram Baran Yadav – all are in a similar way Nepal's reciprocation to the Chinese change in attitude towards Nepal.

Despite India's forewarning of the Prime Minister's maiden visit to China was conveyed but it was undertaken on the plea that it was a non-political visit as the Prime Minister was going to attend the closing ceremony of the Beijing Olympics to be held in the 'Bird's Nest' in Beijing on 24th August. It was against a long done tradition according to which a newly appointed Nepalese Prime Minister should have visited India first. Despite all pretexts the tour was found to have political undertones as an hour long meeting was held between Mr. Hu Jintao -the President of PRC and Mr. Prachanda- the Prime Minister elect of the Federal Democratic Republic of Nepal.

It took place on a day when the President was awfully busy in Olympic schedules. This shows the importance China attaches to Nepal today in return of Nepal's fidelity to China. The President categorically acknowledged this in saying that Nepalese Prime Minister's visit to attend the Olympics closing ceremony within a week after being sworn in, demonstrated the attention Nepal attaches to relations with China. In response to Hu Jintao's remarks Prachanda while describing China as reliable friend expressed that his government was willing to cement cooperation with China and to elevate bi-lateral ties with China to a new high. He did convey the expectation of Nepal from China in bringing peace and economic development in the mountainous Himalayan republic.

There was not anything wrong in Nepal's seeking Chinese assistance but what displeases India in addition to the Chinese tour of Mr. Prachanda was regarding China's pledge to extend a state assistance of $300,000 for the victims of the devastating flood in south Nepal that left over 75,000 people homeless. In the Indian circle this generous assistance of China is been regarded as an 'Indian specific move' since there has been growing allegations in Nepal about India's negligence being responsible for the breach of a barrage in south Nepal that rendered over 75,000 people homeless.

This has caused Indian ire. It has projected the image of China as a 'friend in need' in relation to Nepal. It is reminiscent of a similar situation in late 70s when China accorded recognition to Nepal's 'Zone of Peace' proposal when India was against it. It then brought China closer to Nepal. Today a similar situation has been exploited by China to build its own image before Nepal. Indo-Nepal 'Treaty of Peace and Friendship' of 1950 is now under scrutiny. The new government led by the Maoist leader is to decide whether to scrap or review all unequal treaties with India as the CPN (Maoists) party had promised to the electorate during April 2008. Today there has been growing allegations in Nepal about India's negligence being responsible for the breach of a barrage in south Nepal that rendered over 75,000 people homeless. There are also accusations of India encroaching on Nepali territory and interfering in Nepal's internal matters, including the recent elections. Under these circumstances ascendancy in Sino-Nepal relationship has caused concern to India.

In the previous couple of years Nepal has been found to be a great supporter of China. Two instances are significant in this direction. These are, first, Nepal's support to China in securing the 'Observer Status' in SAARC despite India's unwillingness to it and second, Nepal's action in cracking down anti-China demonstrations in Nepal.

In the 13th SAARC summit held in Dhaka China succeeded in getting an entry in to through Nepal's lobby. Even during the 14th SAARC summit held in New Delhi during 3-4 April 2007 Nepal announced its support for the membership of China in the SAARC. It was too a move against the wishes of India. Further the Himalayan State has shown its loyalty to China in cracking down on Tibetan protest movements with an iron hand in its territory. Since a large section of ethnic Tibetans are living in Nepal and three districts of Nepal are bordering Tibet Nepal's move has been regarded by China as the Himalayan State's support to 'One China' policy of Beijing. Not only had this Nepal in late 80s procured $200 million worth of arms from China.

In go back China has never disappointed Nepal with an exception in 1989 when Nepal could not get China's assistance when it was facing economic difficulties following India's trade blockade in 1988. China was then having internal problems. However, today China has emerged as an economic and military power. China has included Nepal in its Western Development Campaign Plan. It has been consistent in supplying economic aid to Nepal supporting construction of highways and several infrastructural building projects. China's support to King Gyanendra during 2005- 2006 was unmatched. Though it was a strategic failure but China's support to Nepalese authority was a proven fact. However China during that time had been reiterated its earlier stand it took in 1961 by serving a warning to the outside powers not to interfere in Nepal. That was indicated against India's possible ambitious designs. Today, China is eyeing to Nepal's trade and economy as the former has proposed to extend its railway link from Lhasa (in Tibet) to a town i.e. Khasa in Tibet before Nepal's border in five years. This has been done in order to boost trade and tourism with the latter. There is also a proposal to further extend the railway line from Khasa to Kathmandu.

With its extension even to the border Nepal's trade may get a fillip through its northern border. It may be more convenient then to divert it to China instead of continuing with India. It may result in more imports from and trade with China. While Nepal will provide a good market for China's goods at the same time China would like to use Nepal for its strategic use. China is developing its military base and logistics in Tibet. If this Himalayan barrier is breached it may provide an easy access to China to reach India. Not only this, China was reported to had mooted a single Communist party with the polarisation of the two leading Communist Parties viz., CPN (UML) and CPN (Maoists) in Nepal in a bid to get their support in consolidating its position in Tibet.

These developments have complete India apprehensive about China's ambitious designs in South Asia. What India fears is that with Pakistan and Nepal being its supporters and 'all weather friends' may provide strategic advantages to China vis-à-vis India. To add salt to injury China's claim over some parts of Arunachal Pradesh and Sikkim has been an irritant to India and if Nepal is slipped in to the grip of China it will definitely heighten India's security concerns. Therefore China's forays into Nepal have been looked with suspicion by India.

Some analyst have described it as the revival of playing 'China Card' policy by Nepal against India. However Nepal must think the reasons why China is extending its support to Nepal (?). First, it is the Tibet issue. Integration of Tibet (TAR) into China still remains a headache for China.

Nepal being the border of Tibet could play a big role in dissuading Tibetan pro-independence struggle from the side of Nepal. Since three districts of Nepal are adjacent to Tibet where some ethnic Tibetans are living those districts may encourage pro-Tibetan movements involving the external powers in it. Therefore China wishes to please Nepal in eliciting its support in curbing anti-China movements from Nepal's territory.

Second, China fears the spread of insurgency activities in Nepal that may spread to the said bordering districts and thereby makes an outlet to spread to China. Therefore neither China wishes to see Nepal as a failed state neither to be kept under the grip of an insurgent group nor to see an unstable Nepal. Its fear for the spread of insurgency was proved during its support to King Gyanendra. Since the 'anti-government forces/guerillas' as China did term the Maoists earlier are in Power today China has tried to appease Mr. Prachanda through the present deal.

To some analysts this has been view as the revival of the old techniques of playing the 'China Card' by Nepal. However Nepal must not forget that its 'China Card' strategy may not hold good for a longer time.

A lot improvement has taken place in Sino-Indian relationship. India like China's entry into SAARC has got an 'Observer Status' in the Shanghai Cooperation Organisation with the Chinese support. China is also well aware of the Indo-US strategic alliance and China in order to promote its economy would not wish to displease India and the US. Nepal must keep it in mind the situation of 1988-89 when China could not come to its rescue. Despite an opening on its northern side Nepal's economy will not cease to depend on India. Further Nepal will be open to Chinese incursion into its territory at any moment. Further any strain in Indo-Nepal ties will definitely affect

SAARC and BIMSTEC. The need of the hour for Nepal is to have a balanced relationship with both the immediate neighbours. Let a good sense may prevail in Nepal, which should recollect the help and succour that it had received from India during its hard days.

India and Nepal share deep-rooted ties. Even today most of its political leaders are the products of Indian Universities like the Jawaharlal Nehru University and Benares Hindu University etc. Nepal earns in a major portion of its remittances from India. India has been the source of livelihood for a large section of Nepalese. Nepal should remember its woes during the Indian trade blockade of 1988.

Since Nepal trade and economic activities depend mostly on India Nepal should think twice before it takes an anti-India stand. It is a country in transition. It has a lot many problems. It is not the proper time to develop strained relations with India at the cost of its own core interest. It must reconsider its demand to review or scrap the 'Treaty of peace and Friendship' of 1950 with India. From economy to democracy India will be closer and expedient to Nepal. India has been instrumental in bringing development in Nepal through its aid supporting several infrastructural developments. It is reported recently that Nepal is stuck in a major gas crisis with the state-owned Nepal Oil Corporation, which is unable to pay its dues to the sole Indian fuel exporter, the Indian Oil Corporation. This shows India's role in Nepal. In this critical juncture Prudence lies in balancing both the Asian giants. This has been rightly reflected in a statement of Mr. Prachanda on 23rd August 2008 who was reported to have said that Nepal's dealing with both China and India would be based on 'Panchsheel ties/ principles'. This shows political maturity and acumen on the part of Mr. Prachanda in dealing with such an intricate issue. In the recent visit of Prachanda (the official one) to India he was reported to have said that Nepal's relationship with India could not be compared with that of China. This is how Nepal is trying to strike a balance between the two goliaths, which is very essential for leading its transition to its desired end.

TO DEEPEN SINO-NEPALESE COOPERATION NEW IMPETUS TO THE DEVELOPMENT

Li Keqiang said that China and Nepal are the world and in Africa's most populous developing countries, are facing accelerating development and improving people's livelihood task, walking in the mutually beneficial cooperation between China and African countries in the forefront of yesterday with the President, Mr. President Xi Jinping held a rich the outcome of the talks the Chinese side is willing to make joint efforts with Nepal, enhance political mutual trust, deepen trade and investment, infrastructure, energy, agriculture, humanities and other fields all-round cooperation and expand in international and regional affairs, communication and coordination, promote Nigeria strategic partnership sustained and healthy development.

Li Keqiang said that China as a reliable friend and sincere African partners, consistent support Africa in achieving peace, security and development in the international community should fully respect the way the people of Africa to African solutions to African problems in the field of development in Africa more practical in dealing with regional hotspots issues more to promote peace talks, together to promote peace and development in Africa will play a constructive role China is willing to African countries to China-Africa new strategic partnership for the continuous development of new impetus.

Jonathan said that Nepal attaches great importance to relations with China and appreciates China for the maintenance of world peace, stability and development play an important role, thanked China for its help and support in Africa and is willing to expand bilateral exchanges and cooperation to promote new developments in Nepal relations for non-Chinese relations contribute to the development.

NEPAL AND THE SINO-INDIAN RIVALRY

The inevitable passing of the Fourteenth Dalai Lama, the radicalization of the Tibetan diaspora and the fervor of the international campaign to free Tibet are bound to keep the Himalayan dispute on the world's front pages. India, which has sheltered the Dalai Lama and tens of thousands of his followers, today increasingly sees Tibet as a bargaining chip with China in its overall bilateral relationship. Home to some 20,000 Tibetan refugees and wedged precariously between the assertive Asian giants, Nepal is likely to become an even more important theatre.

From Nepal's perspective, at least, the issue of Tibet goes beyond the freedom of a land, the liberation of a culture and a celebration of a way of life. The region always has been a conduit for major external protagonists to pursue wider objectives. The British Empire considered Tibet a critical part of the imperial chessboard, a legacy that lives on in today's geo-strategic milieu where China sees the region as a front rivals are intent on using to contain its rise. The Tibet issue has a peculiar psychological subtext in Nepal. Some of the same people, who profess the greatest admiration for the Dalai Lama and his cause, also hope that Tibet remains under Chinese control. Many Nepalese recognize that an independent Tibet would leave their country without a border with China. They believe such a situation would allow India, which has long invoked its own version of the Monroe Doctrine in the land-locked nation, to tighten its grip.

Although Tibet has been central to the Sino-Nepalese relationship, Nepal's formal contacts with China did not originate through the region. It began with China's quest for Buddhist texts, artifacts and codes from the wider Gangetic heartland. In the mid-seventh century, a powerful Tibetan king extracted consorts from Chinese and Nepalese royal households on the principle of peace through kinship. The two wives helped bring Buddhism to Tibet and opened a direct Himalayan route between Nepal and China, bypassing the more arduous one across Central Asia. As religion and trade began traversing the same Himalayan passes, peace and goodwill began losing ground. As the British sun rose higher over India, Nepal fought two wars with Tibet, precipitating a Chinese invasion. The Nepalese gained peace by entering into a tributary relationship with the Middle Kingdom, a duty they would discharge with utmost diligence. The Nepalese became the last foreigners to pay tribute to the Qing, as the arrangement helped maintain their independence as most of modern South Asia fell under the sway of the British Empire.

Nepal, which fought a third war with Tibet in 1855-56, refused to aid the Tibetans against a British invasion in 1904, but helped secure the withdrawal of the invaders. The diplomatic triumph was short-lived as the tottering Qing formally claimed suzerainty over Nepal.

Seeking to preserve its interests in Tibet - and project its independence - Nepal mediated between Beijing and Lhasa in 1912, after which Tibet enjoyed a period of de facto independence. For all their antipathy for the Qing and for each other, Chinese nationalists and communists pressed their country's claims on Nepal: Sun Yat-sen and Mao Zedong both included Nepal among territories China had lost to imperialism.

The Chinese invasion of Tibet in 1950 impelled the leaders of independent India to restore the monarchy at the top of a multiparty democracy in Nepal to forestall a communist advance southward. On the eve of Nepal's first democratic elections in 1959, Tibetans rose up in a failed revolt against Beijing, prompting the Dalai Lama's flight into exile in India. Nepal's first elected prime minister, B.P. Koirala, sought unsuccessfully to consolidate democracy by asserting Nepalese independence from India and China. When King Mahendra dissolved parliament, jailed Koirala and most of the elected leadership, and abolished multiparty democracy, much more than royal ambition was at play.

Nepal had become a center of Cold War intrigue where the United States and India - the world's two largest democracies - were working to undermine each other as were the communist giants China and the Soviet Union. By the end of the 1960s, Sino-American rapprochement put the two nations on the same side in Nepal for the duration of the Cold War. As the 1980s drew to a close, a new round of unrest in Tibet merged with student protests in Beijing, culminating in the bloody crackdown in Tiananmen Square. The fall of the Berlin Wall inspired the Nepalese to bring down the palace-led partyless Panchayat system, with Beijing a mere bystander. With the kingdom's democracy turning rancorous, Nepalese disciples of Mao launched a bloody insurgency, a convulsion exacerbated by the assassinations of King Birendra and almost the entire royal family in a June 2001 palace massacre.

India, like the United States and Britain, opposed King Gyanendra's February 2005 coup, widely perceived to have enjoyed Chinese backing. Beijing, which accused the Nepalese Maoists of soiling the Great Helmsman's memory, armed the palace against the rebels. Yet a year later, as the royal regime faced massive popular protests, Beijing distanced itself from the monarchy and befriended the Nepalese Maoists. Chinese policy toward Nepal has been marked by much ambiguity, which both Beijing and Kathmandu have benefited from. One school of thought sees limited Chinese interest in Nepal, where phases of Beijing's assertiveness are the exception. In keeping with its foreign policy of unsentimental pragmatism, this school contends, China could easily concede Nepal as part of India's sphere of influence.

Chinese assertiveness, however, is likely to grow as its interests in Nepal go beyond the issue of Tibet to encompass its wider South Asian strategy. Nepal is only country that maintains diplomatic representation in Lhasa and Beijing reminds Kathmandu with ever greater regularity the responsibility that flows with the privilege. Enticing Nepal with promises of greater commercial benefits as part of its massive investments in Tibet, Beijing is intent on committing Nepal to firm political, security, economic and cultural agreements.

Should tradition become a more dominant part of Chinese regional diplomacy - as also seems likely - Nepal's status as a former tributary to the Middle Kingdom is likely to drive Beijing's policy. This is bound to raise anxiety levels in India, whose own relations with China sit uneasily atop planks of cooperation, competition and confrontation that are vulnerable to extra-regional pressures.

WEAKENING SINO-INDIAN RELATIONS

It was a very perturbed Sardar Patel who wrote to J L Nehru on November 7, 1950, pointing out that by our silence at the UN, we had accepted Chinese suzerainty over Tibet. In a forceful letter, Patel, not a man to mince words, warned that "The Chinese Government has tried to delude us by profession of peaceful intentions" but in fact "it is not a friend speaking in that language, but a potential enemy". He then detailed ten steps that needed to be considered to strengthen our internal border security and defenses especially in the North-East. The tragedy is that this letter was apparently never discussed.

Till 1950, India had borders with Tibet not with China and by accepting China's suzerainty we became direct neighbours. Also this concession in effect gave China a border with Bhutan, Nepal, India and Pak-occupied Kashmir. It was in April 1954, India and China (People's Republic of China) signed an eight-year agreement on Tibet that set forth the basis of their relationship in the form of Five Principles of Peaceful Coexistence, or Panch Shila. On this political move, Nehru observes, "in the absence of either the wherewithal or a policy for defence of the Himalayan region, India's best guarantee of security was to establish a psychological buffer zone in place of lost physical buffer to Tibet."

Though India's diplomacy with China in 1950's was Hindi Chini bhai- bhai, but Nehru did not trust the Chine at all. By annexing Tibet, China now had the potential to be a player in South Asia. China and India are two of the world's oldest civilization and have coexisted in peace for millennia. Cultural and economic relations between China and India date back to ancient times. The Silk Road not only served as a major trade route between India and China, but is also credited for facilitating the spread the Buddhism from India to East. The revolt in Tibet in March 1959 leading to the Dalai Lama's flight to India added to China's paranoia. The Chinese thought it necessary to warn India through its ambassador Pan Tzu-Li in a letter to Prime Minister Nehru in May 1959, saying that China would make common cause with Pakistan. This would force India to face diplomatic and military pressure on two fronts. Therein lay the beginning of an all weather affair that is deeper than the ocean and higher than the mountains.

Relations between contemporary China and India have been characterized by border disputes, resulting in three major military conflicts-the Sino-Indian war of 1962, the Cholas incident in 1967, and the 1987 Sino-Indian skirmish. But 1962 and 1965, were landmark years when India was involved in conflicts with both her neighbours. This provided an opportunity for Pakistan to get closer to China and the two have remained locked in warm unusually unquestioned embrace. For China, becoming Pakistan's largest arm supplier to match Indian acquisitions-conventional, delivery system and nuclear weaponry was a convenient hedge against India, and Pakistan thus strengthened by American indulgence and Chinese connivance felt emboldened to hone its assistance to freedom fighters (militant) as a low cost, highly effective foreign policy option.

However, since late 1980s, both countries have successfully attempted to reignite diplomatic and economic ties. In 2008, China emerged as the largest trading partner of India and the two countries have also attempted to extend their strategic and military relations.

Despite growing economic and strategic ties, several issues continue to strain Sino-Indian relations. Though bilateral trade has continuously grown, India faces massive trade imbalance heavily in favour of China. The two countries have failed to resolve their long-standing border dispute and Indian media outlets repeatedly report Chinese military incursions into Indian Territory. In order to become a regional power, China aspires to destabilize India, and for this purpose it maintains good relations with all anti-India elements, whether it is insurgency in North-Eastern India, or Pakistan. To make Pakistan capable to equalize India in power, China gave its nuclear and missile technology. Pakistan is one of the largest users of Chinese military equipment. This has doubled India's harbour of suspicions about

China's strong strategic relations with its arch-rival Pakistan while China has expressed concern about India's military and economic activities in disputed South China Sea. Consequently both nations have steadily built-up infrastructure along border areas.

Pak-India hostility has been well exploited by China as a bridge for accessing West Asia not just as a counter to the US. It seeks geostrategic space and the rich mineral deposits of oil and gas, copper, gold, zinc, lead, iron-ore and aluminum in these countries including Afghanistan and Central Asia. There are reports of Saudi-Pakistan-China tie up on nuclear issues as well. Chinese ambitions extend beyond using Pakistan as a low cost secondary deterrent to counter India. Ayesha, a Pakistani analyst observes, China is an 'empire by stealth' which is "growing steadily without necessarily taking on the socio-political or economic liabilities of its client states." China will invest only in the extractive industries of Pakistan not in the country's development.

China is surrounding India from all the sides, By building a railway station for Pakistan at zero line, would mean that PLA is at stone's throw It is building a naval base in Gwarda on the Makran coast that has great significance and importance for China only if has unimpeded access through Gilgat and Baltistan, from where it can keep an eye on all Indian, European and American vessels passing through Persian Gulf, the recent development where Pakistan is leasing Gilgat and Baltistan to China for fifty years has been a cause of great concern to India authorities. Building of a base in Maldives, developing a civil port in Sri Lanka, building a naval base in Myanmar etc, is adding more fuel to the fire. Whatever is happening with India, India seems to be very much affected by continuous bullying by China, but can India do something to control it? If India won't act, China will take India soft and will either include it in its own influence and try to maintain its monopoly in the region or it will crush India. The need of the hour is that India has to do something, it should have a strong economy first, strong international relations second, and good military third. Then only India can keep its stand otherwise messing with China will be like inviting punishment for India. Had India heeded Sardar Patil's advice in 1950 it would not perhaps been in this state of feeling surrounded by China from all sides?

THE SINO-INDIAN RELATIONSHIP: AN INDIAN PERSPECTIVE

The recent unveiling of a new Chinese passport that contains a map marking territory disputed with India has emerged as a renewed source of tension between the two countries (Sina.com, November 25; *Indian Express*, November 24). While the passport issue is unlikely to be a lasting source of tension, the underlying source of friction—the Sino-Indian territorial dispute—remains alive and well. In the context of their overall bilateral relationship the strategic significance of the territorial dispute, however, is declining amid the rise of both countries as major regional and potentially global powers. This is revealing new theaters of interaction and potential competition.

The changing nature of the Sino-Indian relationship is made evident by the contrast of the current state of bilateral relations with their state during the month-long border conflict that took place 50 years ago. Future hostilities between both countries, however, are unlikely to be confined to their disputed border. Rather, with both countries acquiring more tools and platforms of interaction, renewed hostilities will likely spill over beyond the confines of their bilateral relationship with greater repercussions for the regional and global security architecture. Amid the growing strategic importance of trade and imported resources to fuel their economies, the most likely theaters of this "spillover" are both countries' third-party relations and their growing interests in the maritime domain.

Beijing Leverages "All-Weather" Friends

The potential "spillover" is most evident in third-party relationships. Notably, China's "all-weather" relationship with Pakistan has been complemented by deepening relations with other states around India's periphery (*Far Eastern Economic*

Review, October 2, 2009). These deepening relations have been evidenced in China emerging as a leading trade partner, source of diplomatic support and provider of military hardware to several countries in the region. More specifically, Chinese investment in several strategically important projects—ranging from port projects at Gwadar in Pakistan, Hambantota in Sri Lanka, and Sonadia Island in Bangladesh, a railway link between China and Nepal as well as an oil and gas pipeline from the Burmese port of Kyaukryu to Yunnan—has raised Indian fears that these projects could facilitate Chinese encirclement (*Asia Times*, September 29; April 23; Xinhua, September 10, 2010).

Pakistan is a case in point. Despite growing levels of political, economic and security instability facing the country, more than 60 Chinese companies and 10,000 Chinese nationals in the country working on 122 major development projects demonstrate Beijing's commitment (*Far Eastern Economic Review*, October 2, 2009). Notably, China recently renewed its commitment to the Gwadar port project after the Singaporean Port Authority decided to pull out of the port management and development contract (*Asia Times*, August 29). Despite problems facing the project over land acquisition and security concerns, China has reassumed responsibility for the infrastructure project after financing the port's construction.

Moreover, China is now Pakistan's leading trading partner and economic integration has continued to gain momentum facilitated by their free trade agreement, the establishment of the Pakistan and China Joint Investment Company (JIC) and an agreement to settle trade across the Xinjiang Uyghur Autonomous Region border using the Chinese renminbi as the base currency instead of the U.S. dollar. China's on-going support for Pakistan's civilian and military nuclear power program also has served as veiled criticism of the civilian nuclear power agreement between India and the United States ("The China-Pakistan Reactor Deal and Asia's Nuclear Energy Race," *China Brief*, June 11, 2010; *Times of India*, June 2, 2010; May 13, 2010; *Asia Times*, April 21, 2010).

In Afghanistan, a nascent competition for transshipment corridors is underway with India having constructed the Delaram-Zeranj highway connecting Afghanistan with the Iranian port of Chahbahar. This provides an alternative route to the Chinese-funded Gwadar as a means for accessing the resources and markets of Central, West and South Asia (*Asia Times*, December 4, 2009). The value that both countries place in their relations with Afghanistan is evidenced by China's conclusion of a "strategic and cooperative partnership" with Afghanistan in June less than a year after India concluded a similar agreement in October 2011.

Burma's on-going democratic transition also makes the country a key "battleground" state in the Sino-Indian competition for resources and strategic influence. While India has so far played "second-fiddle" to China in Myanmar, New Delhi's middle-path approach of engaging both members of the former military junta regime and pro-democratic forces is likely to yield dividends as Burma comes in from the cold and re-engages the international community. The liberalization process itself appears to have been driven in part by the desire of the military-backed government to reduce the country's overwhelming reliance on China. This was made evident by the suspension of the Myitsone dam and hydroelectric power project in Kachin state in September 2011 over social and environmental concerns (*The Irrawaddy*, October 2).

Meanwhile, Burmese pro-democracy leader Aung San Suu Kyi's recent visit to India is evidence of a burgeoning Indo-Burmese relationship, which could come at the cost of the Sino-Burmese relationship if the country's democratic transition continues (*Global Times*, November 29). New Delhi has the potential to forge a special relationship by facilitating capacity building on the economic front while strengthening democratic institutions and the rule of law. This will ensure Burma's ongoing reform process remains substantive and sustainable.

Another potential "battleground" state is Sri Lanka, where internal transformation is also emerging as a catalyst for China and India to reorient their relations. Unlike Myanmar where the democratic transition offers opportunities to India to expand its influence, Sri Lanka's authoritarian consolidation has offered China the opportunity to strengthen its presence. Amid criticism of Sri Lanka's human rights record in the conduct of its military campaign against the Liberation Tigers of the Tamil Eelam (LTTE) that culminated in victory over the separatist insurgency in 2009, Colombo has turned increasingly to "non-traditional" sources of diplomatic and financial assistance. Notably, China has emerged as Sri Lanka's leading aid donor, providing preferential loans at subsidized rates and investing in strategically and symbolically important infrastructure projects, such as the Hambantota port project and the Colombo South Harbour Development Project. Beijing also was more forthcoming in providing offensive armaments to the Sri Lankan military in its campaign against the Tamil Tigers and providing crucial diplomatic support to Sri Lanka that New Delhi was unable or unwilling to provide (*Sri Lanka Guardian*, October 29, 2009). This has strengthened goodwill between Colombo and Beijing while souring relations with New Delhi.

Bangladesh and Nepal are not far behind in this competition. China has concluded the second-biggest investment in Bangladesh earlier this year by contributing two-thirds of the cost of a fertilizer factory in Sylhet followed by a private sector power project in Habiganj. This has been accompanied by projects aimed at helping Bangladesh emerge as a regional trade and transshipment hub, including constructing bridges and upgrading road and rail infrastructure in the country, upgrading the airport at Cox's Bazar as well as strengthening the country's commercial shipping fleet. The fact that opposition leader Khaleda Zia followed up a recent visit to China with a parallel visit to India demonstrates how the Sino-Indian relationship has seeped into Bangladeshi domestics politics (*Asia Times*, November 9; April 23).

Meanwhile, the transition of the Nepali Maoists from an insurgent group into a mainstream political party, Unified Communist Party of Nepal (Maoist), with growing influence has fuelled closer relations between Nepal and China. Nepal has exploited this to reduce India's traditionally dominant influence over the country, including putting pressure on India to renegotiate their unequal friendship treaty. Meanwhile, the Nepali government has reciprocated China's advances by becoming increasingly aggressive in its crackdown on Tibetan activists (*Times of India*, March 7, 2010).

Delhi Leverages "Strategic Pivot"

Meanwhile, India has pursued a deepening relationship with China's traditional competitors, including Japan, Vietnam and the United States. Notably, the United States has made a concerted effort to draw India into the East Asia region as a means of balancing China's expanding influence in the region. Calls by U.S. officials for India to go beyond its "Look East" policy and "Be East" alludes to U.S. attempts to embed India into the region (*Business Standard*, February 11, 2011). Although the Obama administration has not yet revived the more confrontational rhetoric of an "arc of democracies" that emerged under the Bush administration, it is nonetheless pursuing a similar agenda amid the ongoing multilateralization of the U.S. security posture in Asia. Evidence of this includes the launch of the U.S.-Japan-India trilateral dialogue in 2011 and Japan's participation in the U.S.-India Malabar joint naval exercises since 2007 (BBC, December 13, 2011).

Meanwhile, India's relations with China's key Southeast Asian rival, Vietnam continue to deepen. India has been conducting joint naval exercises with Vietnam since 2000 and Vietnam has granted Indian Navy vessels permanent berthing rights at Na Thrang port, which has extended New Delhi's "sustainable maritime presence" in the South China Sea (*Times of India*, October 8, 2011). Reportedly, India also has offered Vietnam its indigenously-developed *Brahmos* supersonic cruise missile and training in underwater warfare to support Vietnam's expanding fleet of submarines (*Asia Times*, March 29; August 17, 2011). India also is emerging as an increasingly prominent player in Vietnam's energy sector with Indian state-owned company ONGC Videsh jointly exploring in disputed waters (*Outlook India*, August 3). The fact that India's deepening maritime and energy cooperation with Vietnam coincides with renewed tensions between China and Vietnam over their maritime territorial disputes in the South China Sea signals Sino-Indian competitiveness could "spill over" into Southeast Asia.

Finally, the rapprochement in India-Japan relations has coincided with a deterioration in the Sino-Japanese relationship. To be sure, Indo-Japanese economic interactions remain weak with $14 billion in bilateral trade in 2011 and a target of $25 billion by 2014. This pales in comparison to Japan's trade with China that was close to $345 billion in 2011 (*Economic Times*, May 20; JETRO, February 23). Nonetheless, despite starting from a low base Indo-Japan relations have continued to grow from strength to strength in the economic and strategic domains. India has been the leading recipient of Japanese overseas development assistance (ODA) since 2003 while in 2006 both countries forged a "strategic and global partnership," which has been complemented by a bilateral strategic dialogue since 2007, a free trade agreement in 2011 and bilateral naval exercises in June (*Press Trust of India*, June 4; *Business Standard*, February 22, 2011; Mofa.go.jp, December 2006).

Moving into the Maritime Domain

Beyond both countries' engagement with third parties, the most likely platform of "spillover" in the Sino-Indian relationship is the maritime domain, which has gained strategic importance amid their rise as major trading and resource-consuming powers. This in turn has transformed the nature of their bilateral relationship from a land-based rivalry toward a competition increasingly taking place in the maritime domain. This is rooted in the fact that more than 95 percent of India's exports are seaborne compared to 60 percent of China's exports while 70 percent of Indian hydrocarbons emanate from offshore blocks and 80 percent of China's oil imports transit the sea lanes of the South China Sea and Indian Ocean.

Both countries traditionally have pursued relatively modest maritime security interests confined to playing a supporting role to land-based operations and protecting their respective coastlines. China's focus has been on sea-denial capabilities aimed at deterring U.S. intervention in a conflict in the Taiwan Strait while India has focused on coastal defence and surveillance given the country's porous, poorly-demarcated and disputed maritime border. Both countries' are now pursuing increasingly ambitious naval doctrines, reflecting the need to protect their expanding overseas interests. For instance, Chinese maritime strategists have espoused moving beyond "near-coast defence" toward "near-seas active defence" and increasingly into the realm of "far-sea operations".

China's pursuit of "new historic missions" that entail increasing overseas deployments coincide with the Indian Navy's ambitions to transform itself into "a brand new multi-dimensional navy" with "reach and sustainability" (*Times of India*, December 21, 2011). This will bring both countries' navies into closer contact and ensure that they cross paths more frequently. This was demonstrated in July 2011 when an Indian Navy vessel, the *INS Airavat* allegedly received radio contact from the Chinese Navy demanding the vessel depart disputed waters in the South China Sea after completing a port call in Vietnam (*Times of India*, September 2, 2011). Similarly, the 2009 deployment of a People's Liberation Army Navy (PLAN) naval taskforce to the Indian Ocean has brought China's navy into closer contact with India's strategic backyard (BBC, December 13, 2011). The fact that China and India are two of only six countries with a nuclear submarine capability and two of only ten countries with aircraft carriers points toward a growing interest by both countries to project power beyond their littoral regions.

Constructive Competition

To be sure, competition between China and India is by no means a certainty nor necessarily and a cause for concern. For instance, third-party countries benefit from Sino-Indian competition through improved infrastructure and greater access to aid and investment. If this competition grows fiercer, however, it may drive Beijing and New Delhi to provide more aid to local elites with fewer strings attached at the expense of good governance.

In the maritime domain, given both countries' mutual dependence on trade and imported resources to fuel their economies, they share an interest in protecting sea lines of communication and maintaining freedom of navigation. This potential for cooperation has been demonstrated by China and India coordinating their anti-piracy patrols in the Indian Ocean within the framework of the Shared Awareness and Deconfliction mechanism (*Times of India*, February 2). India has so far outpaced the PLAN in the sphere of protecting the 'maritime commons'. This was demonstrated by the Indian Navy's assistance following the Asian tsunami in 2004, the cyclone that struck Myanmar in 2008 and the evacuation of Indian, Sri Lankan and Nepalese civilians from the conflict in Lebanon in 2006 (*Financial Times*, February 17, 2010;*Times of India*, January 7, 2005).

China is fast catching up in its humanitarian response capabilities as demonstrated by the PLA Navy escorting non-Chinese vessels, including UN World Food Program convoys, through the Gulf of Aden as well as the deployment of a Chinese missile frigate to the Mediterranean Sea in early 2011 to support the evacuation of Chinese nationals from Libya. China's rhetoric of maintaining "Harmonious Seas" and engaging in military operations other than war (MOOTW) suggest that Beijing's potential for cooperation in the maritime domain could grow as its maritime security interests move farther from its coastline (*South China Morning Post*, March 30, 2011; February 26, 2011; *China Daily*, November 27, 2010; "PLAN Shapes International Perception of Evolving Capabilities," *China Brief*, February 4, 2010).

Fifty years on, another war between China and India remains an unlikely prospect. Conflict has been constrained by the fact that their bilateral frictions have been largely strategic rather than ideological. The bilateral relationship lacks the historical animosity seen in the Sino-Japanese or Sino-Vietnamese relationship (*Pragati*, January 6).

Nonetheless, both countries face an increasingly complex and multi-layered relationship amid their growing international diplomat, economic and military clout. The Sino-Indian relationship is more nuanced than the U.S.-Soviet rivalry of the Cold War, interspersed with cooperation, competition and a latent rivalry. On the one hand, a climate of mistrust permeates the bilateral relationship rooted in their unresolved territorial dispute, economic imbalance and resource competition, because of deficient institutional mechanisms for interaction. Both countries, however, see eye-to-eye on a number of global issues ranging from climate change to poverty reduction and relations with pariah regimes, such as Iran, Sudan and, until recently, Burma.

Fuelled by a demographic dividend and both countries' growing overseas interests and capabilities, the Sino-Indian relationship is likely to be among the most potent sources of rivalry between major powers in the 21st century. As both states acquire the capabilities and ambitions to reshape the international system, the relationship is likely to play out on the world stage.

Deterring renewed Sino-Indian hostilities will require both countries to acknowledge the changing nature of their bilateral relationship amid their rise as major powers. This will entail devoting more resources to manage the potential "spillover" of their bilateral relationship into other arenas, including third-party relations and the maritime domain, through more institutionalized forms of interaction. Ultimately, maintaining a cordial bilateral relationship will ensure the continuation of both countries' growth and a stable global ecology than unrestrained competition.

2

India and China Rivalry in Nepal

INTRODUCTION

It is interesting to note that in a whole variety of areas India and China are increasingly approaching a level of peaceful interaction and a mutual dialogue about important issues related to security, the border, trade and civil society exchanges. After years with hardline deterrence and unresolved strategic problems a new era may be emerging where partnership and end their historical animosity against each other.

The improved relation between India and China can best be characterized as one of global cooperation on transnational issues especially vis-à-vis the "West", geostrategic rivalry at the regional level in the form of growing commercial exchange and in some cases bilateral trade, investment and competition (Schmidt forthcoming). These contradictory processes are complicated by some degree of asymmetry between the two Asian giants as China's political establishment does not appear to feel threatened by India while the Indian political class seems to project a sense of insecurity in coming to grip with China's rise in the world system (Bajaj 2011).

Important aspects of the India-China rivalry are illuminated in the Himalayan region and in particular in Nepal. A relatively small and mountainous country - long viewed by Western and Asian policymakers as a strategic backwater - has attained significance as renewed competition between India and China plays out within Nepal's borders. Nepal has always been historically, culturally, economically and politically close to India. The country is also very important for China as it borders Tibet. Beijing's attempt to influence political power in Kathmandu may be viewed as a diplomatic move to establish a buffer zone and thereby checking perceived Western and Indian infiltration to destabilize the region and China itself. The Chinese government is cording and enticing Kathmandu in an attempt to impact policy-making by announcing diplomatic and security offers, huge economic packages and development projects. This is causing alarm in New Delhi as Nepal's traditional and historical Indo-centric foreign policy dependence is gradually shifting on maintaining an equidistance relationship on both fronts.

In traditional neo-realist thinking Dabhade and Pant note, "If we take South Asia as a regional subsystem, then the two major powers whose behavior substantially impacts the foreign policies of smaller states in the area are China and India" (2004: 157-169). In their analysis of Sino-Indian rivalry and penetration of Nepal, they conclude: "Chinese and Indian strategies reflect their respective desires to expand their relative influence over Nepal at each other's expense. Both powers display a lack of satisfaction with the current status quo and have pursued strategies that are aimed at maximizing their share of regional power". However this is not necessarily a zero-sum game where Nepal and other small countries are passive receivers.

On the contrary with a newly installed left-wing government serious attempts are being made to escape this conundrum and re-iterate a more independent line. It is noteworthy that Nepal can be viewed as a country located between two emerging or "would-be" global powers where such normative concepts like democracy, human rights, development and social change entail very different meanings. In China social rights take precedence over political rights. So far it seems that this development model has been able to promote stability and rapid economic growth. While in India, the opposite is the case as democracy in many respects seems to paralyse the political system and in some specific cases promotes an unstable political and social order and a worse human rights record than in authoritarian one-party China (US State Department 2010a and 2010b). However, the debate regarding which regime is best for development seems without end. The authoritarianism versus democracy problematique is not easily solved neither academically nor politically and this has caught Nepal's young democracy in a catch twenty-two.

Theoretically speaking China remains a challenge to the mainstream linear view, which sees democracy, rights and stability as pearls on a string and as the end station of all human evolution on "the end of history". The regime competition between India and China is also a challenge to the political elite in Nepal because of the democratic stalemate and no clear defined political agenda which make it very hard to deliver growth and services and creates a situation where more and more people are longing for an absolutist solution.

The aim of this paper is to explore the rivalry between India and China and how it impacts Nepal in geo-strategic and geo-political terms both theoretically, conceptually and empirically. The foreign policy rivalry between India and China appears not only to influence investment and trade decisions but also to penetrate issues related to stability, governance and political institutions.

What kind of rivalry is taking place? Naturally the focus includes security and geopolitics where Nepal is portrayed as a buffer and there may be direct links with key-players – i.e. political parties and other important domestic actors and entities. However this view will be complemented with an analysis of geo-economic competition over access to hydropower, water and other natural resources. There seems to be some coordination between US and India – but also the World Bank and some other multilateral agencies to implement austerity programmes. Seen from China's point of view Nepal is the key in the Himalayan region to provide security and peace in Tibet but also as provider of access to natural resources. The most imperative motive of Chinese foreign policy towards Nepal is *stability* and the ability to cooperate with any type of government so that it doesn't turn against China's national interests and to curb any impact on the Tibet issue as well.

The main question then is how Nepal is responding to the rise of China and India and the strategies these states are pursuing to preserve their national interests? Was and is it possible for the government(s) in Nepal to take advantage of this situation where the so-called Great powers increasingly seek to influence policy-making and what is the foreign policy response of Nepal? Is it possible to identify the most important social actors and institutions trying to influence the government's position towards the attempts to intrude and persuade and influence the interplay between foreign policy and its impact on stability, democracy and rights in the domestic context? In short Nepal's security perceptions cannot be put into singular but rather reflects a number of political and ideological interests and views of social change and power relations in the region.

Nepal is also different from other nations in the South Asian region where for instance Pakistan's security perceptions center on India as a mortal threat, the United States as an unreliable friend, and China as a steady ally. Nepal is more similar to also landlocked Bhutan in the sense that it has a historical close relationship with India and cultural, political close security ties with India while the China link is more recent and pragmatically based. Nepal has attempted to expand its margin for maneuver vis-à-vis India without contesting its regional dominance. Although the domestic politics are so far marred by fragility and instability, this situation leaves the government with increasing autonomy; leverage and bargaining it can also potentially backfire in the sense that India for instance may sabotage a real rapprochement and appeasement between Nepal and China. Nepal is also dependent on India as the source of access to the sea through the major port of Calcutta – a situation creating a certain degree of vulnerability although Nepal exports are modest and the economy has gone from bad to worse (Shrestha 2011).

Notional Implications

It seems obvious that traditional and mainstream IPE theory is unable to provide the conceptual tools to investigate and elaborate on a full-scale thorough empirical analysis of the issues at stake in the Himalayan power game.

The aim here is not so much to describe Nepal as an objective node or as a passive entity geo-strategically squeezed in between India and China but rather to provide an understanding of what is socially constructed are the meaning of things and their social effects, not the physical existence. Utilizing a critical IPE perspective means an objection towards accepting the actual state of affairs – accepting dependency, inferiority, inequality and unevenness – in Nepal's foreign policy with its immediate neighborhood in South Asia and the Himalayan region. This implies that change is possible for better or worse. Whereas mainstream IP theory takes a foreign policy problem as a given and tries to analyse the policy behavior of those who try and solve it critical theories are more interested in the construction of foreign policy issues as 'problems' that need to be solved.

Mainstream IPE theories tend to look at foreign policy problems as framed by policy-makers and seldom question whether this is a real problem or not and thus they seldom question the purpose behind why policy-makers frame the issue the way they do. Critical theories of foreign policy attempts to uncover the processes through which a foreign policy issue is represented as a problem or a crisis..

Mainstream IPE theory tends to view foreign policy as a practice used to solve problems between countries while critical theory view foreign policy as constitutive of those problems the others take for granted. Hence critical theory wants to understand how specific problems are 'constructed' and studies the process through which 'national interests' are constructed. This also implies that deciding whether a situation faced by the state is a threat to 'national interest' or not, requires interpretation by policy-makers. In contrast to realism, threats are not self-evident. States' national interests in the face of threats are matters of interpretation by policy-makers and social actors and cannot be understand without some historical knowledge.

DANGEROUS POLITICAL FINANCIAL SYSTEM AND THE REVISE OF FOREIGN POLICY

Critical political economy (CPE) is a dynamic perspective on the interplay between geo-political and geo-economic priorities in foreign policy. This approach recognizes a certain degree of nation state diversity, but equally insists that the focus of mainstream neo-realist and neo-liberal theories on national distinctiveness is ultimately misleading in that these established theories lose sight of essential similarities in national models of regulation that are substantially shaped by the external structural imperatives of capitalist accumulation.

CPE goes beyond the perspective of the orthodoxies of neo-realism, neo-liberalism and some structural theories like world-system theory in which "historical change is assumed to follow a predetermined path regardless of historical context and human agency; with the result that theoretical argument dominates and displaces the complexity of history". CPE rests on historical dialectics trying to discern not only the past but with a continual process of historical change and with exploring the potential for alternative forms of state and world order.

The dissolution of the Soviet Union in 1989 spelled the end of the Cold War and thereby the dominance of politics in command turned into economics in command. An important post-1989 effect was the shift from the primacy of military power to a greater role for economic power in shaping global geopolitics. Economic structural change has become the epitomization of globalization and it challenges "deeply embedded socio-cultural and political structures in critical ways that cannot be ignored, provoking dynamic responses of promotion, accommodation, and resistance". The classical interplay and dynamics between exercise of 'political authority', security issues and 'the distribution of wealth and production' cannot be analyzed as exclusive domains but at the present stage of history it is manifested that geo-economics has a dominant position in international relations.

The concept of geo-economics thus came into prominence after the end of the Cold War and it suggests interconnectivity but also unevenness of the economic and commercial opportunities, broader political and international relations, and a blurring of the boundaries of the state to pursue its strategic interests, including through military capabilities. This concept is rooted in the growing importance of economic factors in international relations and in a wish to dig deeper than neo-realism in order to provide an understanding of the nature and sources of power.

The CPE approach does not essentialize the state as a pre-constituted entity or a 'black box' of "national interests" interacting within anarchical international relations. Rather, CPE seeks to understand 'forms of states' as 'state/society complex' and asks how the prevailing order has come about and how it is changing. It is the interplay of particular configurations of contending social forces and alliances, including attempts at integration of a variety of class interests that defines "national interests" and characterizes inherent contradictions in the historical structure. We have to explore the boundaries of the state in its current conjunctures, its historical dynamic and the process of social change. In this way, we seek an understanding of the underlying and prevailing tensions between geo-politics and geo-economics in foreign policy. It is important to ask "who defines national interest" and who has the power to change it?

It is power itself which is becoming more diffuse, diffracted through an increasingly complex, prismatic structure of socio-economic forces and levels of governance. The result is a hollowing out of the state even if it maintains the monopoly over the means of violence over a given territory and this gives space to a plethora of actors and institutions – not least financial capital - capable of influencing foreign policy and social change in Asia and the world. Transnational issues including climate change, terrorism, cyber-warfare, pandemics, rush to secure energy and resource supplies, and difficulties in sustaining multilateral focus in trade and on economic issues through the completion of the Doha Round. All open up the foreign policy field and would, ideally speaking, denote a myriad of actors and influences from formal organizations such as transnational corporations to advocacy networks and think tanks 'epistemic communities' (networks of individuals and/or organizations based on authoritative claims to consensual knowledge). In the end, this blurring of the levels of 'sovereignty' and 'non-intervention' sanctioned by socio-political conflicts – internal and external to the state – concerns the classic problem in international political economy: 'Who gets what, when, where, and how'.

When it comes to the question about foreign policy in India and China these considerations lead to a number of inter-linked issues of strategic importance. For instance, what are the links between energy security (oil, gas and water), trade, FDI and ODA flows in relation to more traditional issues of military security, encirclement and containment? What explains the fact that both countries share mutual interests in a number of global policy areas? While they in the same areas retain a degree of rivalry and competition at the regional level in the Himalayas and more specifically in Nepal?

THE COLLISION OF INDIA–CHINA RIVALRY TO THE HIMALAYAN REPUBLIC

Chinese interest in Nepal can be said to make a U-turn in 2008, when bloody protests erupted on the Tibetan plateau. One of China's core interests in Nepal has been to minimize the political activities of Tibetan refugees, which China views as potential threats to its own security. The extended anti-Chinese protests in the streets of Kathmandu in April and May 2008—immediately preceding the Beijing Olympics—seem to have worried the Chinese authorities. Beijing has consistently linked economic and military aid to Kathmandu's adherence to a "One China" policy, a thinly veiled reference to Nepal's ban on political demonstrations by Tibetan exiles. Over the years, China has increased its aid to Nepal. China has pledged US$ 140 million assistance to Nepal during Prime Minister Wen Jiabao's visit to Kathmandu on January 14, 2012. During discussions with Nepali counterpart Dr Babu Ram Bhattarai, the Chinese leader was also positive to extend support for infrastructure development of the impoverished landlocked country, which may run into more than US$ 5 billion.

China also pledged to construct an international airport in the second largest city, Pokhara, three large hydropower stations in the west and improvements of roads and creating rail networks. This shows the level of importance China has attached to its close door neighbor on the south. On a similar light, India recently also pledges approximately US$ 220 million grants to Nepal for the year 2012-13. Previous year figures show that Nepal received grants worth approximately US$ 130 million in 2010-11 and US$ 117 million in 2011-12. These increasing ODA grants clearly illustrate that India is competing China on all fronts. Actually Indian ODA figures show that it is only Afghanistan and Bhutan who received more grant aid than Nepal who comes in third on the list from fifth in the region.

Similarly, as a sign of growing rivalry between both nations, China last year committed to provide Nepal with US $ 19.8 million in "non-lethal" military aid. This is the biggest amount doled out by Nepal's northern neighbor as military assistance. China had earlier provided US $ 2.6 million in non-lethal military aid and communication logistics worth US $ 3 million. This is a strategic move by Beijing as New Delhi was the biggest provider of military assistance to Nepal, but it stopped supplying lethal military aid since former king Gyanendra Shah's royal takeover in 2005 even though both Indian and Nepalese military has historical ties.

These new intrusions into the security and defence sectors of Nepal's - structurally speaking – most stable political institution sparked a response from the Indian side as New Delhi also gave the nod to resume the assistance during a bilateral talk held between Deputy Prime Minster and Defence Minister of Nepal Bijaya Kumar Gachhadar and his Indian counterpart AK Antony in early 2012. It is noteworthy that "Beijing would rather deal direct with the Nepalese Army than with the government, and this reflects the perceived status and stability of Nepal's army relative to the government".

In another layer of competition over Nepal's security situation was the Indian suspicion around 2009 that the Maoists were collaborating with China to establish a one-party dominated People's Republic by its attempt to influence Nepalese Military. The Maoists' government's move to sack the chief of the Nepalese Army and to replace him with a 'sympathetic general' was perceived as the last straw for India, which saw it as an indirect move by Beijing to extend its influence on Nepal's military. In a late-night decision, President Ram Baran Yadav used his prerogative as the ceremonial supreme army commander to reinstate the army chief. The other political parties in the coalition withdrew their support and Prime Minister Prachanda resigned on May 4, 2009. In Kathmandu this was seen as India directly interfering in the reinstatement of the army chief by lobbying the parties for its interests – a move with huge ramifications for the rivalry between India and China and for the domestic polity in Nepal.

Recently, the power play between China and India for influence in Nepal has turned electric, as China has signed a US$1.8 billion agreement to develop the 760-megawatt (MW) West Seti Project hydropower plant in Nepal. The deal marks the Asian giant's entry into a lucrative sector in the Himalayan nation — water and power — that has been dominated by India for years. It comes in a time when several other major hydropower projects, mainly developed with Indian investment, have stalled for various reasons, including protests by Maoists against the awarding of deals to foreign companies labeling it as "unfair share" of hydropower projects in Nepal. In the beginning of 2012, the Maoists burned the project office of the Upper Karnali Project (900MW), which was awarded to GMR of India.

China's renewed interest in its southern neighbor is not entirely a quid pro quo. In Kathmandu, Chinese tour groups visit the tourist enclave of Thamel and Pokhara, where they frequent Chinese-run restaurants, bookstores, and hospitals. According to the Chinese embassy in Nepal, projects such as the Birendra International Convention Center (now used as Parliament Building) and the capital city's main highway are evidence that "China treats Nepal as its closest neighbor and best friend." Although these initiatives aim to signify the softer side of Chinese-Nepali ties, China ultimately appears most interested in stifling "anti-Chinese" activities on Nepal's soil. Beijing seems less concerned with Kathmandu's political jockeying than with ensuring that the next government is as pliant as the current one. The Chinese strategy has been to focus fewer resources on national politics and more on localized economic aid, such as building schools in politically sensitive border areas. China main concern appears to be stability not who is governing Kathmandu. For China, the ideological difference doesn't make any difference. They had a very good relation with the king. They had a very good relationship with the Nepali Congress party. Beijing also appears to have a good working relation with the present Maoist led government and party and they will have relation with whoever emerges as a stabilizing force in Nepal.

Besides deepening political and military ties, the proliferation of China Study Centers (CSC) across Nepal has also generated a lot of interest and apprehensions in India. According to various news sources in India 'the CSC which started as a benign China-supported informal civil society group in 2000 to promote cultural interaction is growing in membership and has become an effective tool to promote the Chinese perspective on key issues concerning Nepal.' Media Sources has identified more than 33 such centres, most of which are located in close proximity to Nepal's border with India. These provide Chinese language and culture classes and are often manned by volunteers from China. While enabling greater access to information about Chinese social and economic development, these centers also provide a convenient platform for the dissemination of Chinese policy towards South Asia and India's role therein. Similarly China Radio International has launched a local FM radio station in Kathmandu with the purpose of bringing China closer to Nepal. China is providing "volunteer" teachers to various schools in Nepal who give Chinese language lessons to Nepali students and exposure to Chinese culture. These are evidences of Chinese so-called "cultural exchange" initiatives and are part of the soft power component of China's foreign policy.

On the political front, the competition between the two Asian giants is also impacting the political development of Nepal. Even though China has good relations with all political sectors it is unsure about the polity due to the current political stalemate. So unlike India, which has a direct influence in Nepalese polity due to its long-due historical, cultural, economic and political engagement with the monarchy and Congress party, the Chinese strategy seems to establish equidistance relations with the most important political parties and cordially and mutually reinforce its policy direction with economic incentives.

These are testimony that India and China are now in fierce competition in Nepal both in-terms of geo-political and geo-strategic terms. Even though, Nepal's relation with India is a very special relationship, there is negligible Chinese influence on the political front of Nepal as India has always been a traditional ally and force for change in the Himalayan region. But obviously we can see that Chinese influence has been growing in geo-strategic terms. The Indian political and bureaucratic class has over the years neglected to establish broader ties with all political entities and appears to have created a situation of negligence and high-handedness – what critics would call arrogance and supremacy.

NEPAL'S FORECAST AND CHALLENGES AMIDST GREAT RIVALRY

These instances of interference and rivalry bring both opportunities and challenges to Nepal. The biggest challenge so far is to balance the relationship between both India and China. Since for Nepal, both neighbours are equally important. India has been historically and culturally the most important neighbor for Nepal whereas recent posture of China as an emerging economic superpower is equally important for Nepal to boast its economic performance and investments. Thus, for Nepal, maintaining equidistant relationship between these two big neighbours is one of the most challenging foreign policy imperatives and interestingly there are signs of optimism and potential benefits as well.

There is consensus on both sides in India and China that stability of Nepal is in their best interest. Tibet is of vital importance to China, which is why Beijing wants peace and stability in Nepal whereas, due to the historical, socio-economic and cultural relationship between Nepal and India, political stability and economic development is major concern for India as Nepal and India shares open and porous borders. Thus de-stable Nepal is direct security imperative to India.

India has recently redefined its strategy towards Nepal. The current Indian Ambassador to Nepal Shri Jayant Prasad opined on a recent program that "India and Nepal are equal and sovereign states, and in keeping with the spirit of non-intervention in each other's domestic affairs, India does not have preferred electoral outcomes, preferred ruling arrangements or favourites among political parties".

Chinese Prime Minister Wen Jiabao, paid a visit to Nepal in January this year. During his short official visit to Nepal, interestingly encouraged the continuation of Nepal's traditional and cordial relations with India. At the luncheon that Prime Minister Baburam Bhattarai had hosted in Premier Wen's honor at Singha Durbar quoted the Chinese leader as saying that Beijing wishes to see the "continuation of Nepal's warm and friendly ties with India", pointing that relations between China and India are also deepening. Later Indian Prime Minister Manmohan Singh in his meeting with Nepal's Deputy Prime Minister Bijaya Kumar Gachhadar in New Delhi later that month indicated that it is comfortable with Nepal's close relationship with its northern neighbor China, India has said it is positive about recent developments in the Sino-Nepali relationship.

Prime Minister of Nepal Dr. Babu Ram Bhattarai on his first address to parliament as Prime Minister on August 28, 2011, "We should abandon a 'Buffer State Policy' between two giant neighbours China and India" and added "Instead, Nepal should act as a 'friendship bridge' between the two countries". Since Nepal is strategically placed between the two largest growing economies and China has become India's largest foreign trade partner with US$ 60 billion dollars worth of transactions. The bilateral trade is expected to reach US$100 billion. Transportation cost, on average, amount to 10% of the total trade. In other words, in a trade of 100 billion, transportation cost will be to the tune of US$ 10 billion. If Nepal can tap only 10% of the transportation moving from Nepal, the country can generate about US$ 1 billion worth of business annually, a substantial amount for a country like Nepal. As not all goods can be economically moved from one country to another by air or sea route alone, surface route can provide an attractive alternative for movements of goods. However, Nepal needs to develop its infrastructure (road and railways) to handle this traffic in trade. Nepal can seek the assistance from both countries in this respect. Also, development of such an infrastructure will help boost Nepal's bilateral trade with each of these neighbours.

Final Remarks

Given the perceived competitive and in some cases even adversarial potential of Sino-Indian relations, China expects to find itself pitted against India's national interests, possibly even in concert with the US. For India on the other hand, it is critically important to balance China's rising power. By not doing so, India's own increasing role as a regional power would be reduced. This would also have serious ramifications for India's interests in South Asia but also other parts of world like Southeast Asia where there is increasing rivalry and competition between Delhi and Beijing. Reinforcing India's contradictory engagement with the region is the fact that while India has got a seat at the table, it has yet to shape the rules of the regional architecture of which it is a member. Underlying New Delhi's inability to be a proactive shaper of regional security is the fact that it lacks a strategic vision of its regional role. On the other hand, the very diverse set of challenges confronting India in South Asia make it very difficult to adopt overall consistent, universal strategies.

This leads to our observation that Nepal should clearly prioritize its national interests and adopt a policy in managing its relationships with India and China, that best preserves and promotes her national interests.

As the country has recently undergone political transformation, such national interests could be: security, internal stability, economic development, and establishing a sound democratic mechanism. In order to preserve its long term security, it is necessary for Nepal to understand the sensitivity of India and China in terms of their security related issues and adopt policies wisely, following a middle path, that respects the interests of both neighbours without endangering its own sovereign and independent position.

Given the historic role of India in the political transformation of Nepal, India being the largest democratic system, may potentially serve as an example for Nepal to establish democratic mechanisms. Furthermore, given the historic ties of Nepal's major political parties and the military with India, the diplomatic and non-diplomatic involvement of India in establishing conditions in order to institutionalize democratic values, and to bring political stability, has been observed as an asset to mature the democratic practices and political institutions of Nepal whether the example mentioned in this paper of New Delhi's intervention into the military reshuffle can be viewed in this manner remains an open question.

In contrast, China has always expressed that Nepal is capable of solving its own internal problems, and has largely kept itself out of the Nepalese political affairs. The findings of this paper also show a clear preference for stability and order on the Chinese side and cordial working relations with all political parties in Nepal. Implicitly Chinese ODA and its 'One-China' policy with regard to the Tibetan question may be regarded as pressure and a clear attempt to influence the polity in Kathmandu. Another vital national interest of Nepal has been the economic development, which ultimately helps to promote stability.

Nepal has benefitted from the economic assistance of both India and China, and considering the economic rise of both countries such assistance could provide substantial benefits in the future. It would be highly beneficial for India too, if she conducts her external affairs, positively and matures the "standard of diplomatic dealing," towards her smaller neighbours. This could contribute to extracting goodwill and considerable willing respect by pulling surrounding neighbours towards India, which would substantially, facilitates to establish its desire as a regional power and assist in lessening China's influence, "perceived and potential.

SINO-INDIAN RIVALRY PLAYS OUT IN NEPAL

While mocking the severe dependency of Nepal, particularly the politicians, to India and the Indian establishment, it is often joked that if it rains in Delhi, they open umbrella in Kathmandu. While people keep debating whether particular government in Kathmandu is pro- or anti-Indian, the relationship between the two very dissimilar neighbours in South Asia remains highly complex and quite often veers towards trouble.

Nepal's geographical proximity to India apart, the 'dependency' factor has become historic as the latest uninterrupted period of such relationship exists for almost two centuries by now. It was in the fateful Sugauli Treaty of 1815 that Nepal was forced to cede almost one third of its territory in the east, west and the south to the British India thereby also ensuring that the British would not encroach further north.

Ever since, regardless of the nature of regime in Kathmandu and the ups and downs in the formal political relations, the social and economic realities of the Indo-Nepal relationship have remained largely unchanged, with the low-productivity subsistence economy of Nepal being dependent on the industrializing Indian economy. After the Indian independence, the Indo-Nepal Treaty of Peace and Friendship of 1950 was signed, which galvanized the relationship between Nepal and independent India. Even though the calls for amending or even scrapping the 1950 treaty are ccommon and occasionally become very loud in Nepal, the persistent economic dependence on India as a result of chronically under-performing economy and lack of clarity about alternative of that treaty has ensured that the treaty endures even though it can be scrapped unilaterally with a year's time.

Interestingly, the time of the latter treaty between Nepal and India almost coincided with the invasion of Tibet by the newly born People's Republic of China led by Mao Zedong. In the context of new found determination of the Chinese to reassert themselves after the triumph of communist revolution, it became necessary for India to maintain and even strengthen the existing relationship with Nepal. Even now many analysts in India regret the act of their then government which condoned the Chinese act of transgression eventually loosing the important buffer zone between the two Asian giants to China.

With eventual peaceful takeover of Sikkim in 1975, however, and the whole-spectrum dominance that India enjoys in another buffer country Bhutan, some of the scores of loosing Tibet to China were settled, many others argue. By any means, the only effective and strategically important buffer zone between the two rising Asian powers is now Nepal with its whole length separating the northern provinces of India from the Tibet Autonomous Region of China. With increasing economic and military clout of both the powers, the stakes for both in maintaining influence in Nepal have risen significantly.

The increasing importance attached by both the countries to the relationship with Nepal is shown by the fact that both of the new envoys sent to Nepal by India and China recently are senior most till date. Even as successive governments in Kathmandu keep reassuring the Chinese side about Nepal's firm commitment to 'One China Policy' and the Chinese keep praising that commitment, the real and overwhelming concern of the Chinese is somewhat different.

There is no denying the facts that there is steady traffic of Tibetans fleeing to India through Nepal and that there is a significant Tibetan refugee population inside Nepal. Given China's determination to project Tibet as a part of Chinese economic miracle and not the socio-culturally exploited periphery, this flow of refugees through Nepal has become very sensitive issue between Nepal and China while dragging other countries into spotlight occasionally. The other important issue for the Chinese has been, particularly in the recent past, to ensure that the government in Kathmandu should not be so pro-Indian as to threaten the Chinese interests in Nepal.

On the other hand, the core interests of India in Nepal go even further. Even though Nepal, small and landlocked as it is, has historically been dependent on India economically, the cost of having a regime in Kathmandu overtly hostile to India serves worst the Indian interests in Nepal. Unlike Bhutan where India has become hugely successful in harvesting the hydropower in addition to establishing itself as a trusted big brother in all strategic matters, similar attempts in Nepal have brought patchy success at best. The lingering border disputes and the perception in Nepal that India is exploiting Nepal for its weakness and systemically encroaching the Nepali land has all along generated a strong anti-India sentiment in Nepal. It is to take advantage of this sentiment that the politicians in Nepal have time and again resorted to anti-India rhetoric even though there is little prospect of meaningfully confronting India in any front.

On the other side, the Indian elites are not at all enthused by the fact that the leftists and apparently pro-China parties have been constantly gaining ground in kathmandu pushing the traditionally India-friendly parties like Nepali Congress to the corner. And they repeatedly show this displeasure through anti-Nepal rhtoric in India where many draw a parallel between the rise of Maoist insurgency and eventual ascent to power of the Maoist party in Nepal and steadily growing Naxalite insurgency in many Indian states. Above all this, around 800 km long open border between the two countries means that any strife or instability in Nepal obviously tends to spill over to the northern part of India. Moreover, given the eternal hostility between India and Pakistan the issue of Pakistan-based terror-groups using the Nepali land and open border to attack Indian targets has been a constant source of attention and apprehension for India. It is in best interest of India to have a compliant or at least cooperative regime in Kathmandu.

In wider geopolitical context also, the overarching concerns of both the neighbours intersect in Nepal. With increasing warmth in the Indo-US relations and the worsening stand-off with the East Asian countries in the South China Sea, the matters are only worsening for China with the latest news of Indo-Vietnam deal to jointly explore for oil in the waters that China says are 'contested'. Further collaboration between or among other Asian countries that share the apprehension about China's rise can create further trouble. In this context, it only makes sense for China to strengthen relationship with Nepal which despite its tiny size, forms an important buffer with India. All this said, the act of balancing the interests of the south and the north has been a very delicate task for the government in Kathmandu. When the acts of deporting back the Tibetan refugees on China's pressure anger the western benefactors like US, the matters get further complicated.

While the two Asian powers are involved in active exchange of gestures and even threats with each other in 'hot' issues like the Sino-Indian border dispute or the Indian deal with Vietnam, a silent but crucial diplomatic game goes on Kathmandu. With Chinese ambassador to Nepal Houlan recently blasting the "international forces" for instigating the Tibetan movement to contain China's rise, it takes little for these issues to come in the front. With increasing mercury of the diplomatic tensions between the two giant neighbours because of a host of issues ranging from border disputes to increasing Indo-US and Sino-Pakistan proximity to increasingly hot dispute in the South China Sea, striking a balance could be increasingly hard for Nepal.

And so long as Nepal remains mired in dismal economic performance and politics starting and ending at demagoguery, thereby perpetuating its endless dependence on India, little will be Nepal's ability to choose what policy vis-à-vis each of the neighbor best suits its interest. As of now Nepal is focused at just at not offending or annoying any of the neighbours, oblivious to the greater geostrategic rivalries and games.

NEPAL AND THE SINO-INDIAN RIVALRY

The inevitable transitory of the Fourteenth Dalai Lama, the radicalization of the Tibetan diaspora and the fervor of the international campaign to free Tibet are bound to keep the Himalayan dispute on the world's front pages. India, which has sheltered the Dalai Lama and tens of thousands of his followers, today increasingly sees Tibet as a bargaining chip with China in its overall bilateral relationship. Home to some 20,000 Tibetan refugees and wedged precariously between the assertive Asian giants, Nepal is likely to become an even more important theatre.

From Nepal's perspective, at least, the issue of Tibet goes beyond the freedom of a land, the liberation of a culture and a celebration of a way of life. The region always has been a conduit for major external protagonists to pursue wider objectives. The British Empire considered Tibet a critical part of the imperial chessboard, a legacy that lives on in today's geo-strategic milieu where China sees the region as a front rivals are intent on using to contain its rise.

The Tibet issue has a peculiar psychological subtext in Nepal. Some of the same people, who profess the greatest admiration for the Dalai Lama and his cause, also hope that Tibet remains under Chinese control. Many Nepalese recognize that an independent Tibet would leave their country without a border with China. They believe such a situation would allow India, which has long invoked its own version of the Monroe Doctrine in the land-locked nation, to tighten its grip.

Although Tibet has been middle to the Sino-Nepalese relationship, Nepal's formal contacts with China did not originate through the region. It began with China's quest for Buddhist texts, artifacts and codes from the wider Gangetic heartland. In the mid-seventh century, a powerful Tibetan king extracted consorts from Chinese and Nepalese royal households on the principle of peace through kinship. The two wives helped bring Buddhism to Tibet and opened a direct Himalayan route between Nepal and China, bypassing the more arduous one across Central Asia.

As religion and trade began traversing the same Himalayan passes, peace and goodwill began losing ground. As the British sun rose higher over India, Nepal fought two wars with Tibet, precipitating a Chinese invasion. The Nepalese gained peace by entering into a tributary relationship with the Middle Kingdom, a duty they would discharge with utmost diligence. The Nepalese became the last foreigners to pay tribute to the Qing, as the arrangement helped maintain their independence as most of modern South Asia fell under the sway of the British Empire.

Nepal, which fought a third war with Tibet in 1855-56, refused to aid the Tibetans against a British invasion in 1904, but helped secure the withdrawal of the invaders. The diplomatic triumph was short-lived as the tottering Qing formally claimed suzerainty over Nepal. Seeking to preserve its interests in Tibet - and project its independence - Nepal mediated between Beijing and Lhasa in 1912, after which Tibet enjoyed a period of de facto independence.

For all their antipathy for the Qing and for each other, Chinese nationalists and communists pressed their country's claims on Nepal: Sun Yat-sen and Mao Zedong both included Nepal among territories China had lost to imperialism. The Chinese invasion of Tibet in 1950 impelled the leaders of independent India to restore the monarchy at the top of a multiparty democracy in Nepal to forestall a communist advance southward. On the eve of Nepal's first democratic elections in 1959, Tibetans rose up in a failed revolt against Beijing, prompting the Dalai Lama's flight into exile in India.

Nepal's first chosen prime minister, B.P. Koirala, sought unsuccessfully to consolidate democracy by asserting Nepalese independence from India and China. When King Mahendra dissolved parliament, jailed Koirala and most of the elected leadership, and abolished multiparty democracy, much more than royal ambition was at play.

Nepal had become a center of Cold War intrigue where the United States and India - the world's two largest democracies - were working to undermine each other as were the communist giants China and the Soviet Union. By the end of the 1960s, Sino-American rapprochement put the two nations on the same side in Nepal for the duration of the Cold War.

As the 1980s drew to a close, a new round of unrest in Tibet merged with student protests in Beijing, culminating in the bloody crackdown in Tiananmen Square. The fall of the Berlin Wall inspired the Nepalese to bring down the palace-led partyless Panchayat system, with Beijing a mere bystander.

With the kingdom's democracy turning rancorous, Nepalese disciple of Mao launched a bloody insurgency, a convulsion exacerbated by the assassinations of King Birendra and almost the entire royal family in a June 2001 palace massacre. India, like the United States and Britain, opposed King Gyanendra's February 2005 coup, widely perceived to have enjoyed Chinese backing. Beijing, which accused the Nepalese Maoists of soiling the Great Helmsman's memory, armed the palace against the rebels. Yet a year later, as the royal regime faced massive popular protests, Beijing distanced itself from the monarchy and befriended the Nepalese Maoists.

Chinese policy toward Nepal has been marked by much ambiguity, which both Beijing and Kathmandu have benefited from. One school of thought sees limited Chinese interest in Nepal, where phases of Beijing's assertiveness are the exception. In keeping with its foreign policy of unsentimental pragmatism, this school contends, China could easily concede Nepal as part of India's sphere of influence.

Chinese assertiveness, however, is likely to grow as its interests in Nepal go beyond the issue of Tibet to encompass its wider South Asian strategy. Nepal is only country that maintains diplomatic representation in Lhasa and Beijing reminds Kathmandu with ever greater regularity the responsibility that flows with the privilege. Enticing Nepal with promises of greater commercial benefits as part of its massive investments in Tibet, Beijing is intent on committing Nepal to firm political, security, economic and cultural agreements.

Should tradition become a more dominant part of Chinese regional diplomacy - as also seems likely - Nepal's status as a former tributary to the Middle Kingdom is likely to drive Beijing's policy. This is bound to raise anxiety levels in India, whose own relations with China sit uneasily atop planks of cooperation, competition and confrontation that are vulnerable to extra-regional pressures.

SINO-INDIAN RIVALRY FUELS NEPAL'S TURMOIL

Massive torchlight parades, clashes between the police and demonstrators, vows to bring the Nepalese government to its knees, a tottering United Nations peace process, and barely concealed great-power sparring between China and India. Clearly, Nepal is in crisis. This week, a bough of Nepal's Maoists declared the autonomy of the Nepalese state of Kirat, a move that might lead to the total collapse of the Nepalese peace process and the return of the Maoists to insurgency against the central government:

The agitating Unified Maoists Party has declared the Autonomous State of Monday, November 9, 2009. The Maoist Party politburo member and the coordinator of Kirat State Uprising Committee, Mr. Gopal Kirati, amid the presence of hundreds of Maoist cadres, had made the declaration in Diktel of Khotang District.

So far, Western media have reported remotely and somewhat uncomprehendingly on the massive demonstrations in Kathmandu led by the Communist Party of Nepal (Maoist), with a marked lack of interest. This perhaps reflects the shared desire of the Indian, Chinese and Western governments not to inflame the situation with excessive attention and rhetoric. The CPN-

M has vowed to bring 300,000 activists to the capital to shut down the government.

Inexorably and almost invisibly, Nepal has emerged as the focus of the competition between India and China to seize the strategic advantage along the Himalayas.

India moved first, helping to orchestrate the fall of the incompetent and stubbornly independent 240-year-old Nepalese monarchy in 2007. Nepal's King Gyanendra had conducted a bloody, ineffectual campaign against a Nepalese Maoist insurgency, incurring New Delhi's wrath in the process by turning to Beijing for arms.

India's foreign secretary at the time, Shyam Saran, arranged an unholy alliance of the Maoist insurgency and disaffected pro-Indian politicians in Kathmandu. This alliance toppled the monarchy and put a nascent parliamentary democracy in its place, in a scenario reminiscent of the cycle of Indian-inspired unrest that extinguished the monarchy and independence of the Kingdom of Sikkim in 1975. It was assumed that the Maoists, author of a good number of bloody outrages during the insurgency, would emerge from Nepal's parliamentary elections as a relatively unpopular fringe party, leaving control of parliament to a melange of pro-Indian middle-of-the-road parties.

However, in a development that undoubtedly caused India a great deal of dismay and may have even disconcerted the Leninist stalwarts of the Nepalese Maoists, the 2008 elections gave the Maoists - organized as the CPN-M under their leader, Pushpa Kamal Dahal (aka Prachanda) a commanding plurality of 38%, twice as many votes as the nearest challenger.

Prachanda was sworn in as prime minister on August 15, 2008, after months of maneuvering and negotiations. Instead of paying his first official visit to New Delhi - as was the tradition of Nepalese prime ministers under the monarchy - Prachanda jetted to Beijing for the closing ceremonies of the Beijing Summer Olympic Games. He further endeared himself to China with a vigorous crackdown on anti-Chinese demonstrations by Tibetan emigres that had ignited after the unrest in Tibet and in the run-up to the Olympics.

The Institute for Defence Studies and Analyses, an Indian think-tank affiliated with the Defence Ministry, described the accelerated bloom in Sino-Nepali relations under the Prachanda government: In fact, 12 high-level Chinese delegations, including two military teams, visited Nepal in the course of 2008-2009. During these visits, China has repeatedly assured economic, technological and military aid to Nepal. The Maoist-led government was also asked to adopt a "One-China" policy, not to allow Nepalese land be used for anti-China activities, take strong action against Tibetan refugees and grant special facilities for Chinese investments in strategic sectors. Beijing has also initiated track-II diplomacy with Nepal and invited Nepalese scholars to undertake visits to Chinese think-tanks.

Some of the important visits from China to Nepal were:

- February 25, 2009: Assistant Chinese Foreign Minister Hu Zhengyue led a 14-member delegation.
- February 19, 2009: Liu Hongcai, vice minister of the International Department of the Central Committee of the Communist Party of China (CPC), led a delegation to take part in the inaugural ceremony of the 8th convention of the Unified Marxist Leninist in Butwal.
- February 10, 2009: A high-level Peoples Liberation Army (PLA) delegation, one of the largest delegations in two months, arrived in Nepal.
- December 6, 2008: Lieutenant General Ma Xiaotian, deputy chief of General Staff of the PLA headed a 10-member delegation. China agreed to provide US$2.61 million worth of security assistance to Nepal.
- December 1, 2008: China's Foreign Minister Yang Jiechi visited Nepal.
- July 24, 2008: Chinese Vice Minister for Foreign Affairs, Wu Dawei, visited Nepal. He pledged a grant assistance of 100 million yuan (US$15 million) as economic and technical cooperation.

- March 4, 2008: Assistant Minister for Foreign Affairs of China, He Yafei, undertook a three-day visit to Nepal.

Nepal's engagements with China have also increased manifold with the visit of delegations both at state and non-state levels. Apart from visits at the official levels, private visits by political leaders, journalists and academicians are also sponsored by China as part of public diplomacy. During these visits, Chinese authorities have reportedly assured all kinds of support to the Maoist government in its efforts aimed at laying the foundation for a "New Nepal".

For the Nepalese Maoists, growing Chinese engagement is a win-win situation in line with their "policy of equidistance", which has been deliberately adopted to counter-balance India's influence in Nepal.

The increasing level of bilateral engagement also indicates that China is wooing Nepal as a new strategic partner. This has been confirmed by the statements made by various Chinese officials. For example, on February 16, 2009, Chinese Foreign Minister Yang Jiechi said in Beijing that China would prefer to work with Nepal on the basis of a strategic partnership.

In fact, Vice Minister of International Department of the Central Committee of Communist Party of China, Liu Hongcai, said in Kathmandu in February 2009 that "we oppose any move to interfere in the internal affairs of Nepal by any force". Similarly, on November 4, 2008, Liu Hong Chai, international bureau chief of the Communist Party of China, stated, "China will not tolerate any meddling from any other country in the internal affairs of Nepal - our traditional and ancient neighbor.

In passing, it should be renowned that the Nepalese Maoists are not enamored of post-Mao Chinese communism, describing it as "revisionist". Their distaste for China's current leadership was reinforced by the fact that China sold arms to King Gyanendra to combat their insurgency.

The Nepalese Maoists, together with Peru's ferocious Shining Path insurgents, have affiliated themselves with the

Revolutionary International Movement, organized by American Marxist Bob Avakian. Avakian supported the notorious Gang of Four in China and left the United States for France to avoid criminal charges after an obstreperous demonstration in 1979 at the White House sought to disrupt paramount leader Deng Xiaoping's visit.

Prachanda considers his "Prachanda Path" as embodying the line of pure ideological succession from Karl Marx, Vladimir Lenin and Mao Zedong, and the CPN-M's reachout to China was very much a matter of geopolitical necessary, not ideological affinity.

Prachanda had also stated his intention to renegotiate the friendship treaty between Nepal and India, characterizing it as "unequal". In January 2009, he also raised India's ire in a row over the Pashupatinath temple in Kathmandu. The Hindu temple of Lord Shiva is a UN Educational, Scientific and Cultural Organization World Heritage site and also served as the seat of Nepal's national deity.

Traditionally, its priests have been Brahmins from south India, but the CPN-M government engineered their removal (with a helping hand in the form of a mob allegedly provided by the Maoists militant Young Communist League) and replacement by Nepalese priests. Much unhappiness ensued, with the Indians joined in their outrage by ex-king Gyanendra. In the wake of an unfavorable Supreme Court ruling, the Indian priests were reinstated.

The CPN-M government finally came a cropper in May 2009 in a dispute over the resistance of the army chief, Rookmangood Katawal, following the prime minister's orders on the matter of bringing new recruits into the Nepalese army - a sensitive issue that affected the clout and integration status of the Maoists2 forces under the peace agreement. Prachanda removed Katawal, but President Ram Baran Yadav reinstated him the same day. Prachanda declared Yadav's move unconstitutional; the Maoists withdrew from the government and went into opposition. Madhav Kumar Nepal, former general secretary of the

Communist Party of Nepal (Unified Marxist-Leninist) took over as prime minister. Beyond the maneuverings and disagreements - exacerbated by the ambiguity of the peace agreement, the bad faith and suspicion by all parties and, one would speculate, India's desire to wedge the CPN-M's support and cobble together a pro-Indian majority in parliament - was the shadow of Sino-Indian competition.

The Nepalese army enjoys close relations with its Indian counterpart, and Katawal was seen as a pro-Indian force in Nepalese politics. India assiduously tends to its relationships with pro-Indian politicians inside Nepal and the current government is identified as pro-Indian. Even the CPN-M is rumoured to contain pro-Indian assets or even factions.

The current pro-Indian government has attempted, with little success, to soldier on without the CPN-M. Nepal has suffered through six months of political gridlock as a result. The Maoists have insisted they will not return to parliament until the principle of "civilian control" - apparently the supremacy of parliament and the prime minister over the president - is acknowledged.

Prachanda visited China in October at the head of an eight-person CPN-M delegation. It held four rounds of talks with the CCP. In a rather remarkable display of consideration towards an opposition party leader, Chinese President Hu Jintao hosted Prachanda as guest of honor at China's 11th National Games in Shandong and met with him privately for 25 minutes. It is unclear what explicit or implicit encouragement Prachanda received from China. Beijing is probably not interested in inflaming its tense relations with India by openly taking sides in the current crisis.

After Prachanda's visit, the Telegraph Nepal reported :

[Prachanda] revealed that "China has the support to the agitation sponsored by his party". Prachanda also revealed that he has brought only positive thinking from his week-long trip to China. "The outcome of my visit to China is that we need not focus ourselves on agitation and war rather focus on development and peace," Prachanda added. He... maintained that the Maoists2 party agitation enjoys the Chinese support. He however did not reveal what sort of support will the Chinese regime extend to the Maoists2 party of Nepal in their so-called agitation.

What undoubtedly concerns the CPN-M's adversaries inside Nepal is the fact that Prachanda has the resources and ambition to drive events inside the country, even if he is bluffing about the extent of his Chinese support. Telegraph Nepal's report that Nandkishor Pasan, the commander of the Maoist's military force, the People's Liberation Army, is now in China and that a key CPN-M military strategist also plans to go to China does nothing to dispel the impression that Prachanda enjoys China's support for his actions.

In any case, after his return to Nepal, Prachanda announced a program of mass action designed to bring the government to heel and facilitate the CPN-M's return to the government under favorable conditions.

The CPN-M organized mass demonstrations around the country, cutting the highway links between Kathmandu and outlying districts, and leading confrontational marches to the government secretariat, the Singha Durbar. The Maoists also conventional support from a surprising source, the United Nations.

The UN, concerned that Nepal will be unable to generate a new constitution, that the peace process will collapse, and that the aggrieved Maoists will restart their insurgency, has urged the present administration to back down and form a government of national unity with the Maoists.

UN Secretary General Ban Ki-moon's remarks at the end of October in support of a national unity government, made in response to a request to extend the mandate of the UN Mission in Nepal, which is trying to supervise the integration of Maoist forces into the army under the peace agreement. were construed as interference in Nepalese affairs by the current government. Ban's remarks no doubt irritated India and the United States;

the US, while keeping clear of the Nepalese imbroglio and supporting the UN process, is undoubtedly not pleased at the prospect that the Nepalese Maoists - still on the State Department's terror list - will come out on top again.

Now, it is reported that Prachanda approved the declaration of autonomy in Kirat. By doing so, the CPN-M has inched up to, if not actually crossed, a red line that might trigger the collapse of the peace process and a return to the insurgency.

3

Sino-Nepalese Relations: Overshadowed by Federalism

The recent official visit by Maoist honcho Pushpa Kamal Dahal (aka 'Prachanda') to China highlights how keenly China is following domestic developments in Nepal. For the Chinese establishment, Nepal is the soft underbelly of its Tibet (Xinjiang) Autonomous Region. For more than a decade, events here have not been very encouraging. While its giant neighbours to the north and south have been going from economic strength to strength, the economic growth rate here has not even touched 5%. All the political leaders have shown little vision in solving the problems of the country. The political instability per se has been very disappointing for the Chinese leadership and also because it opens possibilities for Indian interference in its domestic affairs. China expects that Nepal adheres strictly to the policy of "equidistance" between Beijing and New Delhi. It is also not amused when leaders proclaim that Nepal champions the 'one China policy' but do little to curb the activities of Tibetan radicals on its soil. Chinese leaders are very much aware that a stable neighborhood is conducive to an enabling environment for their own domestic objectives.

The Chinese leadership also closely followed the antics of the now defunct Constituent Assembly (CA). They were not very happy with the discussions on federalism and ethnic politics, especially the demand for ethnic demarcated provinces/states. The Chinese are fully aware that the Maoists are championing this cause. The Chinese may have sought assurances that this would not lead to a weakening of the body politic. Dahal did not specifically point out this reason, but mentioned other reasons as to why he was invited and given red-carpet treatment. After all, he met President XI Jinping, the Vice President and other top decision-makers, the first politician from South Asia to do so. He also met a key adviser and expert on Nepalese affairs, Professor Wang Hongwei, who plays the same role in China as Prof. S.D. Muni of the JNU University played in India in the "peace process". Dahal claims that he has "emotional and ideological links" with Professor Wang.

One reason that Dahal mention as to why he was invited was the ideological proximity of the Maoists and the Chinese Communist Party. He claimed that his party's seventh general convention had proclaimed a new road for economic development by emphasizing enhanced production and economic growth in a "peaceful" manner, instead of merely talking about revolution. Apparently, the Chinese party leaders had taken this new line positively as ideologically both parties wanted to make the people economically prosperous. This was a tall claim and quite preposterous as the UCPN-Maoist was nowhere near the modernizing campaigns of their ostensible fraternal party. The Chinese most probably would not like to be placed in the same boat as the Nepalese Maoists! However, some in the leadership may expect them to come out again on top in the next parliamentary/CA elections and, therefore, retaining some influence over the Maoists would be a good bet. Dahal has also made the cock-eyed claim that his party alone is capable of governing the nation! The Chinese may also play it safe and invite the leaders of the other 'major' parties.

Another reason mentioned by Dahal was the strategic security of Tibet. Here too he contended and made claims that had no foundation in reality. He alleged that the Chinese wanted to strengthen relations with the biggest political party. He asserted that the UCPN-Maoist was a party with strong public support and ideologically close to the CPC. He forgot that with the dissolution of the CA, the relative strength of the various parties are unimportant and the results of the next elections are still in the stars. Moreover, the CPC fully favours a market-style of economy which the UCPN-Maoist has yet to adopt. He also avowed that he was the chairman of the 'High Level Political Committee' and close contact with him would consolidate political stability in Nepal. By extrapolative argument he extends this to the security of Tibet! This is indeed laughable.

There is completely no doubt that China genuinely supports all efforts to maintain political stability in Nepal and to conclude the peace and constitution-drafting processes at the earliest. Only then would Chinese assistance for economic development bear fruit. In this connection, at the first stage, China was also willing to extend their railway line from Shigatse to the Nepalese border. Dahal's visit must be seen as the first step in strengthening relations with the new order of things in their southern neighbor. The UCPN-Maoist has no cogent arguments to support their stand that ethnic federalism will not result in instability and anarchism. The only reason why the UCPN-Maoist are supporting the various ethnic groups is because they want to garner their support in the coming elections and to consolidate their power.

Dahal and Baburam Bhattarai also want to be accepted as 'progressive bahuns'. There is no doubt that Nepal has many ethnicities with diverse language, culture, history and religion. There is no question of dishonoring this diversity. But the political unity of the country cannot be endangered by allowing only some ethnic groups to have their own provinces/states in a future state restructuring. Some groups have undoubtedly faced discrimination and humiliation, but these can be rectified quickly if the leaders have the political will. Unfortunately, the Maoists and the leaders of various ethnic groups want to go from the present political unity to a form of 'balkanization'. Some narrow-minded and egotistical ethnic 'little kings' are already dreaming of their own future fiefdoms. The Chinese leaders have no doubt realized that the Maoists are on the wrong path with their support of "ethnic federalism" which will not work in a small, fractured country like Nepal. They are, therefore, rightly worried about the future of Nepal under a possible Maoist leadership.

China itself is a model of ethnic harmony. All ethnic groups enjoy all the political rights like the majority Han population. But not all ethnic groups have their own province or 'autonomous region' Languages and culture are not suppressed. However, to preserve the unity of the country Mandarin Chinese is the lingua franca. Similarly, Nepali must remain the common language for all (this is rejected by the ethnic leaders who make the absurd claim of Gorkhali domination). Like in China, all ethnic groups in Nepal have space to develop themselves without having to establish ethnic-identity based provinces with the tyranny of a minority over the majority. This would be worst-case scenario, not only for Nepal, but for China too.

CHINA'S GROWING POWER IN NEPAL: IMPLICATIONS ON TIBETAN REFUGEES

There are more than 20,000 Tibetans residing in Nepal, living with no defined legal status as the Nepalese law does not recognise the rights of refugees under the principal treaties that govern their status under international law. Provided they have a Nepalese "refugee identity certificate" (RC), Tibetans who arrived before 1989 can remain in Nepal with certain limited rights. Most live in an uneasy state of subsistence, principally in a small number of isolated settlements in the Kathmandu valley and Pokhara. Tibetans residing in Nepal are essentially stateless. They are neither citizens nor refugees under the law, and they possess neither the legal status nor the rights with which to improve their welfare. Moreover, legally resident Tibetans cannot travel to certain "restricted" regions of Nepal, typically those near the border with China. Nepal has not acceded to the 1951 Refugee Convention, or its 1967 Protocol, and has no domestic asylum law. In the absence of formal refugee legislation, the Government of Nepal has embraced different approaches for different refugee populations. Given the nearby scenario, the state of Tibetan refugees' condition in Nepal continues to be grim, more or less, due to the Chinese mounting pressure in the region. According to the latest United States State Department Human Rights Report for 2009, Tibetans repatriated from Nepal reportedly suffered torture, including electric shocks, exposure to cold and severe beatings and were forced to perform heavy physical labour...Tibetan refugees in Nepal also witnessed curtailment of freedom of expression as police imposed restrictions on demonstrations and sometimes detained demonstrators.

As China continues to rise as one of the Asian giants and a superpower in the making, its dealings with the Tibetan movement has scaled the borders and one can observe the alteration in international political dynamics on this issue. Regarding Sino-Nepal relations, on the inter-national front there has been mounting concern over the growing economic relationship between Kathmandu and Beijing, and the escalating ignorance of human rights and fundamental freedoms of Tibetan refugees in Nepal.

In the beginning of March itself, when the Tibetan exiles marked the 51st anniversary of Tibet's invasion by China, the Nepal Government deployed more than 500 policemen in Kathmandu. Also, the Chinese authorities snapped most links, including the Friendship Bridge, between the former Buddhist kingdom and its neighbour Nepal.

It also insisted to control Nepal's nearly 1800 km open border with India, to tab the Tibetans' movement from this side. Moreover, the detainment of Thinley Gyatso by the Nepal Police also hit the news headlines. Gyatso is considered as the unofficial messenger of the Dalai Lama. In addition to this, recent months have witnessed the Nepal Police conducting raids in areas around the Tibetan religious shrine of Boudhanath, a major pilgrimage destination for Tibetan Buddhists. Besides, at least about 25 Tibetan refugees, imprisoned in Nepal for protesting against the Chinese occupation of their homeland, began a hunger strike, demanding their release. However, the Nepal authorities have made it clear that the 'protests against friendly nations such as China will not be tolerated'.

China's power on Nepal is not a new issue, especially when it comes to the Tibetan question. Historically, the Nepalese royals used to have a close and cordial relationship with China. As per the historical records, in the eighteenth century China and Nepal signed the Sino-Nepalese Treaty, to put a halt to Kathmandu's adventurism in Tibet.

The accord was in itself marked by Chinese political domination in the region. During twentieth century, after a lot of crests and troughs in the relationship, both the countries concluded a treaty based on the "five principles of friendly relations". In contemporary times, both the countries are working together to gain economic prosperity, and to contain India's emerging status in Asia. The very foundation of Nepal's policy towards China is to counter India's influence in the region. Moreover, Nepal supports the 'One-China policy', which considers both Tibet and Taiwan as inseparable parts of China and forbids its territory to be used for anti-China propaganda. With the collapse of the Nepali monarchy under King Gyanendra in 2006 and the ascendance of the Unified Communist Party of Nepal (Maoist) and the Unified Communist Party of Nepal (Marxist-Leninist), Nepal has been constantly working on to cultivate deeper economic ties with China. One glaring example of Sino-Nepal relations and its influence on Tibetan refugees was witnessed during the Beijing Olympics in 2008, when the Nepal Government came down heavily on the Tibetan refugees' protest against China.

Exhibiting a alike trend of Beijing's escalating influence in Kathmandu, the International Campaign for Tibet Report 2009 brought to light the growing influence of China over the Nepali Government, judicial system, civil society and media. It further revealed how the Tibetans are experiencing a rise in harassment and extortion, more restrictions on their movements and greater difficulty in securing education and jobs than ever before. As the situation continues to remain the same, the United Kingdom's 12th Annual Report on Human Rights has voiced its serious concern about the Tibetan refugees' freedom of expression in Nepal. According to media reports, there is an increasing despair among the community in Kathmandu, particularly among the most vulnerable, that is, those without papers. The Nepali Government had made a decision that all Tibetan shops, restaurants and businesses be officially registered. To do that, one needs 50,000 Nepali rupees ($ 500) and proper residence status in Nepal.

The issue of Tibetan refugees has forever made headlines in the international community who look forward for the resolution of the issue. International entities like the United Nations (UN), United States (US), European Union (EU) and international donors are playing a vital role in providing relief to the Tibetan refugees. For over three decades and six presidential administrations, the US has remained steadfast in its "One-China" policy. Reiterating the one-China principle and recognising that Tibet is part of the China, the US Government under the leadership of President Barack Obama in 2009 supported the early resumption of talks between Beijing and representatives of the exiled Tibetan spiritual leader, the Dalai Lama. Moreover in 2009, US Secretary of State Hillary Clinton vowed not to let human rights concerns hinder cooperation with China. However, in 2010 the US State Department singled out China alongside Iran, Cuba, North Korea and Myanmar as among the worst rights abusers in 2009, which led to a series of terse exchanges between the US and China. In February 2010, the Obama Administration invited the non-governmental organisations to submit their proposals to run a one-year-long project supporting the Tibetan refugees in India, Nepal, and to a lesser extent, Bhutan. Proposals targeted solely or predominantly to the Tibetan refugee population in Nepal come to about $ 250,000. The programmes for Tibetan refugees focus mainly on protection, including prevention and response, to gender-based violence, health and nutrition, livelihoods and education, water and sanitation sectors in Nepal.

Over the years, the European Parliament has followed proceedings in Tibet closely. In 2009, the European Parliament has also urged China to negotiate and resume talks with the Dalai Lama's representatives with a view to bringing about a "positive, meaningful change in Tibet", not ruling out autonomy for the region, a solution that Members of the European Parliament (MEPs) believe need not compromise China's territorial integrity. In its key demand, the Parliament urges the Chinese Government to consider the Memorandum for Genuine Autonomy for the Tibetan People of November 2008 as a basis for substantive discussion leading towards positive, meaningful change in Tibet, consistent with the principles outlined in the Constitution and laws of the People's Republic of China.

The resolution called on the European Union (EU) Council Presidency to adopt a declaration on the same lines. Again in March 2010, the MEPs held a debate on the current situation of Tibet and voiced their concerns about the human rights situation. During the debate EU Commissioner and Vice-President of the European Commission Maros Sefcovic said: The EU position does not leave any room for misunderstanding. Therefore, let me stress: the EU respects the sovereignty and territorial integrity of China, including Tibet. We respect the 'one China' policy... However, we have always supported peaceful reconciliation through dialogue between the Chinese authorities and the representatives of the Dalai Lama. This dialogue has to be constructive and substantive, addressing all core issues such as the preservation of Tibet's unique culture, religion and traditions and the need to achieve a system of meaningful autonomy for Tibet within the Chinese Constitution.

China has played an important, if at times hidden, role in the Nepali Government's crackdown on Tibetan demonstrations. The unusual number of statements from Nepali leaders reiterating the ban on "anti-China" activities suggests increasing pressure from Beijing. China has long claimed that the bedrock of its foreign policy is "non-interference" in the internal affairs of other countries. Yet it has directly involved itself in Nepali affairs. China's ambassador has publicly exerted China's influence on the Nepali Government through strong and frequent statements, calling for the arrest of protesters and urging the government to take strong action. With the Chinese influence creating deep impression on the Nepal's politics, the Tibetans refugees in Nepal face another challenge for their survival.

CHINA–NEPAL RELATIONS

The bilateral relations between the Federal Democratic Republic of Nepal and the People's Republic of China have been friendly and defined by Nepal's policy of balancing the competing influence of China and Nepal's southern neighbour India, the only two neighbours of the Himalayan country.

Nepal, Tibet and China

Nepal's historical relations with China (and Tibet) have been shaped by conflicts over territory and the control of Tibet. After the Nepal-Tibet-China War (1789-1792), Nepal was forced to sign a treaty stipulating the payment of tribute to China after the latter defeated Nepalese forces in Tibet. China refused Nepal's request for assistance during Anglo-Nepalese War (1814–16), and the latter's defeat led to the establishment of the British Empire in India, the dominant power in the region. Nepal continued to try to balance the influence of China and British India. Through the tenth quinquennial mission to China (1837), Under the leadership of Chautariya Pushkar Shah, the Nepalese government had requested for the Ching court to either send troops or send subsidy of twenty million rupees to oppose British, but the Nepalese delegation was said to have met with a stern refusal of its petition for monetary aid, and opposition to the furtherance of hostility by Nepal against the British. Nepal invaded Tibet in 1855, but the Nepalese-Tibetan War ended soon after China intervened, the Treaty of Thapathali, concluded in March 1856, recognized the special status of China and Nepal's commitment to help Tibet in the event of foreign aggression. In the 19th century, Nepal aligned itself with the British Raj in India and supported its invasion of Tibet in 1908. When China sought to claim Tibet in 1910, Nepal sided with Tibet and Britain and broke relations with China after Tibet drove Chinese forces out in 1911.

Diplomatic Relations and Nepalese Neutrality

The 1950–1951 Invasion of Tibet by the People's Liberation Army raised significant concerns of security and territorial integrity in Nepal, drawing Nepal into a close relationship with extensive economic and military ties. China ordered restrictions on the entry of Nepalese pilgrims and contacts with Tibet, and increased its support for the Communist Party of Nepal, which was opposed to the Nepalese monarchy. The 1950 Indo-Nepal Treaty of Peace and Friendship that had established a close Indo-Nepalese relationship on commerce, defence and foreign relations, was increasingly resented in Nepal, which began seeing it as an encroachment of its sovereignty and an unwelcome extension of Indian influence; the deployment of an Indian military mission in Nepal in the 1950s increased these concerns.

In 1955, Nepal established diplomatic relations with the People's Republic of China and exchanged resident ambassadors by 1960. In 1956, both nations signed a new treaty terminating the Treaty of Thapathali of 1856 and Nepal recognised Tibet as a part of China. In 1960, Nepal and China signed a boundary settlement agreement and a separate treaty of peace and friendship. Nepal also began supporting the change of China's seat in the United Nations. In 1961, Nepal and China agreed to build an all-weather road connecting the Nepalese capital Kathmandu with Tibet. During the Sino-Indian War of 1962, Nepal maintained neutrality.

Economic and Strategic Relations

In the 1970s King Birendra of Nepal proposed Nepal as a "zone of peace" between India and China and in the 1980s, Nepal began importing Chinese weaponry in contravention of its 1950 treaty with India and has since sought to establish extensive military cooperation in a move to reduce perceived Indian influence. When the United States, United Kingdom and India refused to supply arms to the regime of King Gyanendra of Nepal, who had assumed direct rule to suppress the Maoist insurgency during the Nepalese civil war (1996–2006), China responded by dispatching arms to Nepal, in spite of the ideological affinity of the Maoists with China. After the peace process and national elections in Nepal in 2008, the new Maoist-led government announced its intentions to scrap Nepal's 1950 treaty with India, indicating a stronger move towards closer ties with China. In 2007-08, China began construction of a 770-kilometre railway connecting the Tibetan capital of Lhasa with the Nepalese border town of Khasa, connecting Nepal to China's wider national railway network.

Human Trafficking and Sex Trade

China is considered an emerging sex trafficking hub for Nepali girls Since the policy of an open border between China and Nepal, a large number of Nepalese women and girls in recent years have been sold into prostitution or as brides to Chinese men.

CHINA-NEPAL TIES ARRIVE AT NEW HEIGHTS

Nepal proved itself unwilling to allow a repeat of the mass Tibetan demonstrations that were held here from March to September 2008. Although the energy and numbers of last year's demonstrations surrounding the anniversary of the failed Tibetan uprising and Dalai Lama's flight into exile were not present this year, Nepalese riot police still took forcible measures to prevent a group of approximately 200 Tibetan demonstrators leaving the Boudha district of Kathmandu. A British activist named Daisy Karen Wood who attempted to dodge police and enter the Chinese Embassy carrying balloons and a Tibetan flag was quickly arrested.

Nepal's desire to quickly suppress events that would embarrass China, its massive northern neighbor, comes as no surprise. Ties between the two countries have been increasing in recent months. Nepalese Premier Pushpa Kamal Dahal Prachanda plans to travel to Beijing in mid-April or early May and sign what is being called the "Comprehensive Treaty" which will replace the 1960 "Peace and Friendship Treaty" between the two countries. The signing of the treaty will be followed by

China donating US$16.4 million in economic aid and becoming Nepal's chief international backer.

Historically, relations between Nepal and China have been relatively good. For centuries Nepal sent tribute bearing missions to China and acknowledged its superior regional force. The tension that did exist originated out of the perceived threat from India and contention over Tibet, which lies just 114 kilometers from Kathmandu.

Following China's refusal to give military assistance to Nepal during the Anglo-Nepalese war of 1814-1816, Nepal invaded Tibet in 1854. China quickly intervened and the Treaty of Thapathali was signed between the two countries in 1856. Nepal recognized China's supremacy in the region and agreed to provide assistance if Tibet was ever invaded by a foreign force.

When an armed British mission arrived in Tibet from India in 1905, however, Nepal did not intervene. Having come under the influence of British India after its loss in the Anglo-Nepalese war, Nepal went as far as to tell China that it would assist the Tibetans if they ever declared independence, provided it was within British interests. When the Tibetans used the chaos of the 1911 Revolution to expel the Chinese, Nepal broke ties with China altogether.

Relations were re-established in 1955 when the Chinese began sending soldiers into Tibet. With the British gone from India, Nepal recognized Tibet as a sovereign part of Chinese territory and in 1960, a year after Tibet's failed uprising and the Dalai Lama's flight into exile, the two countries signed the Treaty of Peace and Friendship, cementing strong ties that continue today.

Now the new "Comprehensive Treaty" will bring the two countries even closer. The treaty puts into place agreements that China will not attack Nepal and will respect its sovereignty, while Nepal will solidify its acceptance of the "One China" policy. Under the policy Tibet, Taiwan, and Hong Kong are stated as indisputable parts of Chinese territory, and Nepal will not allow anti-Chinese activities on its soil.

Nepal proved its willingness to fulfil such promises in the days surrounding the 50th anniversary of the March 10, 1959, Tibetan Uprising. The day after a visit by Chinese assistant foreign minister Hu Zhengyue, who arrived in Nepal last month leading a 14-member delegation, 27 Tibetans monks were arrested in Kathmandu. Eighteen were released and nine turned over to the United Nations and deported to India. The streets around the two Chinese embassies in Kathmandu were also closed off, declared "protest-free zones", and staffed with police who had orders to arrest anyone demonstrating nearby. Additional arrests of Tibetan activists were carried out and demonstrators were quickly confronted.

China welcomes these closer relations, with the additional support for its "One China" policy and assistance in controlling the more than 20,000 Tibetan refugees living in Nepal. The refugees, if they ever gave up the aging Dalai Lama's method of peaceful negotiation, could use Nepal's difficulty to control its northern border to launch attacks on Chinese forces in Tibet - something which Khampa fighters did with short-lived US Central Intelligence Agency support in the late 1960s and early 1970s.

China views the establishing of closer relations with Nepal as an important step in its competition with India for regional influence. "China now seems to view Nepal as a vital bridge toward South Asia as part of strategy of encircling India," said Nepal expert Sanjay Upadya.

However, Nepal's interest in expanding relations with China is more complicated. The country has long sought to balance the interests of India and China, the two regional powers it lies between. Since the signing of the Indo-Nepalese Treaty of 1950, India has come to heavily dominate Nepalese politics. While the treaty acknowledges Nepal's sovereignty, clauses in the agreement give India a greater amount of control over Nepal than the Maoist government would prefer.

It is the overbearing influence of India that has pushed Nepal's Maoist government decisively towards China. The shift has been so strong that Premier Prachanda went as far as to break the long-standing tradition of Nepalese heads of state making their first foreign trip to India, instead visiting China, ostensibly to attend the opening ceremony of the 2008 Summer Olympic Games in Beijing.

The move toward China does not necessarily mean that Nepal is breaking ties with India - the government rather seeks to decrease Indian influence. As Nepalese journalist Narendra Prasad Upadhyaana said, "It is not that China is ideal. It is only to neutralize India. Historically, socially, and culturally Nepal is closer to India. On a political level however the Maoist government wants to avoid being controlled by India as much as possible."

This new partnership with China comes at a time of great necessity for Nepal. The country is facing growing insecurity which many experts in Kathmandu believe could escalate into a crisis within the next year. With the decade-long civil war resulting in the overthrow of the monarchy, Nepal is facing the challenges of a newly democratic nation that has innumerable political groups and organizations vying for a tiny amount of resources amid growing insecurity.

The country's police and army have become polarized, with different groups supporting the Maoists, opposition forces, and even the return of the monarchy. A number of journalists have been attacked in the past six months. Amid simmering discontent within the Maoist Army, which refuses to integrate with the regular army and continues to recruit soldiers, the expected flood of returning immigrants from jobs in the Middle East and Malaysia due to the global financial crisis makes Nepal's immediate future seem grim.

Perhaps the most dangerous threat to the country's stability, however, is the deteriorating situation in the southern Terai region. Members of the Tharu indigenous group recently declared a 14-day strike, shut down roads, and engaged in near daily clashes with police that left four people dead. The Tharus were demanding to be recognized as distinct from the Madhesis, the ethnic group that most indigenous people from the Terai are lumped into. Government negotiation ended the strike only after the situation had become so tense that police were ordered to escort petrol trucks through checkpoints and the price of fruit and vegetables in some Kathmandu markets had nearly doubled.

Though the strike has ended, the Tarai will continue to be an issue for Nepal. The indigenous groups demand that a new constitution divide the country into ethnically based autonomous states, something that could spell disaster as many of the ethnic groups in Nepal do not even acknowledge the others' right to exist.

The idea of "ethnic federalism" will not be given up easily though. According to Dr Om Gurung, an indigenous rights leader in Kathmandu, the establishment of ethnically based autonomous federal states was a key promise of the Maoists during the civil war. Recently, however, the government has begun backing away from the promise, and most experts believe that such a system would set the stage for future conflict. Indigenous leaders are adamant, however, that Nepal's diverse nature requires such a system.

Dangerously, after the Maoist victory in the civil war and their subsequent international recognition, organizations in Nepal realized that agitation and violence does indeed work as a means of achieving political goals. With 70 identified armed groups operating across Nepal, most the wings of political organizations, the government and safety of the people are severely threatened. How the indigenous groups will choose to assert themselves if their demands for autonomous states are not met is still unknown.

Unless the government manages to control this growing unrest, the Maoist revolution may in fact prove to have just been the catalyst for a longer struggle for territory, resources, and representation in Nepal that the country will have to face as it struggles over the course of the next year to write a new constitution and make the difficult transition from a country at war to a country at peace. This is a desire that can be assisted by a closer relationship with China. Over the past years China has proven itself willing to give large amounts of no-strings-attached cash and support for infrastructure building to countries that support its "One China" policy and allow it to expand its growing global influence. This is in contrast with most Western countries which demand that aid goes to specific projects and require greater oversight regarding where the funds end up. While the lack of transparency in Nepal means that much of the aid will be lost due to corruption, there is enough being offered that some effect will be felt by the population.

Along with the $16.4 million donation, after the signing of the "Comprehensive Treaty" China will add an additional 770 kilometers to the Kathmandu-Khasa highway in Tibet, effectively linking Nepal with China's massive internal railway system. Additional roads connecting Tibet and Nepal will be built and Chinese products are increasingly replacing Indian products, something that most Nepalese appreciate because of the lower cost. "China's products are sound to our pockets," said Nepalese journalist Narendra Prasad Upadhyaana.

The additional access to China is also expected to stimulate economic growth in Tibet, something that the Chinese government considers key to making the Tibetans drop their demands for autonomy. Larger groups of tourists coming from Nepal, and Tibetan salt being sold to Nepal, certainly may lessen some of the Tibetans' anger towards China, but it will not quite be the salve that the Chinese government wants it to be. As one Tibetan activist in Kathmandu said, "China does not have human rights. Nepal is following that. They are bending over for China and letting the Chinese control the police and treat the Tibetans here like animals."

The closer relationship with China is also not being viewed favorably by Delhi. Earlier this month several Nepalese opposition politicians left for India, claiming the trip was for health reasons. Their visit coincides with the presence of Nepal's disposed King Gyanendra, who has been in India since last month for a wedding.

Although the Indian government allowed the Maoists to overthrow the monarchy, the new preference for China is making India reconsider its support. This is something that the Maoists must have expected. They are, however, reacting nervously to the opposition visit to India. "A new pact is being signed in New Delhi against the Maoist government," said the Janadisha newspaper, a mouthpiece for the Maoist Party.

"Delhi is encircling the Maoists," said Nepalese journalist Narendra Prasad Upadhyaana. "India brought them to power and now suddenly they have gone to the Chinese. And India and China still do not have cordial relations."

SINO-NEPAL RELATIONS: ECONOMIC AGENDA FOR A 21ST CENTURY STRATEGIC PARTNERSHIP

The fundamental question we, as Nepalese, must ask ourselves is this: is China a threat or an opportunity for Nepal? This author believes that it's an opportunity not just for Nepal but all of South Asia. And that is why all South Asian nations welcomed it into the SAARC as Observer—albeit India reluctantly: since, other than the George Fernandez who sees China as an undiluted threat, India is yet ambivalent. Being still undecided as to what, where and how much cooperation, coordination, competition, conflict or just communication for confidence building? Asia has emerged as the new geo political and geo-economical power house of the globe after around 300 years of imperialism and colonialism with total marginalization of the once flourishing Asian economies; exploited and left to forcibly trade with the metropolitan country only as slaves.

This structural change has been made possible, firstly, by the post-WW II rise of Japan from the ashes with its spellbinding economic miracle and its judicious adaptation of tradition with modernity during 1945-80. Japan laid the seeds of Asian geo-political and geo economic independence and self reliance: and implanted geo-psychological self confidence by virtue of its modernization found on its own civilization and cultural ethos. Thereafter, the four modernization drives of China, since the late 1970s to this day, rendered China as the world's factory for manufacturing of mass based, high quality consumer goods with intermediate technology maximizing economies of scale with economies of scope. And, since the 1990s, with the initiative of Prime Minister P V Narasimha Rao in India, Asia's renaissance is irreversible as India, reluctantly, launched its economic and financial reforms by dropping the ideology of Nehruvian socialism that engulfed Nepal too.

China is an opportunity for Nepal and South Asia –at least the Hindu Kush Himalayan regions of it—because, with China's new economic and development policy, the centre of gravity of its economic growth has and will move towards the hinterland of South West China and Central Asia from its currently dominant eastern seaboard. In the process, unfolding right before our eyes, unimagined opportunities with many new Silk Routes. It may be hypothesized that the 'centre' of Asia, henceforth, shall be in the regions of Tibet, Qinghai, Guansu, Sichuan, Kunming and Xianjian, which are all in the immediate neighbourhood of South and Central Asia. Nepal assumes a new geo strategic importance as the buffer between China and India –the Gangetic plains. Especially, as the huge defence build up in the Tibet plateau and the construction of the Karakoram highway and railroad connection from Beijing to Lhasa— and soon beyond to the borders of Nepal and Sikkim—make it that much more strategic, in depth and width, in the 21st century as compared to the 19 and 20th centuries.

China's high speed railway plan seeking to connect Kunming to Europe via the Central Asian Republics will, coupled with its plan to build gas and pipelines to meet its energy needs, will add a new dimension to regional connectivity by integrating Europe with Asia by land. Undoubtedly, one may expect Turkey and Russia to be a part of this process as the BRICST nations playing a major role in the 21st century multi polar world. China has already started an informal strategic partnership when it announced that it was to fund a $ 3 billion investment plan to build Lumbini as a world peace city to honour Lord Buddha in much the same manner as the Vatican and Mecca are to Christians and Muslims. This news is of immense geo psychological significance for all Nepalese as they now are starting to look North, so to speak, from the psychosis of an India locked, land-locked nation with no access to the High Seas. By all accounts, this investment decision signals a radical shift in Chinese foreign policy involving not just state to state diplomacy but, also, people to people diplomacy with space being given, henceforth, to Buddhism and Confucianism in Chinese society.

For a solid strategic partnership, given that 85% of Nepalese are Hindus, it behoves China to diversify its people to people diplomacy to embolden the world Hindus geo psychologically by allowing them to build a Holy City in the area of Mt Kailash and Lake Mansarovar funded by the global Hindu diaspora. With such acts of enlightened spiritualism forthcoming, China will surely win the hearts and minds of the Hindus, Buddhist and Bon peoples with its soft power, high voltage cultural diplomacy to build world heritage sites with or without UN engagement. Having the UN agency and the active involvement of the UN Secretary General, Ban Ki Moon, is a far sighted idea as it is in Nepal's interest to become the Zone of Peace and a neutral state with guarantees from the UN Security Council and all regional powers.

It may be underscored here that Nepa'sl ZOP concept was endorsed by 116 nations except India and its ally the erstwhile USSR. US Secretary of State, Hilary Clinton, while visiting India recently, has wisely recalled the relevance of the Congress of Vienna, 1814-15, for the emerging multi polar world of the 21st century to garner world peace and security. Hopefully, global diplomacy post NATO withdrawal from South Asia, will move towards a Congress of Kathmandu, a s the capital of SAARC, to create not one but three Zones of Peace in South Asia: namely, Nepal, Afghanistan and Kashmir. Failing this South Asia will become even more dangerous place than President Bill Clinton had originally imagined. Should the Congress of Kathmandu materialize it will liberate South Asia from the deadly stranglehold of its colonial history and raise it to being a Super Power on par with the US and China— if not greater. All it needs is for the Congress of Kathmandu is for SAARC to invite Russia and Turkey as Observer nations.

Political parties in Nepal must forge a national consensus on its foreign policy anchored on strategic partnerships with Bangladesh, China and India and a clear vision on its role in multilateral and regional diplomacy. One would hope that UN, WTO and SAARC would be core pillars of its foreign policy and we accede to as many international treaties as relevant. In particular Nepal must push all the coastal states to accede to the New York Convention on Land Locked States 1965 and ensure that as a land locked of the 21st century it provides transit rights to all its neighbouring states and also its peoples that wish to go to a third country as refugees.

Foreign policy must never be allowed to be hostage to any province of Nepal. It matters not which (ethnic or regional) province Lumbini falls under: an d if it does, then, political parties best agree to declare such heritage sites, be they cultural or natural, as central territory just as they would declare Special Economic Zones or Export Promotion Villages or Zones as falling under central jurisdiction.

Nepal sorely needs to develop new growth zones beyond the Kathmandu Valley and the Bagmati corridor. Pokhara, Lumbini and Mt Kailash-Mansarovar are solid opportunities to usher regional balance. They are the 'golden eggs' for Nepal's tourism and sooner it takes shape the better. One may suggest that Special Autonomous Development Authorities should be created in the spirit and letter of people-public-private -partnerships (4Ps, not 3Ps). Perhaps others for the proposed SEZ at Panchkhal, which should be a SAARC- SEZ that will allow value adding by all South Asian nations for exports to China. By no means should a moratorium be considered, as suggested by Kanak Mani Dixit, since the development show must go on, so to speak. The Prime Minister's Office must take full command over these programmes as it is likely to be hostage to bureaucratic bungling as it is heavily politicized and serves as fiefdoms of various bilateral and multilateral aid agencies.

Let Secretary General Ban Ki Moon and our UN Permanent Representative negotiate on the intricacies of whether the Lumbini Project should be managed by UNIDO or UNESCO or whatever. However, what Nepal should be seeking from China is to relocate its labour intensive manufacturing into the Pokhara- Lumbini growth axis to replicate the "flying geese" that Japan had set out for East and South East Asia to drive their industrialization process and eradicate poverty. What could be better for Nepal socially and economically than utilization of our human capital here in Nepal than to have the youth migrate overseas.

China has provided Nepal duty free access along with all other Least Developed Countries. A strategic partnership would necessitate that it be given new meaning with an Integrated Commodities Agreement (ICA) where a few commodities are targeted for exports to China seeking all manner of backward and forward linkages so as to transform the rural economy. One may use the FNCCI's One Village One Product concept for this bilateral export strategy. Nepal's competitive advantage lies in water resources, tourism, agriculture and agri-manufacturing, (including herbs, forestry, fisheries, floriculture and livestock), water and soil and mountain engineering (dams, roads, tunnels, irrigation); education and health.

It may be interest to China to joint venture with Nepalese educational institutions to set up a China-Nepal University for Multiculturalism, Science and Technology with the vision to bring, under one roof of learning, the Himalayan peoples to discover ways and means to create a green economy founded on their cultural heritage and eco-diversity. Development of nanotechnology to grapple with the challenges from climate change and finding ways and means to conserve and store energy could be other areas for strategic partnership along with advancement of herbal medicine. Exploration of minerals, gas and oil and collaboration in telecommunications and IT and soil engineering, land reclamation and disaster management will be mutually beneficial. China has the two largest banks in the world. It is time to have a Chinese branch bank in Nepal and similarly for a Nepali bank to be established inChina. A joint venture to start a Nepali Reinsurance Corporation would be extremely beneficial for Nepal's balance of payments as well as its insurance industry. Along with opening of bank branches, it would be most advantageous if China could provide a soft medium term loan to Nepal to permit it to move to a managed floating exchange regime with India such that the advantages of import substitution is not lost to it, which has indirectly been subsidizing Indian imports to Nepal with an undervalued foreign exchange rate.

In conclusion, the Budget Speech of 2005 lays down the correct vision for a Nepal in the era of the Asian renaissance : as a secular Hindu state wholly subscribing to social pluralism and political devolution; ; as a transit economy between South and central Asia; as a bridge country between two great civilizations; as a South Asian capital within SAARC; as the financial and arbitration centre of South Asia; as a regional centre for peace and disarmament; as the voice of the Himalayas in the world to save Planet Earth, and last but not least—as a boy politic that pragmatically yields the lead role for economic growth to the private sector based on dialogue, consultation and partnership with strict application of the rule of law and independent regulation of market forces.

What is a miss is political stability without which nothing will materialize— except Nepal being reduced to absurdities of inclusive politics in an ideological battleground over run by foreign intelligence agencies and a mafia economy of cartels and syndicates threatening regional peace and security. What is also amiss are national institutions for its international identity which can only be projected by Hinduism, Buddhism and the Monarchy restored. These three institutions will guarantee national unity, sovereignty, independence, pluralism and democracy—and the Congress of Kathmandu internationally guaranteed its territorial integrity and neutrality. A new Sino-Nepal Treaty of Peace and Friendship is eminently desirable.

Asian visionary statesman, Lee Kwan Yew, foresaw Tibet and Nepal as the core strategic fulcrums of Asia which is about to take form as we harness our vast water resources and opt for clean energy, land and river transportation; and seek culturally relevant solutions to global warming and global unhappiness in a world blinded by materialism and corrupted by infinite greed where money power has disenfranchised and alienated citizens of the traditional liberal democracies.

NEPALESE AUTOCRATS PLAY A CHINA-CARD

Why could Nepalese autocrats play a China-card effectively in the regional politics for continuing their unjust and undemocratic regime? Whenever Nepal had democratically elected governments, the Chinese autocrats lost the partners in autocratic governance giving way to the democratic countries such as India, the US, the UK and other European democratic governments to have more influence on the elected governments in Nepal than the Chinese Government. Naturally, often the Chinese Autocratic Proletarian Government got sidelined, and found ignored by elected governments in Nepal. The elected governments in Nepal tended to loosen their control over the Tibetan refugees in Nepal, and let them freely travel and engage in their activities for freedom in Tibet. Hence, the Chinese autocratic proletarian government always found democracy in Nepal as a threat to their oppressive rule in Tibet.

Whenever the Nepalese autocrats played the China-card, the first victims were the Tibetans fighting for freedom from the autocratic rule of the Chinese proletarian leaders, and another victim, of course, was the democracy in Nepal. This was true in 1960 when the former king Mahendra played the China-card to kill the infant democracy, and in 2005 when the current king Gyanendra played the China-card to throttle the flourishing democracy.

After the unification of small kingdoms and principalities into a present-day Nepal, King Prithvi Narayan Shah said, "Nepal is a yam sandwiched between two large stones." He was referring to India to the South and China to the North as two large stones, and Nepal as a yam in between them. He left his advice to his future generations to follow the policy of not aligning with only one side - either to the north or to the south in other words to achieve a good balance between them.

In balancing between the two powerful countries - one to the south and another to the north, the rulers of Nepal had sometimes played one against another when the situation favorable to do so arose. For example, in 1960s, king Mahendra played a China-card effectively for suppressing the opposition political activities on the borders with India. King Mahendra told the then-Indian Ambassador Shriman Narayan "Your Excellency, I am obliged for the sincere steps you have taken to bring about peace on our southern border. There are still a few stray cases of trespasses and conflicts here and there. But I do realize that it is not very easy to control such incidents completely along the long Indo-Nepal border of several hundred miles. I am sure your honest efforts would continue. On my part, I and my government have now decided to request China to abandon the eastern sector of the East-West Highway and initiate a fresh survey for another road somewhere in the middle regions of Nepal." At that time, Indian authorities did not want Chinese closer to Indian borders.

Indian Ambassador, Shriman Narayan replied, "I personally visited the Indo-Nepal border quite extensively and asked the district authorities to restrain effectively the Nepalese citizens from indulging in undesirable activities against the king and his government from the Indian soil. I also met a number of workers of the Nepali Congress in Uttar Pradesh, Bihar and Bengal and plainly told them that India would no longer allow them to operate against the friendly kingdom." King Mahendra suppressed the voices of Tibetan refugees in Nepal, and stopped any political activities of them from Nepal against he Peoples' Republic of China in 1960s. Later on, King Birendra also eliminated the Khampa rebels fighting against the Chinese rule in Tibet from the northern border of Nepal in 1970s.

Before taking over the executive power on February 1, 2005, King Gyanendra shut down the offices of Representatives of Dalai Lama and of Tibetan Refugees in Nepal. Obviously, this was done to keep the Chinese Government happy. The king was sure that India and the western countries would not support his actions of usurping the power from the elected government. So, he wanted to keep at least one neighbor happy and in his favour.

Then came the February-1 putsch staged by King Gyanendra keeping the whole country in darkness for a whole week by snapping communication lines and closing the media. Describing it as an internal matter, Beijing refrained from taking any stand on the King Gyanendra's February-1 takeover. Thus, China has taken a friendly attitude toward the king in Nepal. India, the US, the UK and the international community as a whole condemned the putsch and suspended the military supplies to the Royal Nepalese Army. The king could not convince the international community that his army would not use the arms and ammunition against the people fighting for fundamental human rights and democracy in the country. So, the embargo remained. Pursuant to the Nepal-India Treaty of 1950, Nepal needs to consult with India to import arms and ammunition from the third party country. At that time, Nepal and India had this treaty done to cater the needs for countering the threat from the People's Republic of China that had captured Tibet by force in 1949. Pursuant to this treaty, India could halt or check any arms and ammunition passing through its territory to Nepal. India did not have any means to check the arms supply to Nepal by China if they came from China to Nepal through Tibet. Nepal could not receive weapons from Pakistan despite Pakistan's strong desire to supply weapons to Nepal after India, the US and the UK have suspended arms supply to Nepal since the February-1 move of the king because India could certainly stop any arms going to Nepal through its territory. The Nepali monarch desperately sought arms from China, and received 18 truckloads of arms and ammunition from it. According to media reports, the Chinese army escorted eighteen trucks carrying arms and ammunition to Nepal's border where plain-clothes Nepalese troops took over in November 2005.

Supplying lethal weapons to Nepal, China not only demonstrated its disregard for suppression of democracy, civil liberties and human rights but also added fuel to the further bloodshed in Nepal. It is understandable that the Chinese communists have no regards for democracy, civil liberties and human rights as the communists believe in subjection of individuals to the dictatorship of the proletariats. However, supplying lethal arms, the Chinese government added fuel to the political conflict in Nepal and had shown disregard for human blood.

'The Indian Express' wrote: the continuing Chinese arms supply to Kathmandu is more than a tactical threat to India's attempt at promoting democracy and stability in Nepal. The time is running out for the Indian Government to get its Nepal act together and compel King Gyanendra to pay the costs of the China-card he has chosen to play against India. Much like his father, Mahendra, who cozened up to Beijing in the early 1960s amidst rising Sino-Indian tensions, the present monarch thinks he can hustle India into legitimizing his power grab. Unable to engineer a split in the coalition between India and the Anglo-American powers, King Gyanendra has put all his eggs in the China basket. This was evident at the regional summit earlier this month in Dhaka, when Nepal became the most vocal supporter of immediate Chinese affiliation with SAARC.

Academic Govinda Bhatta wrote in 'Jana Bhawana' that of media reports are any indication; foreign powers are making the Chinese military assistance to Nepal an excuse to intervene in the Nepali's internal affairs. Efforts are on to implicate Nepal in the international strategic campaign against China. Such campaigners have been saying that Nepal has tilted toward China and that there is increasing Chinese influence in Nepal. But, the fact remains that Nepal has not changed its foreign policy. We still believe in the policy of neutrality and non-alignment.

Sandhaya Jain wrote that by choosing to isolate King Gyanendra of Nepal and support discredited and thoroughly corrupt politicians and the Maoists after last February's palace coup, the Indian Government adopted a disastrous policy on Nepal. After Prime Minister Manmohan Singh and his team decided to suspend arms supplies to the Royal Nepal Army needed to combat the Maoist terrorists, King Gyanendra has been forced to look toward China. Ironically, India broke up its long-standing policy of non-interference in the internal affairs of another sovereign state successfully lobbying the US and the EU for putting pressure on the King for restoration of democracy.

On Sunday, December 11, 2005, former Nepalese Minister for Industries and senior leader of the Communist Party of Nepal (United Marxist-Leninist), Keshab Badal told The Hindu (independent Indian newspaper) in Kolkata, "We urge the Indian Government not to lend any support to the Nepal Government that could end up with the latter turning even more repressive towards the movement for democracy in Nepal. We seek the sympathy of the Indian Government in our endeavors to replace the monarchy in Nepal with a democratic republic. The Government headed by the King is stockpiling arms and procuring weapons in preparation for the bloodiest civil war in the country."

On Sunday, December 11, 2005, leading a four-member delegation, Indian Foreign Secretary and Former Indian Ambassador to Nepal, Shyam Sharan arrived in Kathmandu for a three-day visit to Nepal.

On Tuesday afternoon, December 13, 2005 before returning to New Delhi, addressing a press conference on the Indian embassy premises at Lainchour in Kathmandu, Indian Foreign Secretary Shyam Sharan said, "there has been no change in the India's stance on the early restoration of multi-party democracy and constitutional monarchy in Nepal. Restoration of peace and stability and economic recovery in Nepal is not only in the interest of Nepal, but also in the India's interest. Unity among constitutional forces is essential to achieve the goal of peace and stability in the country. India is always ready to support all efforts aimed at bringing a peaceful resolution to the problems confronting Nepal." In his 10-minute long press conference, concerning the military assistance to Nepal, Secretary Sharan said, "At the moment we do not have Indian arms coming to Nepal but other aspects of our cooperation to Nepal including the RNA (Royal Nepalese Army) is continuing. For example, training for RNA is still continuing." On his meeting with King Gyanendra, Secretary Sharan said, "His Majesty conveyed to me that he remains committed to multi-party democracy and constitutional monarchy and that there should not be any doubt in his commitment." While answering reporters' queries, Secretary Sharan said India and China were not competing in Nepal, but both want a stable and prosperous Nepal."

On Thursday, December 15, 2005, 'Daily Times' online (a new voice for a new Pakistan) reported from New Delhi, India, quoting 'The Asian Age' newspaper that on Tuesday speaking to reporters on his return from a three-day visit to Nepal, Indian Foreign Secretary Shyam Sharan said, "We would trust that India and China are not seen as somehow competing with each other for any kind of influence in Nepal." He said, "India believes both New Delhi and Beijing share a common 'objective' of seeing the return of peace and stability to Nepal."

India has called on China to stop supplying arms and ammunition to Nepal and join international efforts to force King Gyanendra to restore democracy following his takeover in February. Indian Foreign Secretary Shyam Sharan, said on a visit to Nepal: "The international community has taken a position in order to foster the process of reconciliation among political forces here and we would hope that not only China but other countries join in that effort." "Nepal's efforts to lure a largely Tibet-focused China into showing it can play a role in south Asia may not be worth angering India. Feeling in New Delhi is already quite anti-king," a western diplomat said.

Foreign Secretary Shyam Sharan hinted that India's relations with Nepal have resumed after a deep freeze of almost ten months but it was not the business as usual yet. Secretary Sharan said his visit to Nepal was follow-on to the meeting between King Gyanendra and Prime Minister Manmohan Singh in Dhaka. At that meeting, both the king and the Prime Minister agreed to be in touch at different levels. Although Secretary Sharan refrained from making any comment on political overtones, he managed to convey the message to all persons he had met in Nepal that occasional "pin-pricks" by Nepal, such as procuring arms from China, would only complicate the relations between two countries.

On December 19, 2005, Indian Defence Minister Pranab Mukherjee said that the arms supply and military training provide by China and Pakistan to Kathmandu was a concern, and the Indian government was addressing it through its diplomatic missions in both those countries "A problem is there. We have taken it up diplomatically. Let us see how it can be resolved," said Mukherjee.

Deputy Director of the Institute for Defence Studies and Analyses, a leading security think tank in India, Commodore C. Uday Bhaskar said, "India should mount a wholehearted politico-military initiative to ensure that Nepal's military orientation remains with India. "There is a strategic dimension to India's relationship with Nepal and it has to be handled carefully," Bhaskar told IANS. An expert on South Asia at Jawaharlal Nehru University, S.D. Muni said, "I understand the matter has been taken up diplomatically. India's foreign secretary went there with a clear message but if it is more than just a one-time affair, then we have to put pressure (on Nepal)."

After a virtual embargo of arms imposed by New Delhi on the king's army, there has been furious military-diplomatic activity among Nepal, China and Pakistan. After an October-visit to Beijing where he struck a deal for the supply of certain weapon systems from China, Nepal's Army Chief of Staff General Pyar Jung Thapa returned from Islamabad on Saturday, December 17, 2005; where he was offered comprehensive training capsules for the RNA soldiers. On Sunday, December 18, 2005, in a press release, the RNA's Department of Public Relations (DPR) said that the delegation of the People's Liberation Army (PLA) of China led by Deputy Commander of Chengu Military Region Command Lieutenant General Gui Quanzhi met RNA Chief of Staff General Pyar Jung Thapa. Four other senior military officials of the PLA and the Chinese military attaché were present on the meeting at the RNA headquarters. However, no details about the meeting were given.

The cash-strapped RNA paid US$80,000 to buy 18,000 grenades and four million rounds of 7.62mm bullets from 'Poly Technologies Incorporated' in Beijing by November 15, 2005 while ignoring to pay off the older debts to India that have mounted up to over US$26 million. In a surprisingly prompt transaction, the consignments arrived in the Nepalese capital Kathmandu on November 22 a week after the payment was made. India had been selling weapons and equipment to the RNA at a 70 per cent mark-off before it suspended military supplies to Nepal in February 2005 to show concern over Nepalese King Gyanendra's power grab with the help of the army. Defence sources in Nepal said that the prompt payment to the Chinese company was made due to the commissions involved. A section of senior officers in the RNA had been unhappy with the Indian military aid, as it bypassed the commission agents.

China has increased its activities in various aspects of the Nepalese life. For example, Chinese People's Association for Friendship with Foreign Countries (CPAFFC) and Nepal-China Executives Council (NCEC) signed a Memorandum of understanding (M. O. U) on Sunday, December 25, 2005. On behalf of their respective organization, Secretary General of CPAFFC, Zhu Changbing, and General Secretary of NCEC, Rajendra Nakarmi signed on the document. According to the M. O. U, both the CPAFFC and the NCEC shall cooperate on the promotion and expansion of cooperation in the field of trade, tourism and cultural exchanges, and shall act as facilitators to promote and strengthen investment and entrepreneurial relationship between Nepal and China.

Vice-chairmen of the Council of Ministers Kirti Nidhi Bista met Chen Haosu, a visiting Chinese delegation leader and Chairman of CPAFFC. "Nepal-China relations, having a long and illustrious history of friendship, excellent relationship and exchanges, have taken a new dimension and reached a new height after the establishment of diplomatic relations on Aug. 1, 1955," said Bista at the meeting. "Nowadays, mutual understanding, respect and trust, and treating each other equally have become salient characters of China-Nepal relations," said Chen Haosu at the meeting. Leading a 12-member delegation of CPAFFC, Chen arrived in Kathmandu on Thursday, December 22, 2005 for a five-day-long visit to Nepal.

On December 26, 2005, Minister of State for Information and Communications Shrish Shumsher JB Rana inaugurated the three-day Nepal-China postage stamp exhibition held to mark the 50th anniversary of the establishment of diplomatic relations between the two countries at Nepal Art Council in Kathmandu. On the occasion, Minister of State Rana affixed the first cancellation mark on the commemorative stamp on Nepal-China diplomatic relations. (Nepalese media)

A Nepalese non-governmental friendship organization called China Study Centre (CSC) has set up its Eastern Region Chapter (ERC) in Biratnagar, about 400 km east of Kathmandu. "The founding of the CSC's Eastern Region Chapter (ERC) is of great importance because Biratnagar is a very important city in Nepal for its status of industrial area, trade centre and the second largest town of the country," said Chinese Ambassador to Nepal, Sun Heping at the inaugural function of the ERC. He said, "Therefore, there are more opportunities for China-Nepal trade cooperation and will surely bring the entrepreneurs in eastern part of Nepal closer to China. This newly founded ERC will play an important role in eastern Nepal to bridge the two countries in disseminating information on both China and Nepal."

On the occasion, Chairman of the ERC of the CSC, Jana Bandhu Karki said the founding of the ERC is a symbol of Nepal's efforts on strengthening the relationship with its "good partner and a growing economic power", China. Founded in 2000, the CSC has already set up its branches in Nepal's major cities such as Khandbari, Chitwan, Dhulikhel, Pokhara, Butwal, Lumbini and Nepalgunj.

On January 03, 2006, Xinhuanet reported that the Chinese Ambassador to Nepal said that China accorded a high priority to the construction of the proposed Koshi-Lhasa Highway linking

Nepal's eastern zones with China's Tibet Autonomous Region. At an interaction program held by the Morang Trade Association, Chinese Ambassador to Nepal, Sun Heping said, "We have given this highway a high priority. Among the 10 highways that link Nepal with China, this was the most important highway. However, the Nepali Government needed to request the Chinese authorities officially for the construction of the highway." In addition, the Chinese Ambassador to Nepal said that the request to open a Consulate General's Office in Biratnagar could be considered after consultations with the government. "All of the businessmen of the eastern zones have been calling for Chinese help in the construction of the highway because it will benefit trade between China and eastern Nepal," said Kishor Pradhan, central member of Federation of Nepalese Chambers of Commerce and Industry.

King Gyanendra toyed with a plan to let China and Pakistan open consulates in the sensitive Indo-Nepal border areas; the (Indian) Government communicated its strong displeasure to Kathmandu. China is apparently ready to open a consulate at Biratnagar at the border between eastern Nepal and Bihar. Pakistan, not to be left behind, is keen to open shop at Birganj in central Nepal region that also borders Bihar. While King Gyanendra might hope that his threat to draw in China and Pakistan closer to him would force New Delhi to soften its policies, the indications are that the move could further undermine the limited support the monarchy enjoyed in New Delhi.

The (Pakistani) Foreign Office has warned the (Pakistani) Government that India and Nepal were in the process of finalizing a "secret extradition treaty" that might endanger safety of Pakistanis there as the agreement would give full power to New Delhi to get hold of any Pakistani national working or visiting Kathmandu. The (Pakistani) Foreign Office has proposed to the (Pakistani) Government that as a "counter step" Pakistan should immediately sign an agreement with Nepal to save its own citizens from being extradited to India from Kathmandu. In the light of Foreign Office and Interior Ministry's joint proposal, Foreign Office officials confirmed the cabinet has approved singing of an agreement with Nepal in one of the recent meetings presided over by Prime Minister Shaukat Aziz.

In a New Year's Day message to Chinese Premier Wen Jiabao, Indian Prime minister Manmohan Singh said that the two populous Asian neighbours must make 2006 the year of India-China friendship in line with the pledge made last year. Prime Minister Singh also said both India and China have made progress in negotiations over thorny issues such as a border dispute, which resulted in a brief but a bloody war in 1962. Indian foreign ministry officials said that Chinese Premier Wen replied to the Indian Prime Minister Singh's New Year's greeting on an equally positive note. "China is ready to work with India to continuously deepen the contents of our bilateral relations and push forward the China-India strategic and partnership in an all-round and in-depth way," said Premier Wen in his message. A formal ceasefire line has yet to be established following the war but the unsettled border has remained largely peaceful following agreements signed in 1993 and 1996. India says China occupies 38,000 square kilometers of Indian Territory in Kashmir while Beijing claims that the 90,000-square kilometers Indian state of Arunachal Pradesh belongs to China.

Ingratiating to Beijing, King Gyanendra has been using his father's policy of playing India off against China. Critics point out that this policy was made at a time when Nepal's two giant neighbours had just fought a bruising war in 1962. Today, China and India are bhai-bhai (friends) again; this strategy is hopelessly outdated. However, India's lingering memory of being 'stabbed in the back' in 1962 is so strong there is growing alarm that South Block's diplomacy toward Nepal has been 'pushing Kathmandu into the Chinese fold'. Until recently, conventional wisdom has been that rapprochement between China and India meant the two weren't competing with each other in Nepal or elsewhere. While many still adhere to this view, some aren't so sure any more. In fact, those who talk about a benign China are now often labeled in the Indian press as 'Beijing apologists' and part of a 'pro-China lobby'.

King Gyanendra's strategy of obtaining military aid and buying arms and ammunition from China and Pakistan has worked brilliantly to stoke fears in New Delhi about Nepal going over to the other side. Even though the recent $1 million military grant and the 18 trucks of grenades and bullets from China last month may not have been substantial, its prominent coverage in the Indian media stoked suspicions again. However, the Sino phobia is restricted to a relatively small section of the military-intelligence establishment and the political opposition. A large number of people in the political and business sector is more worried about how India can keep pace with China's blistering economic growth and emulate its success in wooing foreign direct investment.

Indian Ambassador to Nepal, Shiv Shankar Mukherjee said India had very high stakes in Nepal and was very concerned with the latest developments in Nepal. Ambassador Mukherjee said that the constitutional monarchy should remain the symbol of unity, continuity and integrity of the nation and should not compete with the political parties for power. "The most sane, non-violent and practical way out is for the palace to reach out to parties and together bring Maoists to mainstream," said Ambassador Mukherjee. Responding to a query on the Indian embargo on arms supply to Nepal, Ambassador Mukherjee said, "We had helped Royal Nepalese Army to battle insurgency. After February 1, 2005, it was no longer the previous situation." Ambassador Mukherjee did not see it that Nepal was trying to use "China card" against India. He, however, said, "We expect all members of the international community, including China, not to add to complications."

Referring to the interview by Indian Ambassador Shiv Shanker Mukherjee to the private television in Kathmandu, Former Army Chief of Staff and Member of the Standing Committee of the Privy Council, Satchit Shumsher Rana said, "It is against diplomatic norms to give unwanted advice to the King." Mr. Rana also said, "If the King had been active in politics, he would have opened a political party and the seven parties (agitating against the king's direct rule) would have been wiped out." In a press-meet in Beijing, Indian Foreign Secretary Shyam Sharan said that he had held talks with his Chinese counterpart li Jhaoji on the Nepalese politics and the situation evolving there.

Secretary Sharan disclosed that he had conveyed India's concern over the deteriorating economy and political upheavals in Nepal, and the Chinese arms supply to Nepal in the recent days, as it would compound the political problems and prolong the ongoing Maoist insurgency, to his Chinese counterpart during the meeting. Secretary Sharan said that the Chinese made it clear to him that the China's policy toward Nepal is non-interference in the internal affairs of Nepal.

The Nepalese king deals a fake-China card. All sides except for the palace laugh off the bid to pressure India. The monarchy sought to manipulate India by threatening it with the China card. Sometimes there is a hint of arms supplies from Beijing and at other times a possibility of allowing them to open a consulate on the Indo-Nepal border.

However, it is clear that there is no China card that Kathmandu can play. The Nepalese democratic political parties are dismissive of it, Western diplomats are impatient with any such suggestion and Indian diplomats certainly do not believe in its existence. A European diplomat based in Kathmandu explained: "There is no China card.

But the perception of the China card is more important than the card. It is a classical case of manipulation by the palace. If people believe that there is a China card, the king's purpose is served." The "China card" seems all about trying to force India to help legitimize the king and his actions. Even if a consignment of weapons did come from Beijing, Chinese diplomats are now backtracking. General Secretary of the Communist Party of Nepal (United Marxist Leninist), Madhav Kumar Nepal said, "I told the Chinese ambassador that if they are indeed arming the RNA, then it is not good. He told me that they have not provided any weapons." The Chinese ambassador conveyed the same message to President of the Nepali Congress, Girija Prasad Koirala. President Koirala confirmed this and added, "India should rid itself of the mental make-up arising out of the 1962 war with China. That situation cannot be repeated.

It is the king who is trying to play on that fear psychosis by showing the China card. All these cards will fail. India need not get bothered with this." President Koirala said he was aware that the Indian diplomats were in constant dialogue with the Chinese and there was a lot of understanding between them. "We also appeal to the Chinese and the Pakistanis not to fish in Nepal's troubles and do anything that appears to help the autocratic king. That will not benefit Nepal and destroy the prospects for peace," said he.

4

Indian, Chinese Posturing Deepens Nepal's Federalization Dilemma

The anticipated process of state restructuring in Nepal, ranging from an increasingly polarized populace for and against ethnicity-based federalization to the consistent ineptitude of political leaders failing to lead from the front to seek a meeting point between conflicting interests. But the increasingly prominent posturing of Nepal's two giant neighbours on these issues threatens to sabotage the whole process and push Nepal further into chaos.

"When the uneasy relationship between two Asian giants degenerates into a confrontation, Nepal will find it extremely difficult to balance its relations with them. In such a situation, weaknesses in Indo-Nepal relations would be open to exploitation by unfriendly elements." This is how Col. R. Hariharan, a retired Indian Military Intelligence Specialist associated with the Chennai Centre for China Studies, sums up the predicament of Nepal's foreign policyamid the changing nature of relationship between the two rising Asian powers.

Writing on the Journal of Defence Studies under the heading of "China's Expanding Footprint in Nepal: Threats to India", Dr. Satish Kumar, Assistant Professor at one Indian university writes: "The strengthening of bilateral ties between the two countries is quite natural. But China's overstepping in Nepal has a real and concrete strategic impact on India's Himalayan security."

These two statements reflect the increasing realization on the Indian side of the intensifying Asian tug-of-war that the latest interactions between Nepal and China are something qualitatively different from those in the past when India used to take its influence in Nepal for granted. From the geopolitical view, China's increasing influence in Nepal can be viewed as a part of its increasing assertiveness in general and India's attempts at retaining the centuries long influence in the tiny northern neighbor is also understandable. These are indeed the recurrent themes of the interactions that have been taking place between Nepal and either of the two neighbours over past many years.

To date, as can be explained by discrepancy in terms of economic, political, and military power, politicians and diplomats from Kathmandu have contributed little towards shaping the relationship of Nepal with either of the two neighbours. Rather, the motives and actions of either New Delhi or Beijing have shaped and reshaped those relationships. This makes even a small overture by either of those capitals to Kathmandu very significant as the other capital is likely to view the same with alarm and suspicion.

As a result, it has been long felt in Nepal that the politicians in Kathmandu have miserably failed in preserving the core national interests vis-a-vis the neighbours by either deferring to their interest unnecessarily (usually when they are at power) or antagonizing them through hollow rhetoric towards mean political gains (obviously when they are in streets). This phenomenon is much more prominent in relation to India, which does not hesitate being seen taking sides in confrontations between various actors and institutions in Nepal; unlike China, which plays more subtle and covert role. In this backdrop, the preferential treatment of different political parties and leaders by either of the two neighbours is not uncommon. Over past many months, the conflicting positions of the two neighbours in the question of thorniest issue in Nepal's transition have increasingly come to the fore: the yet undecided process of state restructuring that is supposed to follow the implementation of the new constitution. While India visibly prefers the ethnicity-based federalization of the state with as much autonomy to the southern plains of Terai (that is increasingly identified as 'Madhesh' as more preferred political unit) as possible, same possibility has become a matter of ominous concern for China which prefers stabilization of Nepal with as little change in status quo as possible. The matters went nearly out of hand of Kathmandu politicians drawing strong protest from people about two months back when one Indian diplomat reportedly prompted the Nepali politicians in the southern plains of Madhesh to bring a "storm of protest" for identity of the plains.

The situation was problematic enough even when the Constituent Assembly (CA) was in existence until two months ago, with the assembly fumbling to get the job of writing the constitution done on time amid the failure of political forces to agree on issues crucial to state restructuring. After the tragic collapse of that institution with its failure, the uncertainty has increased and the problems seem to only multiply for everyone, from Nepali politicians to the governments and diplomats in the two neighbours.

In this context, some of the latest developments in Nepal need special mention. Mohan Baidya, the president of CPN-Maoist (that was formed after splitting the Unified CPN (Maoist), the largest party in erstwhile CA), recently completed his 10-day trip to China. On return, he was unequivocal on passing a message from Beijing that China was "against any foreign interference in Nepal in the name of federalism". It could be clearly read in the statement that the Chinese side had tried to woo Baidya away from the stance of ethnicity-based federalization, something his party has remained mum about since its birth, even though most of the leaders had been strongly advocating the former before the split.

The wording and intention of the message from Beijing aside, Baidya's engagement with China is sure to create discomfort in his former party, the UCPN (Maoist) which is still in power in

Kathmandu amid many difficulties and confusion. At one front, the UCPN (Maoist) has been known for inconsistency in its foreign policy characterized by India-bashing while at the street and India-embracing once in power. Indeed, the current government led by Dr. Baburam Bhattarai in alliance with the Madhesh-based regional political parties is said to be one of the most pro-India governments in recent past, even though many analysts portray it as merely pragmatic government.

At another front, the Maoist party before split was the vociferous advocate of identity-based federalization of Nepal, mainly because that had been the slogan around which it had galvanized the support of masses from marginalized communities during its decade long 'People's War'; a position which now increasingly raises China's discomfiture. In principle, the post-split UCPN (Maoist) still maintains that position, but in absence of any mechanism to move forward in the issue of state restructuring, they can afford to continue sending the ambiguous message on the issue for the time being even as the confusion around the whole political process intensifies.

In the meantime, K. P. Oli, another seasoned politician from another communist outfit CPN (UML), has reportedly pleaded to the highest authority in New Delhi to hear the grievances of the opposition parties in Nepal, who bitterly criticize the Maoists for clinging to power after collapse of the CA instead of seeking the alternative of 'national unity government'. The fact that Oli even presented himself as the prospective PM of Nepal in a foreign capital tells a lot about the role New Delhi plays in shaping the outcomes of power tussle in Kathmandu.

Ironically, while the Bhattarai led government in Kathmandu is believed to be enduring because its stances on crucial issues are more pro-Indian than those of past governments, Oli has tried to precisely outsmart the former on the same front by convincing the Indian establishment. Indeed, during the tenure of Madhav Nepal as PM in the recent past, the alienation of the Maoists by an alliance of almost all non-Maoist forces with blessings from India had led to rude India-bashing by the former.

But now some deep paradoxes have developed in Nepal's political arena surrounding the issue of state restructuring. First, with vocal opposition of the identity-based federalization, the erstwhile center-right forces like CPN (UML) and Nepali Congress (for whom India's blessing was 'usual' and 'natural' as opposed to the leftist Maoists who apparently favored closer ties with China) have pushed themselves into increasingly awkward position with India. While it is yet to be seen what policies the UCPN (M) adopts after ouster from power some day in future, their natural course seems to be more convergent with the one India would wish for them to follow. This is sure to prompt Beijing to distance itself from their once-trusted party, something the newly formed CPN-M wishes very badly.

Coming to domestic considerations, the calculus of vote politics is such that the issue of federalization of the country can no way be sidelined and stances of political parties on this particular issue are going to matter more than anything else in the upcoming polls, savagely polarized by the intense and often violent debate over many months before the fateful dissolution of the CA. Political parties advocating the ethnicity-based federalization of the country are likely to garner votes of people from ethnic groups that felt marginalized in the past, while those against that process are sure to be favored by high-caste people from the hills who have been dominating the state machinery till now.

Thus the issue of federalization, while becoming that of prime concern for the neighbours, has come to be vital for near as well as remote future of the political forces in the country.

And exactly for the same reason, the whole debate surrounding state restructuring in Nepal has been sabotaged and degenerated into the vicious tug-of-war between and among the vested interests. The verbal duels among politicians to appease a particular section of population apart, the real and constructive debate to seek the optimum mechanism to address the grievance of the people is altogether missing. While extremist views for and against the ethnicity-based federalization spread among the populace like wild fire further polarizing the people, political parties are as busy wrangling for the chair of PM in Kathmandu as ever.

It is not hard to follow the developments in Kathmandu and see whether Beijing's interests get upper hand or those of New Delhi do, but the tussle makes the negotiated settlement of divisive issue of state restructuring in Nepal increasingly untenable.

Not that either Beijing or New Delhi is to be blamed for the misfortune; it is natural for them to advance their own interests. It is the myopia and ineptitude of the leadership in Kathmandu that fails to reach the crux of the problem Nepal faces. Rather than travelling to Delhi or Beijing for blessings, they should be in dialogue among themselves and with the masses to convince them that a compromise means as much losing something as gaining something and negotiated settlement is the only way to better future as opposed to the polarization along extremist lines.

Nepal is obviously vulnerable to the tectonic shifts going on in world politics, and changing dynamics of the Sino-Indian relationship is going to impact the future of this small country. But so long as the politicians in Kathmandu keep seeking the blessings of one neighbor or the other to outpace their rivals as a more convenient alternative to painstaking negotiations and compromises at home, Nepal is going to look more like a battlefield of increasingly acrimonious regional powers rather than a sovereign and independent nation.

Add to that the chaos resulting from the leaders following the whims of crowds rather than judiciously leading them in issues as sensitive and divisive as state restructuring that makes a perfect recipe for a disaster.

Yet all hope is not lost. Nepal's best way forward is a comprehensive dialogue on all issues including state restructuring among the political powers and all other stakeholders, something that was amiss in the attempts to sort out those thorny issues last time around, followed by political mechanism acceptable to all. On federalization, a settlement may not entirely conform to the wishes of either India or China but they will be happy to live with a stable Nepal regardless of whether their interests are preserved or not in the particular process. In the long run, that is indeed in best interests of all the parties.

'CHINA ENCOURAGES VENTURE IN NEPAL'

The two sides reviewed the time-tested Nepal-China friendly relations and noted with satisfaction that since the establishment of diplomatic relations in 1955, China-Nepal relations have been growing in a consistent, steady and healthy manner. The relationship is characterised by equality, harmonious coexistence, ever-lasting friendship and comprehensive cooperation. The two sides maintained that China-Nepal relationship is of vital significance to both the countries. Deepening bilateral friendship and cooperation serve the fundamental interests of the two countries and the two peoples, and are conducive to peace, stability and development in the region and the world at large. The two sides decided to further promote Nepal-China friendly relations of Comprehensive Partnership of Cooperation Featuring Ever-lasting Friendship on the basis of the Five Principles of Peaceful Coexistence.

The two sides reiterated their commitment to respect each other's independence, sovereignty, territorial integrity, choice of social system and development path chosen in light of their respective national conditions, and respect and understand each other's major concerns and core interests. The two sides further reiterated that they adhere to the principles of the United Nations as enshrined in the Charter, five Principles of Peaceful Co-existence, non-alignment and non-intervention in each other's internal affairs, and develop friendly exchanges and cooperation on the basis of equality and mutual benefit. Both sides agreed to share development experiences and technological advancement, and enhance all round cooperation so as to achieve mutual development and prosperity.

Both sides believed that high-level contacts are of special importance to the development of bilateral relations. The two sides agreed to maintain the momentum of high-level mutual visits, and have meetings between the leaders on the multilateral occasions. The two sides agreed to make full use of the existing mechanisms, including the diplomatic consultations and the Nepal-China Joint Economic and Trade Committee Meeting. The two sides also agreed to form a Consultation Mechanism at the level of Minister for Foreign Affairs.

The Nepali side reiterated that there is only one China in the world, and the Government of the People's Republic of China is the sole legal government representing the whole of China. Both Taiwan and Tibet are integral parts of the Chinese territory.

The Chinese side reiterated its commitment to the policy of non-interference in the internal affairs, and expressed firm support to the efforts made by the Nepali side in upholding its independence, sovereignty, territorial integrity, national unity and stability. As a close neighbour of Nepal, the Chinese side is pleased to see the progress achieved in the peace process in Nepal and sincerely hopes that Nepal will realise peace, stability and prosperity including the drafting of a new constitution in the near future. The Nepali side highly appreciated the goodwill shown by friendly neighbour China at this historic transition.

The two sides agreed to further intensify cooperation in socio-economic development, promotion of trade and tourism, hydropower, transportation infrastructure development and other fields on the basis of equality and mutual benefit. The Chinese side agreed to expedite the implementation of various development projects, including the upgrading and expansion of existing Ring Road of Kathmandu and Tatopani Dry Port. An Agreement on Economic and Technical Cooperation was signed between the Government of Nepal and the Government of the People's Republic of China.

The two sides agreed to enhance cooperation to ensure the construction of the Upper Trisuli 3A hydropower project with concessional loan of the Chinese government. The Nepali side welcomed Chinese participation in the construction of Pokhara

International Airport, and the Chinese side took a positive attitude to this.

The two sides congratulated the official opening of the second Nepal-China land route of Syaphrubesi-Rasuwa Gadhi Road. Both sides agreed to give full attention to the geographic proximity, and improve connectivity, particularly, the land transportation infrastructure between the two countries, to facilitate bilateral exchanges, cooperation and business ties.

The two sides maintained that the Tibet Autonomous Region of China and Nepal should make full potentials and take their respective advantages to strengthen people to people exchanges in the border areas, and to promote trade, tourism, and the flow of goods and services to expand mutually beneficial cooperation.

The Chinese side stated that China encourages and supports competent and well-established Chinese companies and enterprises to promote investment and joint ventures in Nepal, and will provide financing assistance including loans of concessional nature, to mutually agreed projects. The Nepali side stated that Nepal appreciated and welcomed the offer made by the Chinese side. During the visit, a Memorandum of Understanding on Operationalisation of Loan Mechanism was also signed between the Ministry of Finance of the Government of Nepal and the Export-Import Bank of China. The two sides agreed to continue discussions regarding the bilateral Agreement on the Business Investment Promotion and Protection of Investment.

The two sides believed that strengthening border areas management and development serves the common interests of both the countries. Both sides agreed to make joint efforts to build a boundary of peace, tranquillity, friendship and cooperation. The two sides signed the Agreement on the Management of Ports in Nepal-China Border Areas and the Agreement on Trans-frontier Pasturing by Border Inhabitants. The two sides applauded the cooperation between the Ministry of Public Security of China and the Ministry of Home Affairs of Nepal, and agreed to improve the meeting mechanism between law-enforcement authorities of the two countries, and to deepen cooperation on border management and law-enforcement capacity-building, so as to uphold peace and stability of China-Nepal border areas.

The two sides were pleased with the momentum of bilateral people to people and cultural exchanges and announced the year 2012 as "Nepal-China Year of Friendly Exchanges". The two sides agreed to promote exchanges and cooperation in the areas of culture and education and between youths, media, think tanks, scholars and friendship groups of the two countries.

The two sides signed the Agreement on Cultural Cooperation, and agreed to enhance cultural exchanges and cooperation. Both sides believed that China Festival held regularly in Nepal by the Chinese side has promoted cultural exchanges between the two countries, and agreed to continue the Festival.

Both sides also agreed on the mutual visits between their cultural and arts group. Both sides noted with appreciation that since the establishment of the youth exchange mechanism in 2009, the youth delegations of the two countries have realised mutual visits. The two sides also agreed to expand tourism cooperation and support each other's promotional activities in their respective countries.

The two sides positively view and support each other's participation in regional cooperation, and agreed to strengthen coordination and cooperation in various regional cooperation mechanisms. The two sides believed that the official visit of Premier Wen Jiabao to Nepal took Nepal-China relations to a new height. It also served as a milestone in the annals of Nepal-China bilateral friendly relations and cooperation. The Chinese side expressed its appreciation to the government and people of Nepal for their gracious hospitality.

Premier Wen Jiabao extended an invitation to Prime Minister Baburam Bhattarai to pay an official visit to China at a mutually convenient time. Prime Minister Baburam Bhattarai accepted the invitation with delight.

NEPAL-CHINA BORDER SEPARATION : TOKEN OF FRIENDSHIP

Nepal and China have a common border of 1,414.88 kilometer presently. It runs west to east from Zanskar range passing through various ranges such as Gurans Himal, Byasrishi, Nalakankar, Chandi, Gorakh, Kanti, Gautam, Mustang, Peri, Langtang, Phurbichyachu, Rolwaling, Mahalangur, Chamlan, Umbak and Janak Himal ranges. Boundary business between the two countries starting from the boundary delimitation agreement to boundary treaty, demarcation of pillars, preparation of strip-maps and signing on the boundary protocol have been completed within a short span of time. Timely and successfully completed Sino-Nepal boundary business is considered as the symbol of friendship in the history of Nepal.

Nepal and Tibetan area of China are neighbours since time immemorial. If we have a look on the history, Nepal's contact with Tibet proper began in the seventh century. Economic, social and cultural contacts have been started from that period, though there were some hostilities between Nepal and Tibet. Some of these cases were below standard of the Nepalese coins circulated in Tibetan markets, dissatisfaction of Nepal's trade interest to Tibet, ill-treatment to the Nepalese traders stationed at Lhasa, adulterated salt exported to Nepal by Tibet etc.

Historic Border Treaties

In the past history of some centuries, there were some confrontations between two countries especially in the economic and trade affairs. With this context, there were border conflicts in some trade and transit points. But agreement and treaties were made time to time to settle those conflicts amicably. As a result, Khasa Treaty (September 1775) was performed to maintain the borderline in its previous position. Kerung Treaty (2 June 1789) was signed to retard Nepal back from the invaded Tibetan land to its former borderline, Treaty of Betrawoti (5 October 1792) was to prevent an unprovoked dispute with the intention of possessing the territories of the other, and Treaty of Thapathali (24 March 1856) was to restore Taglakhar, Chewur Gumba, Kerong, Jhunga, Kuti and Dhakling by Tibet and to withdraw all the Nepalese troops that may be on this side of the Bhairab Langur range.

After the agreement of Thapathali also named as Nepal-Tibet Treaty of Peace-1856, Nepal had no conflicts and disputes with Tibet. Since then, customary borderline was maintained and economic, social and cultural relations were developed smoothly. China always wished to see Nepal as a prosperous neighbour and friendly nation. As a consequence, diplomatic relation between Nepal and China was established in 1955 and also there was an agreement on trade and cross-border transit in 1956. Sino-Nepalese Treaty of Peace and Friendship was signed in 28 April 1960 to promote the friendship on the basis of Panchasheel and Nepal treated the Tibetan affair as an internal matter of China and has consistently supported the policy of one China.

Developing Border conformity and Treaty

To develop relation and friendship furthermore between the two countries, Sino-Nepal Boundary Agreement (21 March 1960) was signed by two Prime-Ministers, Bishweshwor Prasad Koirala and Chou En-Lai. The main objective of this agreement was to respect the existing traditional customary boundaryline and to delineate and demarcate it scientifically. With the effect of this agreement, Boundary Treaty (5 October 1961) was made between two nations and it was signed by two heads of the states, His Majesty the King of Nepal Mahendra Bir Bikram Shah Deva and Chairman of the People's Republic of China Liu Shao-Chi. It was regarded as a symbol to consolidate as a boundary of peace and friendship towards strengthening peace in Asia and the world.

Border Delimitation

The mandate of the treaty was to conduct necessary on the spot investigations and surveys and made certain adjustments in accordance with the principles of equality, mutual benefit, friendship and mutual accommodation. Three sessions of the

Joint Boundary Committee were held in Beijing and Kathmandu to delineate the boundary in detail from one point to the other in various sectors and segments of the boundaryline, before formally signing on the treaty.

In connection to execute the treaty, boundary delineation was made on the basis of existing traditional customary line with the technical principles of determining the water-parting line to connect snow-capped high altitude mountain peaks, passing and crossing through mountain passes and spurs, saddles and cols, rivers and rivulets, pastureland and river basin or valleys. The most important aspect adopted was to maintain certain adjustments in accordance with the principles of mutual accommodation on trans-frontier cultivation of lands and trans-frontier pasturing by the inhabitants of certain border areas. After the transference of the areas to the other party, be definitely considered citizens of the country to which the area belong. Any inhabitants of these areas who do not wish to become citizen of the country to which the area belong may retain their previous nationality by making declaration to that effect within one year of the enforcement of the agreement. Concrete rules were laid down regarding choice of nationality, the legitimate rights of those who decide to retain their previous nationality and protection and disposal of their property.

After the signing service of the Boundary Treaty, editorial of the People's Daily (Peking 13 October 1961) wrote it as an unparalleled enthusiasm of the Chinese people with the Nepalese to celebrate the birth of this boundary of peace and friendship between China and Nepal. It was also expressed sincere gratitude to the Nepalese friends who have contributed to the creation of this boundary for the sake of the future generation of the Chinese and Nepalese people.

Boundary Separation

To implement the boundary treaty, the most important work was to demarcate the boundary line, to establish and construct the main boundary pillars and markers and also the erection of reference pillars physically on both the sides of the frontier.

During the demarcation, boundary delineation was followed as mentioned in the treaty of 5 October 1961. However, some adjustments were made through friendly consultation in such sectors where the boundary lines as shown in the maps of the two sides did not coincide and where divergence occurred as to the appraisal of the conditions under which jurisdiction was actually exercised.

In the context of the boundary demarcation, some of the maps produced by both the sides were not coincided in 35 places on the Sino-Nepal borderline. But it was settled forever in accordance with the principles of equality, mutual benefit, friendship and mutual accommodation. Besides, it was adopted by both the parties; the Five Principles of Peaceful Co-existence and in a spirit of fairness, reasonableness, mutual understanding and most importantly respecting each other as Nepal and China have the equal rights and status in the international spheres.

Sagarmatha was Claim by China

In connection to the boundary delineation, China had claimed that Sagarmatha (Chomolungma) belonged to her, while Prime-Minister B.P. Koirala visited Beijing on 21 March 1960. But Koirala refused to entertain the claim. During the discussion, Chinese side mentioned that Everest is the British name and Chomolungma is the Tibetan name since long. These names are written on the maps published by the respective countries. But there is no word for it in the Nepalese language. In reply, Nepal side responded that Sagarmatha is its Nepalese name. But the Chinese thought it was of recently named. In counter response, Nepal briefed that the emerald Nepalese historian Babu Ram Aacharya named it colloquially as Sagarmatha in 1938 after the research and investigation, though we have not yet published the map with our own language and script. Eventually, China was not satisfied one hundred percent with all these answers and they proposed to rename the mountain as "Friendship Peak." But Nepal did not agree on it. Finally it was agreed to name as Sagarmatha in Nepal and Chomolungma in China, after the cordial discussions.

Regarding the question of Sagarmatha, two parties exchanged the maps. The delineation on the maps of the two countries was different. The Chinese maps which were drawn on the basis of Chinese historical situation show the mountain within Chinese territory, while the Nepalese maps drawn on its historical facts show the mountain on the boundary line between two countries. Finally Chinese side agreed to follow the Nepalese delineation, which shows the mountain on the boundary line, with the northern half belonging to China and the southern half belonging to Nepal, respecting the water-parting line.

As a result, the dispute of Sagarmatha was settled and ended while the visiting Prime Minister Chou En-Lai made a statement in Kathmandu that "Sagarmatha belongs to Nepal." This statement was made in a press conference at Singha Darbar Gallery Hall on 28 April 1960 at 10.30 P.M. And it proved as an action of the principles of mutual accommodation and real friendship with mutual understanding of the degree of sensitivity and gravity of the problems.

There may be an underlying curiosity that how Sagarmatha belongs to Nepal and why the world has recognized that Sagarmatha lies in Nepal, whereas the northern half of the mountain belongs to China! The simple answer is that the northern face of Sagarmatha on the Chinese frontier has very steep slope and it is very difficult to stand the mountaineer on the border ridge, whereas the southern face into the Nepalese frontier has less steep.

The most important geographical fact is that there is a small sloping terrace having 6 by 7-ft. on the Nepalese side just south of the water-parting borderline and this is the highest portion of the mountain. Those who accent on the top of Sagarmatha also from the northern (Chinese frontier) route, they must step on to the Nepalese sloping terraced area to conquer the summit of Sagarmatha. Until and unless the expeditioners climbing from northern face step on to the Nepalese side i.e. the highest part, they are not regarded as the conqueror of Sagarmatha. To mount the victory flag on the summit and even to put off the expeditioners' bag and to take the pictures as the conqueror, the mountaineers must have to stay into the Nepalese frontier. With all these facts Sagarmatha belongs to Nepal and it is recognized by the world.

NEPAL-INDIA-CHINA TRI-JUNCTION POINTS, YET TO BE FIXED

Regarding the tri-junction of the western end, Chinese Ambassador to Nepal Zeng Xu Yong told in a program organized by the Reporter's Club that Lipulek was regarded as the tri-junction boundary point among Nepal, India and China by which Kalapani lies in the Nepalese territory as the boundary agreement between Nepal and China was signed three and half decades ago. However, old documents were ignored at that time which depict the Nepalese border up to Limpiyadhura, the origin of the river Mahakali (Kantipur Daily, 3 September 1999). With all these facts, it is sure that the length of Nepal-China borderline will be further extended and its final total length will be nearabout 1,464 km, after the finalization of the tri-junction points at Limpiyadhura and Jhinsang Peak. But nobody knows even the approximate period of the finalization of these triple-points, because it needs the consent of India indeed, as an inevitable fact.

Border Protocols

After the completion of the joint boundary demarcation physically on the ground, Boundary Protocol was signed on 20 January 1963 by Chinese Vice-Premier and Foreign Minister ChenYi and Vice-Chairman of the Nepalese Council of Ministers and Foreign Minister Dr. Tulasi Giri. After the elapse of fifteen years, joint inspection of the boundary line was made with the repair, maintenance and construction of the damaged pillars. In the same way Second Boundary Protocal was signed on 20 November 1979 by the Nepalese Foreign Minister K.B. Shahi and the Chinese Foreign Affairs Minister Huang Hua. Nextly, Third Protocol was signed on 6 December 1988 by the respective Foreign Ministers, Shailendra Kumar Upadhyaya from Nepal and Qian Qichen from Chinese side to renew the last protocol, after the completion of the joint inspection and maintenance of the borderline. These are the images of the true friendship between Nepal and China.

Concluding Remarks

Now it is high time to make the fourth protocol, because twelve years have been elapsed since the third protocol was signed. There might have been damaged and disappeared some of the main boundary pillars and reference pillars or markers due to landslide, flood and snow. So it needs to formulate a joint inspection committee to erect the missing pillars and repair the damaged ones. Nepal-China friendship will be further consolidated as one of the good neighbours with the inspection and maintenance of Nepal-China borderline at an interval of a decade. This is the common interest of both the nations. Nextly, it is expected that Nepal will execute positively to open two more trade routes at Kimathanka (Dingri) and Mustang (Liji) in a very near future as already agreed by both the nations. It will help to promote not only the trade and economic activities but also to strengthen furthermore the cordial friendship between the people of Nepal and China.

NEPAL AND INDO CHINA RELATIONS

Nepal, the only Hindu Kingdom in the world, underwent major transformation in its political landscape with the overthrow of monarchy ....years ago. The Maoists, backed, motivated and funded by China became a force to reckon with when they started a violent agitation. Ever since overthrow of the monarchy, the democratic process in the country has come under severe strain. Nepal's two immediate neighbours, India and China have apparently shown keen interest in the likely political outcome – an interest which has guided both the nations to protect their interests in the erstwhile Kingdom.

Nepal has been without a government since June 30, when former prime minister Madhav Kumar Nepal stood down under pressure from the opposition Maoist party to pave the way for a new power-sharing administration. Since then, political leaders have been unable to agree on the shape of the new government and six earlier attempts to choose a new prime minister have failed, with neither of the two candidates securing an absolute majority. The Maoists, who fought a decade-long civil war against the state before transforming themselves into a political party and winning a 2008 election, hold the largest number of seats in parliament, but not enough to govern alone.

Now, the political crisis in Nepal further deepened as the Parliament failed to elect the Prime Minister even after the sixth round of the prime ministerialelections on Sunday. Prachanda, Chairman of the Unified Communist Party of Nepal — Maoists (UCPN-M), secured 240 votes, almost double the tally that his only rival — Ramchandra Poudel of the Nepali Congress. However, he fell short of the minimum requirement by 60 votes. The ongoing constitutional crisis has been continuing for the last two months. Both the candidates failed to garner support from the 601-member Constituent Assembly. Prachanda got 240 votes, but 101 parliamentarians voted against him. Poudyal could manage only 122 votes. 206 parliamentarians remained neutral.The date for next round of election has been fixed for September 7.Nepal's Madhesi ethnic minority who hold 82 of the 601 seats in parliament, enough to secure a victory for the Maoists, hold the key to formation of the government. This is te reason for the "buy" theory.

Amidst reports of a mega Chinese delegation, comprising 21 members, reaching Nepal to meet the political party heads, the political activity after Prachanda's recent failure to secure the Prime Ministerial post has heated up. The delegation is headed by He Yong, vice-premier and secretary at the secretariat of the 17th Central Committee of the Communist Party of China. This when a wiretap on Saturday alleged that the Maoists have sought Rs 50 crore from China to "buy" lawmakers to get their supremo elected to the coveted post in what is now called the audio tape scandal . In the audio-tape leaked to the media outlets, apparently UCPN-Maoist foreign department chief Krishna Bahadur Mahara is heard holding a conversation with an unidentified Chinese official seeking Rs. 500 million to buy off lawmakers to ensure Maoist supremo's win in the prime ministerial election. Now the maoists as well as the two largest ruling parties – the Communist Party of Nepal-Marxist Leninist and Nepali Congress – apparently invited the delegation to visit Nepal.

The media as well as the parties' reaction to the imminent visit shows up the anti-India hysteria building up in Nepal. Even vefore the elections, Prachanda began blaming their current arch enemy Indiafor the failure, accusing India's external intelligence agency Research and Analysis Wing (RAW) of plotting to ensure Prachanda's failure in an election already marred by charges of floor-crossing, horse-trading and backstabbing.

India, however, has taken note of the reports of alleged Chinese monetary interference in the on-going Prime Ministerial elections in Nepal. "New Delhi has taken note of the reports," sources said here today, two days after allegations of a Maoist leader trying to buy MPs with the help of a Chinese "friend" surfaced

When the Indian government's special envoy Shyam Saran had visited Nepal last month, it created bitter animosity and accusations of Indian intervention, especially by the Maoists and royalists. Indian commentators underline that Nepal is passing through a very "critical phase" and in such circumstances, China's interference into the internal affairs of Nepal will not only be a threat to the future of the neighbouring country but also the security of India.

This news, coming on the heels of reports of Chinese military presence in Gilgit Baltistan and their renewed efforts of incresed political and military activity in Bangladesh and Burma is worrisome for India. Indian political parties have asked for a close vigil on the "developments" in Nepal. Some how this vigil is not enough.

China 's four-fold policy to strengthen its bilateral relations with Nepal has been articulated as: "First, accommodate each other's political concern. Second, enhance theeconomic cooperation on the basis of mutual benefit. Third, boost people-to-people and cultural exchanges. Fourth, strengthen the coordination andcooperation in international and regional affairs." This report brings out the extent of Sino Nepal cooperation in all these fields with their attendant security implications.

China is matching its strategy with deeds to gain the confidence of the Nepali people by participating actively in the socio economic changes bringing about a political change. The assistance is graduallybound to manifest in Nepal leaning far too left and creating unmatched security dilemmas for India. There is a suggestion in an article in IDSA that India should invest $ one billion in Nepal, find alternatives to Mahakali agreement and engage in nation building in Nepal to counter the Chinese influence. Despite its sincerity, the article falls short in suggesting that India apparently has already missed the bus in Nepal as it has in Burma and Bangladesh. The smaller nations no longer want a big brother who can not be consistent with its commitments and appears to dominate them without participating in their genuine growth. This when China has pulled all stops to pursue it's five fingers policy in Nepal.

China does not need Nepal to pursue any military strategy against India. It is well disposed as of now in Tibet but another finger won't hurt. This needs shift in Indian paradigms of dealing with its neighbours on its periphery to marginalise the impact of the fingers – lest they are used assiduously for ulterior motives. Yes ofcourse, this should be a win win situation for our neighbours but in the long run, this investment is likely to yield high returns. Indian moves have to be borne out of a genuine farsighted policy and not ploys to counter China on its periphery.

As if that was not enough, the Pakistan media is already celebrating the growing Chinese influence over Nepal.

"If the Chinese have complete control of the country, there is no denying the fact that Pakistan will have free access to carry out anti-India activities from Nepalese soil and there is bound to be a chain reaction that in the long run would put immense burden on India to bear" as per a report in merinews. India needs to play it's cards well by keeping Nepal engaged constructively.

CHINA AND INDIA AS DRIVERS OF REGIONAL GROWTH

There is little doubt that China's rapidly growing exports to countries outside of Asia-Pacific in Asia has generated equally rapid growth in imports by China from other Asian and Pacific countries, not just from its neighbours in East Asia but also from Australia, India and Indonesia. According to Perlez (2003), Japan's current "recovery is being driven by a surge in exports to China. Australia's healthy economy is being kept that way by Chinese investments in liquid natural gas products. China is now South Korea's largest trading partner... In Indonesia, Malaysia and the Philippines (and to a lesser extent in Thailand)... China's main interest is to scoop up what it can for its modernization. Indonesians call this new relationship with Beijing as 'feeding the dragon.'" Although India is by far the largest (and rapidly growing) market in South Asia, it is yet to have a major impact on the trade of its neighbours in South Asia in spite of the creation of the South Asian Preferential Trade Area (SAPTA) in 1997. To a significant extent, this reflects the hostile relations between India and the next largest market in South Asia, viz. Pakistan. Pakistan is yet to grant a most favoured nation status to India. Unless the relations between the two normalize, the prospects of SAPTA are not bright. However, India-Sri Lanka bilateral trade and investment have grown rapidly since the conclusion of a free trade agreement between the two became operational in March 2000. Recent signs of a warming of Indo- Pakistani relations, if they lead to their normalization, could make India the engine of growth for South Asia, as China already is in the Asia-Pacific region.

Foreign Direct Investment

China receives a much larger flow of net foreign direct investment (projected at $57 billion in 2003) than India's (under $4 billion in 2001-02). In Srinivasan (2002), I discussed some of the reasons for this difference. In short, as Luce and Kynge (2003) succinctly point out, "whether it is China's cheaper, more reliable power supply or the more rapid turn around at its ports,

China remains an incalculably better environment for most manufacturing than India, which is slowly waking up to this." This environment and the bureaucratic obstacles at all levels of government in India in large part explain the huge flow of FDI to China relative to India. The Indian government has recognized FDI as key for achieving the Tenth Plan target of 8% annual growth and appointed a steering committee on FDI in 2001. It reported in 2002 with several recommendations for making India more attractive as a destination for FDI.

Exchange Rates and Foreign Reserves

Although China's trade surplus with the United States has been growing, its overall trade surplus is modest since it is running a growing trade deficit with Asia-Pacific countries that offsets in large part its trade surplus with the US. The economic logic that only a country's overall trade and current account balances have economic significance and not its bilateral balances with any one or a subset of trading partners, has never been understood by politicians anywhere, and in particular, in the US. As Japanese trade surpluses created an anti-Japan backlash in the eighties, it is now China's turn to be at the receiving end of US pressure. China has accumulated a substantial (projected at $383 billion by the end of 2003) foreign exchange reserves, exceeding its annual imports. India has done the same—its reserves, around $92 billion at the end of 2003, exceed by a substantial margin the likely imports of $60 billion. The issues of the appropriate level of reserves, and whether both countries have accumulated far too much relative to what would be needed to smooth volatility in export earnings and import expenditures and to contain any potential financial crisis like the one experienced by East Asia in 19975. Since neither the renminbi nor the rupee is convertible on capital account and capital controls are in place in both countries, prima facie the probability of an exchange rate crisis of the type experienced by countries with open capital account and fully convertible currencies is very low. This is not to say, of course, that a balance of payments crisis (BOP) that makes the prevailing exchange rate unsustainable cannot arise—after all, despite capital controls and an inconvertible (on capital account) rupee, India experienced a severe BOP crisis in 1991, which resulted in the devaluation of the rupee and other policy changes. Still, given that partial insurance from other sources of external funds (e.g., from the IMF) is in principle available, should self-insurance through reserves be pushed as far as the current level of reserves in China and India seem to have done?

Any attempt to determine the appropriate level of reserves has to be based on an analysis of the appropriate exchange rate regime for either country, and the related issue of whether the benefits from integration with the global financial markets outweigh the costs. Without doing such an analysis myself, let me cite Kenneth Rogoff of Harvard, the former Economic Councillor and Director, Research Department of the IMF, on the issue:

My interpretation of the evidence not just from Asia but from the whole world, from Europe's experience, from floating rates, from the Bretton Woods system, is that policy makers vastly overrate the risks of having volatile exchange rates and vastly underrate the indirect costs that can come from all the policies that they have to try to suppress them. Certainly I wouldn't say that India has gone too far at the moment in accumulating reserves, it has a very strong position but I think all the countries in Asia are reaching a point when they have to start asking the question how much is enough, that basically a lot of the reserves that the Asian economies are accumulating—even outside of Japan—we are talking about close to a trillion dollars, are basically low interest rate loans from the emerging markets to United States and Europe, and this is very costly. There are opportunity costs to the domestic economy. How much is enough and at what point should one risk letting the exchange rate appreciate. Knowing the multilateral aspects of it, I realize that there are some outside the IMF who call for greater flexibility in Asian currencies in order to strengthen demand from the rest of the world. I think that is an issue worth considering but it is not the one I want to focus on. From the Asian economies' own perspective, and this is true for India, it is true for China, it is true for virtually all the countries in the region, moving to a regime of greater flexibility would be something that is advisable, would not bring the cost many policy makers fear, and in fact would allow the economies to reduce the level of recession and that would have many positive growth effects (Rogoff 2003). Rogoff's conclusion does not imply that US pressure on China to revalue the renminbi was justified or that India should also let its rupee appreciate, but only that greater flexibility in exchange rates would be appropriate in both countries.

The Indian exchange rate regime is one of managed float (although Rogoff prefers to characterize it as a crawling peg), and it does allow some flexibility. It is possible to argue that the Indian central bank (i.e., Reserve Bank of India) has inappropriately intervened to prevent the rupee from appreciating, and this has cost the Indian economy in terms of foregone growth. But this is an argument that the flexibility inherent in the managed float regime has not been utilized appropriately. It is not the same as arguing that India should immediately make the rupee fully convertible and adopt a regime of clean float. The latter argument is not persuasive for the simple reason that domestic financial sector reforms are incomplete, and it is risky to open the capital account under the circumstances.

In any case, there is no country in the world, developed or developing, that allows a clean float of its currency. On the other hand, there are long term benefits from a convertible currency and by credibly committing to a fully convertible rupee for at a not too distant and specified future date, the pressure to complete the financial sector reforms by that date would become significant. What about China? Again, the problems in the financial sector, particularly the overhang of NPLs are serious, and an immediate revaluation might worsen the problem. Besides, it has not been established by anyone, least of all by the US Treasury, that the current renminbi-dollar exchange rate is too far from a long-run equilibrium rate. If it is not, and China moves to a floating regime, that US Treasury might find, to its surprise, that the exchange rate does not move from its current level! Unfortunately, China is likely to succumb to the pressure to revalue if newspaper reports (*Financial Times*, February 10, 2004) are to be believed.

It is not unlikely that if India's reserves continue to climb, and outsourcing gathers further momentum, there would be charges of "currency manipulation" against Indian authorities, as the Chinese are currently being charged with. China and India should cooperate in resisting such accusations and pressures and decide on their exchange rate policies in their own interests.

Finally, as Rogoff rightly points out, by continuing to accumulate reserves in terms of US dollar assets, China, India and other Asian countries are financing US current account deficits. As Alan Beattie (2003) points out: "In theory, Asians' role in financing the US current account deficit could give them enormous economic or even political leverage, since a sudden shortfall in capital inflows would spark a slide in the dollar and possibly a sharp rise in interest rates." But he rightly concludes that: "A wholesale flight from the dollar, if it drove up interest rates and forced the US into a rapid tightening of consumers' belts, would also hurt one of the principle buyers of Asia's exports." Chinese and Indian policy makers are sophisticated enough to realize this and can be expected to slow the accumulation of reserves, if appropriate, and allow greater exchange rate flexibility in due course.

INDIA'S SECURITY CONCEPT ON ITS CHINA POLICY

Earlier sections of this book explain changes in India's post-Cold War security concept and adjustments to its China policy. In the process of this discussion, we have distinguished two phases of adjustment to both the post-Cold War India security concept and China policy, and established that these changes were more or less simultaneous. We have also found that India's China policy reflects its security concept; in other words that adjustments to the content of India's China policy correspond to continuities and discontinuities in India's security concept. It may be said that this consistency demonstrates the important influence India's security concept has had on its China policy.

Policy-making, in any event, is the linking of concepts and policy; in other words, concepts, through government policy-making, crystallize into policy. Exploring the evolution of the Indian policy-making class and mechanisms, therefore, also benefits understanding of the manner in which security concepts of different eras and phases have influenced India's China policy.

India's foreign policy behaviour during the Cold War was largely determined by a few predominant personalities, both its foreign and security policies having long been dominated by Nehru and Indira Gandhi. The two leader's views on China had decisive influence on India's China policy. When considering India's defeat in the 1962 Sino–Indian Border Conflict and the open wound it represented to both the Nehru family and the INC, their adoption of an unyielding tack toward China was the sole political means of saving face. Sino–Indian relations consequently remained in stalemate for nearly 30 years. When Rajiv Gandhi replaced his mother in 1985, he seemed at first to follow her line on foreign policy. The rapidly changing international situation, however, forced him to veer from it, and specific improvements in Sino–Soviet relations compelled his adjustments to India's China policy. Soviet leader Mikhail Gorbachev urged Rajiv Gandhi during a visit to India in 1986 to improve relations with China, saying it would suit Soviet interests, and hinting at a press conference that the USSR would no longer be willing to provide support to India in the event of Sino–Indian conflict. In this situation, Rajiv Gandhi considered that India on its own would be powerless against a threat on two fronts. He was hence forced to change his preparations for a two-front war, as it was apparent that dispelling tensions along the eastern front through reconciliation with China would allow him to concentrate India's energies on the western front with Pakistan.

The Nehru family's stately bearing was absent after the Cold War, and the INC's power had declined. The insularity that had characterized India's foreign policy-making process since independence, however, did not change. The nation's foreign and security policy stayed in the hands of the prime minister and cabinet from 1991 to 1996, during which time the views of Prime Minister Rao and leaders of the INC government on security and foreign policy matters were decisive, and the influence of parliament, think tanks and academic institutions was negligible. It is notable, however, that Rao's background as home minister, defence minister and external affairs minister throughout the 1980s, as well as his status as the Congress Party's elder statesman, signified that he was a loyal adherent of Nehruvianism, and unrepresentative of any new type of thinking. The transformation of India's security concept during the Rao administration, therefore, can be understood as entirely the result of external forces.

As earlier mentioned, changes in the international and domestic situation compelled Rao to change his understanding of national strength. He began emphasizing the strategic influence of economic strength and promoting restoration of the economy as a matter of urgency in withstanding security threats in the aftermath of the Cold War. This passive reaction to a complex situation gave the impression of India's overall foreign policy as passive and defensive. India adopted a focused approach to diplomacy during this period, directing its energies towards restoring the economy but maintaining a low profile in international affairs, as expressed in its China policy. Rao continued and furthered Rajiv Gandhi's adjustments by focusing on stabilization of Sino–Indian political relations and establishing tranquil borders as means to ensuring the recovery of India's domestic economy.

Two major changes occurred in India's foreign policy-making process during 1998. The first was the BJP's assumption of office that ended the long-standing INC power monopoly, and established foundations for a clean break with the traditional security concept. Although the BJP's domestic policies had a relatively ideological slant and promoted a Hinduist revival, the party was pragmatic as regards foreign policy. In contrast to the Congress Party, it dared to confront history, criticise India's previous foreign policy and introduce new thinking. Jaswant Singh, successively the Vajpayee government's External Affairs Minister and Finance Minister, published early in 1999 a book entitled *Defending India* in which he systematically describes his new security concept. Various views were thereafter expressed in government-issued articles. The BJP was obviously preparing to move on from the passive security concept of the Rao era. The second major change was India's refinement of its foreign policy-making mechanism. The November 1998 establishment of the National Security Council symbolized India's casting off of the influence and control of personality-based policy-making in favour of scientific research, inquiry and decision-making, and comprehensive long-term planning. The introduction by National Security Advisory Board subordinated to the National Security Council of scholarly authorities, reporters and former government and military officials demonstrated how much more open India's foreign policy-making process had become.

The BJP differed in its approach to China policy from both that of the Cold War era Nehru family, with its 1962 complex, and the early 1990s Rao government, which had been wearied and bound hand and foot by domestic and international pressure. The BJP's seizing of this historic opportunity confirmed India's rise as the nation's long-term strategic goal and placed its relationship with China on the strategic level. In other words, the BJP saw the Sino–Indian relationship as an important influence on India's rise. Although the two nations would be dealing with historically significant problems, they could be seen as a starting point.

The gradual opening of India's foreign policy-making process, moreover, made way for a vibrant exchange of ideas regarding China policy, which fell roughly into three groups: the first held that Sino–Indian cooperation suits both sides' interests and that post-Cold War China has no intention of making an enemy of India, desiring instead friendly relations and strategic partnership; the second that China is a long-term strategic threat to India because China's strategic objectives lie in establishing hegemony over Asia, which necessitates India's containment and, therefore, limitation of Indian influence. India, therefore, should adopt diametrically opposed policies; and the third group, situated between the two, held that the two nations could simultaneously rise to become main Asian powers and that competition and cooperation could coexist. Discussions on how to evaluate and understand China by Indian scholars and strategic circles are ongoing. After frequent debates among Indian National Security Council groups, the third, middle-ground viewpoint seems to be gaining acceptance.

When the INC regained power in 2004, a variety of factors led the new government to carry on with the previous administration's security concept. The new INC government's China policy was its predecessor's legacy, because the rise of India's international status during the BJP coalition government left the INC powerless to dispute the success of the previous government's foreign policy. The INC's democratized and more youthful leadership team was also willing to jettison historical baggage and look to the future. Although the Nehru family's leadership role within the Congress Party remained uncontested, the influence of Prime Minister Manmohan Singh and Foreign Minister Mukherjee on foreign and security policy could not be disregarded. Moreover, the liberalization of India's foreign policy-making process was superimposed against a long-standing civil service system which ensured continuity of policy. In other words, many masterminds of BJP foreign policy still active in the external affairs ministry, defence ministry and other relevant functional departments under the INC, as well as in consultative committees, the media, think tanks and other non-functional departments, continued to exert influence.

Substantial changes occurred in India's China policy after the end of the Cold War whereby the nation's long-standing (1962–1988) antagonistic approach became one of reconciliation and engagement. These adjustments originated to a great extent in changes in the sub-continent's post-Cold War security concept, manifest in two major shifts which effected two major phases of adjustment in India's China policy. The new post-Cold War

China policy nonetheless retained traces of the former, programme, imbuing it with a duality that reflected the overlap of India's old and new security concepts.

A change in India's security concept first became apparent during the period from the end of the Cold War to 1998. The first phase of adjustments this change triggered in India's China policy was evident in the sub-continent's extended concept of military might as national strength to one encompassing economic factors, and acknowledgement of the strategic value of economic strength in countering what it perceived as the looming threat of marginalization within the international community. Restoration of the domestic economy hence became a main measure through which to resist security threats in the post-Cold War era. Having made this shift in foreign policy objectives towards economic recovery, India set about creating a favourable environment within which to achieve this goal. Overall implementation of a China policy of preserving stable Sino--Indian relations by guaranteeing border tranquillity was vital to achieving this strategic objective. India consequently focused on the feasibility of reconciliation and, in view of China's reflective, inward-looking mood, no longer viewed China as an enemy. As regards India's specific policies, while focusing on the establishment of a progressive means to guaranteeing tranquil borders, thereby stabilizing Sino–Indian relations, India at the same time sought communication and cooperation in other areas. To avoid provoking China, the Indian government made tactical adjustments to its approach to Tibet from that of exploiting the issue and causing uproar to handling the matter in a low-key manner.

The new developments apparent in India's security concept in 1999 brought with it the second phase of adjustments to India's China policy. Indian leaders considered that the nation's security environment had improved to the extent that it constituted a strategic opportunity for India to rise to global-power status. This change in thinking and understanding caused the second shift of objective in India's foreign policy from that of improving the economy to the grand goal of global-power status. It corresponded to India's acknowledgement of the crucial nature of the Sino–Indian relationship and change of focus from border tranquillity and stable political relations to comprehensive considerations of how the two nations' relationship would strategically affect India's; rise. These insights compelled a shift of objective in India's China policy towards making China a positive factor in the sub-continent's rise; also recognition that this objective could be accomplished only by maintaining a stable basis for Sino–Indian relations. Official introduction during this phase of a comprehensive security concept signalled India's adoption of a more pragmatic, comprehensive handling of its relations with China. The specific steps it adopted were: increasing economic cooperation with China, thus benefiting India's economic development and stabilizing bilateral political relations; strengthening military communication and security dialogue, thus deepening understanding of China's strategic intentions towards India, increasing mutual trust, minimizing misunderstandings and avoiding conflict; and seeking Chinese support in its quest for a permanent seat on the UN Security Council, which would expand India's political power and international prestige.

In the course of research, however, it became apparent to the author that India's security concept did not undergo a thoroughgoing change after the Cold War ended, as elements of the Cold War approach remained in place. Although India's security concept extended after 1988 to include both military and economic security, the ultimate purpose of national defence as regards a fundamental guarantee of security nonetheless remained that of increased military strength to safeguard national unity and territorial integrity. India abandoned its strategy of pursuing security through alliances, yet still viewed parity and the principle of checks and balances as hallmarks of its national defence. Influenced as it was by traditional concepts, post-Cold War India's China policy was imbued with vigilance. Even though India did not perceive China as a threat in the short term, it was nevertheless concerned that the swing in balance of power between the two was not in its favour, and that China constituted a potential obstacle to India's rise. Indian leaders consequently embarked on a race against China to expand comprehensive national strength, particularly military force, including India's nuclear capability, as the means to a balance of power. India at the same time sought to offset Chinese influence both regionally and globally through development of strategic relationships with the United States, Japan and other nations. The sub-continent also remained vigilant in the long-standing issues of border disputes and Sino–Pakistani relations, and maintained pressure on China in this regard.

Changes in post-Cold War India's security concept were thus the result of both domestic and foreign factors. The first change during the early post-Cold War period was triggered by passive reactions to transformations in the nation's domestic and international situation that, in turn, prompted a passive transformation of thinking and understanding, manifest in passive defensiveness of India's foreign policy, specifically its China policy. The security concept that appeared during the late 1990s was comparatively proactive. The expanded strength of India's domestic economy and improvement of its external environment compelled a new understanding of security issues, as expressed in the proactive change in its security concept. This assertiveness was manifest in strategy and in an active, enterprising foreign policy. Seizing the historic opportunity to realize India's rise had become the common security objective of both major Indian political parties. Decentralization of political power and expanded openness of the foreign policy-making process, however, caused India's old and new security concepts to bind into one, and the resultant duality of India's hybrid security concept since the Cold War's end is reflected in its China policy. As India's dual security concept will continue into the foreseeable future, the duality of its China policy will be difficult to change.

INDIA'S CHINA POLICY

Certain scholars believe that India's China policy has undergone three major phases of adjustment since the end of the Cold War: the pre-1998 phase policy of reconciliation; the 1998–2000 phase policy of hostility; and the 2000 to present phase policy of engagement. The second phase around the time of the 1998 nuclear tests featured harangues from the Indian government regarding the 'China threat' and a brief deadlock in Sino–Indian relations. The author, however, believes that two, rather than three, phases of adjustment are applicable to an explanation of the state of bilateral relations between China and India in the post-Cold War era.

When considering India's overall strategic aims at the time of the 1998 nuclear tests and the implications and specific actions of its subsequent China policy, it is difficult to pinpoint two 180 degree-policy shifts in the course of just two years. Facts demonstrate that India named China as a threat at the time of the 1998 tests as a matter of expedience to acquiesce in the anti-China stance of certain parties in the United States and other Western nations; it was a ploy whose purpose was to divert attention from and rationalize the nuclear tests, thereby dispelling any notion of sanctions.

It should be borne in mind, however, that India's understanding of comprehensive national strength deepened after the Cold War, as did its leaders' belief that nuclear arms and credible nuclear deterrence were hallmarks of a superpower. Entering the nuclear club was consequently a stride towards achieving one of the sub-continent's greatest national aspirations. The Rao government, which pursued a China policy of reconciliation and engagement, had made preparations for nuclear tests but stopped short of carrying them out for fear of the potential burden on the newly recovered economy of international sanctions.

Prime Minister Vajpayee and other political leaders repeatedly and publicly expressed soon after the 1998 tests that India had no wish to hold China as an enemy or a threat, stating, to the contrary, their desire for reinforced friendly relations. At no point during this period did diplomatic engagement between India and China cease. Indian External Affairs Minister Jaswant Singh's visit to China in June 1999 demonstrated that the Sino–

Indian relationship had recovered in the space of a year from any damage that the nuclear tests had inflicted upon it. That becoming a nuclear power while maintaining stable relations with China were post-Cold War India's strategic goals was also implied by the sub-continent's explicit moves towards repairing its relationship with China. The 1998 nuclear tests constituted no fundamental change to India's China policy and should, within the scope of Sino–Indian relations, be regarded as a minor episode. Moreover, the shift of India's China policy in 1988 was not prompted by any change of security concept; Prime Minister Rajiv Gandhi's trip to China that year was motivated by the fact of Sino–Soviet reconciliation. Changes in security concept explicitly propelled India's; post-Cold War China policy adjustments. This book, therefore, primarily examines developments and changes in India's China policy after the Cold War. It holds that a substantive change indeed occurred; specifically from one of hostility and antagonism during the Cold War (especially 1962–1988) to reconciliation and engagement thereafter. This policy change, however, was by no means instantaneous but characterized by gradual, phased development. Two, rather than three, phases of adjustment tally with changes in India's post-Cold War security concept.

India's China Policy from the End of the Cold War to 1998

Indian leaders believed after 1962 that hostilities between China and India were inevitable, and viewed China as a major enemy. Prime Minister Indira Gandhi considered Sino–Indian antagonism as going far beyond border disputes, and that China was pursuing the more 'complex' policy of pressing India on all fronts and, moreover, displacing the sub-continent by establishing its own dominant position in the Asian power hierarchy. The goal of India's China policy during this period, therefore, was to ensure its supremacy over China in Asia and, in the event of armed conflict, to avoid repeating mistakes that had led to its defeat in the 1962 Sino–Indian conflict. India's policy at the time can be so summarized: strengthen military capability and deployment; seek aid from major powers, respectively, the United States, United Kingdom and USSR;

and support Chinese separatist forces. After the Cold War ended, however, changes in India's domestic and international situation brought tremendous challenges, and its position as regards China and its related policy goals showed clear adjustments.

India considered China as a nation going through a reflective, 'inward looking' period and, as such, had no intention of attacking the sub-continent. In the short-term, therefore, it constituted no threat. The goal of India's new China policy was to maintain stability in Sino–Indian relations, ensure peaceful borders and create conditions suitable for India to gather its resources and restore economic and military strength. The specific policy adjustments were as follows.

Achieve Simultaneous Progress in Solving Border Disputes

For almost two decades after 1962, India made resolution of border disputes a pre-condition for normalizing relations with China. Its insistence in this regard was the main reason for the longstanding chill in Sino–Indian relations.

Although the two nations restored ambassadorial-level diplomatic relations in 1976, and in 1981 agreed to begin talks on the border issue, this principled standpoint did not change. Upon meeting with visiting then-External Affairs Minister Vajpayee early in 1979, Comrade Deng Xiaoping proposed an agreement that would provide 'a package solution' for relevant border disputes. He said that if it were not possible completely to resolve border disputes at an early date, he would consider cooperation in other areas. But it was not until 1988 during Rajiv Gandhi's trip to China that the Indian government accepted this suggestion and formally initiated the process of normalizing bilateral relations which the successive Indian governments pursued and implemented after the Cold War ended. It is notable that during the time the two sides promoted negotiations on border issues they also exchanged high-level visits in which the two nations signed cooperative agreements in such areas as trade, technology, education and culture, and that cooperation between them grew ever greater in depth and breadth.

Shift Strategies on Border Talks

As India needed a peaceful, stable environment in which to concentrate on economic recovery, securing Sino–Indian borders was its primary goal in the early 1990s. Because of India's; pre-1988 insistence on not normalizing Sino–Indian relations until the border issues were settled, there were suspicions that the sub-continent was 'taking improvements in bilateral relations as a bargaining chip through which to force China to yield in border disputes'. India consequently insisted in the talks that began in 1981 on its own position as regards a segmented solution to the issue. India's objective understanding of the complexity of the Sino–Indian border dispute after the Cold War and of realistic strategic considerations and needs prompted an adjusted strategy for these talks. This was manifest in its suggestion of a gradual solution to border disputes: the first step would be to stabilize the Line of Actual Control (LAC) situation and eliminate disagreements over its demarcation; the second to reach agreement on preserving peace and tranquillity along the LAC; and the third to take measures to establish mutual trust along the LAC.

This accomplished, the two nations could then address substantive problems in their border dispute. This tentative plan enabled India and China to approach a consistent position whereby the two sides worked to achieve a solution to Sino–Indian border disputes and create an atmosphere of reasonableness and peace. The two nations made progress, signing in 1993 the Agreement on Maintenance of Peace and Tranquillity along the Line of Actual Control in the Sino– Indian Border Areas, and in 1996 the Agreement Between the Government of the Republic of India and the Government of the People's Republic of China on Confidence-Building Measures in the Military Field Along the Line of Actual Control in the India–China Border Areas. India saw these two agreements as on the one hand ensuring the two sides could resolve border disputes peacefully without resorting to violence, and on the other that border disputes would not inhibit the development of their bilateral relations.

Tibetan Issue and do not Provoke China

Leaders of India's independence movement had at the time of the British Raj followed the British colonialist concept of Tibet as a 'buffer region' between India and China. After winning independence, therefore, the Indian government supported from the very beginning the so-called 'Tibetan independence movement'.

At around the time of the founding of the People's Republic of China, India seized the opportunity offered by China's political upheaval to promote the international standing of the local Tibetan government and thwart China's liberation of Tibet. New Delhi continued unremittingly in its efforts to convince China's central government, even during the 1950s heyday of Sino–Indian amity, to give Tibet substantial autonomy and to reduce to the greatest extent possible the size of its garrison there. After the insurrection of 1959 the Indian government was more overt in its support of Tibet, giving asylum to fugitive rebels and propping up the so-called 'Tibetan Government in Exile' established by the Dalai Lama in 1960 in the Indian city of Dharamsala.

India further incited and encouraged Tibetan independence activities after the Sino–Indian conflict of 1962. In truth, Indian leaders considered their support for exiled Tibetans' separatist activities as an effective containment against China. But when Prime Minister Rajiv Gandhi visited China in 1988 he issued the statement: 'The Indian side reiterates the long-standing and consistent policy of the Government of India that Tibet is an autonomous region of China and that anti-China political activities by Tibetan elements are not permitted on Indian soil,' which implied India's change of approach from that of support for Tibetan independence.

Indian leaders reiterated this pledge after the Cold War ended and imposed limits on Tibetan fugitives' anti-China political activities. For instance, Indian officials would generally contact the Dalai Lama and leaders of the so-called Tibetan government in exile before a visit by Chinese leaders to India,

requesting that they refrain from Tibetan protests, demonstrations or other anti-Chinese behaviour.

Yet, differences still exist between China and India on the issue of Tibetan autonomy. Although, proceeding from the requirement of preserving stable Sino–Indian relations, the post-Cold War Indian government has been low-key in its support of the Dalai Lama and other Tibetan fugitives, this does not signify a substantial change in its strategic treatment of the Tibetan issue.

5

Sino-Nepalese Relations: Factoring in India

The end of the decade witnessed another state visit to China in December 2009 by Nepalese Prime Minister Madhav Kumar Nepal, the atmospherics of which were markedly less grandiose in the overall-all leveraging of Sino-Nepal relations and appeared to focus more on mundane concerns reflected by the signing of just two accords on Bilateral Economic and Technical Cooperation and a Memorandum of Understanding on Youth Exchanges. Following the abolition of monarchy in 2007 and with Nepal thus in a period of transition, the Chinese government has naturally tended to proceed with some caution and avoided alignment with any one political force, not knowing which party is clearly preponderant in Nepal.

This position has perhaps come into sharper relief after the much anticipated second visit to Beijing by former Premier Pushpa Kamal Dahal aka 'Prachanda' failed to materialize in May 2009. Though the immediate reason behind the cancellation of the visit had to do with the controversy surrounding the sacking of the Nepal Army Chief of Staff Rookmangad Katwal and Prachanda's subsequent resignation, it can also be argued that the agenda of the visit itself was overly ambitious and perhaps premature given the nature of politics of that time. It is obvious that the intensity of Sino-Nepal relations has oscillated during the course of the past decade on account of momentous events such as the assassination of King Birendra in June 2001 and transition to King Gyanendra, the People's Movement of 2006, the abolition of the monarchy and advent of republicanism and the complexities of the Nepalese peace process, land-mark events of the past decade which have all drawn sober official reactions from the Chinese government. However, it would appear that the overarching logic for Nepal in advancing relations with China has always rested on the premise that Nepal would not just accelerate interactions with China but would also open up to the broader canvas of Central Asia, Southeast Asia and even East Asia and thereby create new opportunities to promote its national development and prosperity.

The extent to which this logic impacts upon global geopolitics is debatable, but to say that such a process is detrimental to Indian interests and security concerns requires reevaluation in light of tightening Asian integration and also the notion of 'dynamic equilibrium' which has been employed to characterize Sino-Indian relations and which obviously have a bearing on regional developments. Similarly, remarks in April 2010 by Indian Foreign Minister S.M. Krishna in Beijing that India and China 'must always remember that the two countries are each part of the other's immediate periphery [and] that... both seek a secure and peaceful environment that allows them to focus on domestic growth prospects [and that we must] encourage progress in our neighborhood [so] we will be more secure and stable' (Krishna 2010)—would seem to point to a slightly reduced degree of Indian concern, for example, in the face of Nepal's desire to expand cooperation and connectivity with China and thereby wider regions. It would appear that some sections of the Indian strategic community are also thinking along these lines.

KEY ASPECTS OF MODERN SINO-NEPALESE RELATIONS

The most profound developments in contemporary Sino-Nepal relations are represented by the rapid pace of changes in the western sector of China encompassing the Tibet Autonomous region and also the Xinjiang Uyghur Autonomous Region. The completion of the Qinghai-Tibet Railway is a quintessential example of this, as is the nature of infrastructure development in Xinjiang which could in the near future have particular relevance for North-West Nepal.Such transformations in China's western regions have taken place with great intensity in the past decade and present Nepal with numerous opportunities to expand ties with China and beyond, especially in terms of physical connectivity. Indeed, Sino-Nepal relations are moving forward in a rather organic and irreversible manner.

Nepal shares a boundary of over 1,400 kilometers with Chinese territory (specifically with the Tibet Autonomous Region). Despite the fact that the Tibet issue has continued to crop up especially in Sino-US relations, Nepal's consistent espousal of the One China policy has rendered it a 'non-issue' in Nepal. Protests in Kathmandu by Tibetan activists notwithstanding, and in spite of very limited support for these protests by a small section of Nepal's civil society, by INGOs and some sections of the diplomatic community based in Kathmandu, no government in Nepal has broken with this policy. Further, Nepalese do not necessarily conflate Nepal-China relations with the Tibet issue.

Rather, what figures prominently in Nepal's imagination with respect to China is her expanding clout and achievements which are 'brought home' to Nepal on an almost daily basis via radio, television, internet, vehicular and air traffic, and also the movement of people and students. The likely impact of China on Nepal will be substantially amplified by 2013 when the Tibet Railway is expected to arrive at the border. It is true that Chinese soft power is increasingly being felt in Nepal, but one is rather confounded when only suspicions are cast on China and Nepal, for instance, when Confucius Centers are established in Nepal or when China Radio International launches a local FM radio station in Kathmandu(Bhattacharya2009), without conceding that Nepal stands to gain a great deal as well in terms of knowledge and information, in the same way that Nepal benefits from local radio broadcasts of the BBC World Service, from the Alliance Française, the Goethe Institute or the British Council, and from the availability of TV channels in Nepal in various languages such as Russian, German, English, French, Korean, Japanese, Arabic, Bengali, Hindi and so on. The Nepalese Service of China Radio International, as a matter of fact, has been operating in Nepal since 1975 and now has more than 500 CRI listener's clubs and millions of listeners in the country(Embassy of People's Republic of China in Nepal 2004).

Comments by a former Chinese ambassador to Nepal are instructive: 'Nepalese listeners of China Radio International (CRI) played an important role in disseminating information they got from CRI of China's latest developments to their relatives and friends so [as to] further understanding of each other'. The diffusion across Nepal of more information about China combined with increasing numbers of Nepalese students in China, as also the steadily increasing movement of peoples between the two countries is creating an organic and natural momentum that is bringing the two countries closer together. Furthermore, increasing air, vehicular and cargo traffic between the two countries is rapidly promoting Sino-Nepal economic relations as well.

Trade between Nepal and China has registered significant increases in recent years. Exports from Nepal to China in the fiscal year 2005-06 stood at approximately US$12.8 million; by fiscal year 2008-09, the figure had more than doubled to US$26.4 million. However, it must be acknowledged that China is still only the fifth largest export market for Nepal behind India, US, Bangladesh, and Germany. On the other hand, China is currently the second largest importing country to Nepal behind India and here staggering increases have been seen. For instance, in fiscal year 2004-05, imports from China stood at approximately US$183.7 million but by 2008-09 the figure was close to US$469 million, translating into a significant balance of trade deficit for Nepal of around US$443 million(Trade and Export Promotion Centre2008/2009). Finally, China is also one of the largest bilateral donors to Nepal, ranking sixth in terms of official development assistance to Nepal, providing about US$12 million every year.

On the political front, for China at this point in time, perhaps the single greatest concern in terms of Nepal is related to political stability. The reasons according to Han Hua of Beijing University are, 'simply because it is likely to have a spill-over effect on the security environment in China's frontier areas. For Beijing, Nepal's strategic disposition is of tremendous value to its South Asia Policy and to the stability in its frontier region (Han 2006)

In examining Sino-Nepal relations, the bulk of international commentary tends to focus narrowly on the Tibet issue without acknowledging that Nepal possesses its own logic in building a strong partnership with China, among other reasons because of the varied opportunities that lay in the broader China-India-Nepal triangle which Kathmandu seeks to nurture. At the same time, Sino-Nepal relations have been adversely affected to a certain extent due to protests launched by Nepal-domiciled Tibetan activists, precisely at a time when Nepal requires strong support from its neighbours to consolidate its own fragile peace process. While reports have claimed that an expanding Chinese presence in Nepal would be especially alarming to India, given that India and Nepal share a long and porous border such reports have failed to identify the reverse aspect of this argument, namely that China is also affected unfavorably by the same open border. Thus, the questions that routinely fail to get addressed concern the reciprocal advantages deriving from Nepal-China relations as also from Nepal-China-India relations, and failure to acknowledge these is to ignore truly historic developments currently underway in the very heart of Asia.

China-Nepal-India Trilateral Collaboration – A Potential Railway Axis

A great deal has already been written in Nepal about the considerable economic and trade benefits that will accrue to both Nepal and China in light of the extension of the Tibet Railway to the Nepalese border by 2013. It is worth considering this statement about the early history of American railroads, 'The rails carried more than goods; they provided a conduit for ideas, a pathway for discourse...The completion of [this] great railroad... gave birth to a transcontinental culture. And the route further engendered another profound change. Here was manifest destiny wrought in iron...Distances shrank, but identification to land and fellow [peoples] grew in inverse proportion' (PBS Online 2003). Admittedly, to quantify the economic benefits of a truly historic endeavor that seeks to link by rail two countries like Nepal and China separated by the tallest mountains in the world is a much simpler and less speculative exercise than to talk about the broader transformations that this would engender. However, just as the American Trans-continental Railroad or the Trans-Siberian Railway and others wrought profound and epochal transformations whether political, economic, social, or cultural—the Tibet-Nepal Railway is also set to do the same, though of course the environmental and other drawbacks of this have also to be acknowledged.

To turn to a larger concern, it should be mentioned that in spite of reported plans in the pipeline for a high-speed rail link that intends to connect China and India, specifically Kunming in south-western China to New Delhi(Krishnan 2010), the fact is that a railway line that connects China with India via Nepal is something which could materialize much more rapidly. In fact, once the Tibet Railway arrives at the Nepal border, the total length of the 'missing link' that would connect the three countries would stand at just 220 kilometers (Raxual in Bihar to Kathmandu 80 km, and Kathmandu to Kodari on the Sino-Nepal border, 140 km).

As has been pointed out before, this would represent the achievement of an earlier vision of the British Royal Geographical Society dating back to around 1885 to establish a rail link between India and China. Clearly, in achieving this, several objectives would be met simultaneously, namely the further cementing of Sino-Nepal relations and of Indo-Nepal relations and perhaps more importantly, the establishment of a cooperative trilateral axis that would cut vertically across the heart of Asia and naturally transform Nepal into an earnest 'Zone of Peace'. For Nepal in particular, if it becomes a transit state between India and China, some have argued that foreign investors could very well see greater prospects in investing in

Nepal. The Nepalese Foreign Ministry has noted that 'multinational companies may [decide to] produce in large quantities to capture the big markets of two gigantic economies. It might increase the possibilities of [amplification] in foreign investment in service sector industries [and] the creation of investment opportunities will [likewise] strengthen the tax base' (Nepal 2006).

India Feature in Sino-Nepal Relations

It is a truism that the India factor is pivotal in Sino-Nepal relations (just as the China factor is pivotal in Indo-Nepal relations). This becomes clear if we simply account for the fact that India is by far the largest trading partner for Nepal both in terms of imports and exports and the country's largest trade deficit is with India currently worth a staggering US$1.73 billion(Government of Nepal, Ministry of Commerce and Supplies, Trade and Export Promotion Centre, November 2009).For better or worse, India has also been closely involved at nearly every juncture of Nepal's modern political history.

Nonetheless, what has been amply demonstrated by events of the recent and more distant past is that to achieve true and long-term stability in Nepal (which is vital from a security perspective for both China and India) there must be a high degree of convergence and coordination between these two, the most populous countries of the world that sandwich Nepal with a population of just 27 million.

The narrow geographic space Nepal occupies as a sovereign state between India and China can be thought of as being both very consequential and quite inconsequential. It is consequential in the sense that, from a security standpoint, excessive and to that extent, unhealthy, jockeying and competition by China and India in Nepal (and the instability that must follow) would not bode well for either country in the face of this geographic reality. It is however inconsequential, in the sense that genuine cooperation between China and India in the Nepalese theatre can be relatively easy to achieve, and there are multiple ways to do so, the China-Nepal-India railway being just one example.

The main argument here from a Nepalese perspective is that sustained cooperation between its two neighbours on the question of Nepal would almost certainly constitute the key ingredient of the country's long-term stability and prosperity.

It would be appropriate here to highlight two old Chinese proverbs which can be normatively employed to discuss Sino-Nepal relations within the context of what is referred to as the 'India factor', the 'US factor' and 'Other External Power' factors. The first proverb says that 'better good neighbours near, than relations far away', while the second states that 'distant water won't quench your immediate thirst'. Indeed, Nepal's relations with both China and India stand unambiguously as the cornerstone of the country's foreign policy.

From the perspective of Kathmandu, however, the problem is that it is not enough for Nepal merely to have 'good neighbours' in the form of Beijing and New Delhi. That is to say, at a certain level, it may be largely irrelevant if China and India are 'good' to Nepal without also being good to each other. To evoke another Chinese proverb, 'it never rains on your neighbours without you getting your feet wet'.

To put it differently, if dark clouds hover over Sino-India relations, Nepal will certainly suffer the consequences, no matter how good each neighbor is to Nepal itself. As a matter of fact, the rampant instability we have seen in Nepal over the past decade can be traced somewhat broadly to miscommunication and disjointed efforts by China and India in the Nepalese arena. And this instability has spawned a very unfortunate and undesirable phenomenon which is precisely Nepal's sort of compulsion to cultivate 'relations far away' to address her many development challenges. During these years of sharp turmoil, substantial foreign aid and assistance supplied to Nepal by countries in many case continents away, has still not delivered stability to Nepal, and stability being the principle 'thirst' of the Nepalese people, it has in fact been borne out that distant water does not actually quench your immediate thirst. The case must be made therefore that in light of the centrality of the 'India factor' in Sino-Nepal relations (and vice-versa), ultimately genuine cooperation and partnership between the three countries must be the basis of the process to ensure stability in Nepal and therefore security for both China and India.

Shift in China's South Asian local Strategy?

Finally, with regards to the question of the shifts in the dynamics of China's South Asian regional strategy within which Sino-Nepal relations are arguably embedded, one should begin by acknowledging overarching processes of contemporary Chinese foreign policy. China's interactions with South Asia in the form of SAARC are quite limited and lackluster, relative to China's diplomatic engagements in its other peripheral regions such as in Southeast Asia, Central Asia and beyond in Africa and the Pacific Island region. China is presently merely an observer in SAARC, just as the US, Japan, the European Union, Australia and Iran are, though China's relations with virtually all South Asian states are steadily acquiring much greater depth, situated as it is in geographic proximity to the region unlike the other observers.

However, if one examines China's relations with Africa, for example, what is evident is that not only have these relations advanced rapidly and embraced a diverse range of issues, they have also been institutionalized and regularized within the 'Forum on China-Africa Cooperation'. The same is true for China's relations with Pacific Island countries in what is called the 'China-Pacific Island Countries Economic Development and Cooperation Forum'. It is thus somewhat of an anomaly to find that in spite of the aforementioned geographical reality, institutionally, linkages between SAARC and China are considerably weak at the present time. Therefore, the question must be posed as to whether and how China wishes to institutionalize relations with SAARC in ways more consistent with Chinese diplomacy as evidenced in other parts of the world. This would give a clearer picture as to whether there is any significant shift in China's South Asian regional strategy. The fact that China dispatched senior Vice Foreign Minister Wang Guangya to lead the Chinese delegation to the 16th SAARC Summit in Bhutan in April 2010 is significant in this regard, given Minister Wang's current major role in policy planning at the Chinese Ministry of Foreign Affairs. Minister Wang's comments in Bhutan are also noteworthy and suggest that China is indeed looking at cooperation with SAARC in nothing short of historical terms.

At the Opening Ceremony of the Summit on April 28, 2010, in a speech entitled 'For Friendship, Cooperation and Common Prosperity', Minister Wang said that 'today's world is undergoing major changes, adjustments and development. Asia, including South Asia, is witnessing a steady rise of its international standing and influence. Cooperation between China and SAARC thus faces a historical opportunity. China is South Asia's biggest neighbor. Our traditional friendship boasts a history of more than a thousand years. Our good-neighborly relations are deep-rooted. With a combined population that accounts for over 40% of the world's total, we have a major responsibility to promote world peace and development. We all face the task of growing economy and improving people's livelihood. There is a lot we can learn from each other. There is even more we can do together. All in all, we have everything it takes to foster greater cooperation – the right time, favorable geographical conditions and most importantly, support from our people'.

Finally, it can be argued that China's South Asia regional strategy, as well as various dimensions of its policy in Nepal are really part and parcel of greater macro trends in Chinese diplomacy. It therefore, comes as somewhat of a surprise when analysts outside Nepal take a simplistic view by interpreting any kind of traction in Sino-Nepal relations as being directed against a third country or as a deliberate attempt to disrupt extant geostrategic balances. Obviously it cannot be denied that the rise of China and indeed the rise of India, are profoundly altering old geostrategic patterns and constellations, but to ascribe ill-intentions to the motives of both Kathmandu and Beijing in their desire to expand Sino-Nepal relations is to miss the point. To a large extent current Nepalese political leaders have also been unable to properly consolidate the larger China-India-Nepal triangle, because in practice they have not always been consistent in hewing to the quite forward-looking principle of Nepal serving as a 'Zone of Peace' which was articulated by King Birendra. It should be acknowledged that the overall political dynamics of Nepal over the past decade have been very complicated, that political leaders have not risen above their narrow agendas of advancing their own personal and party interests, and that they have appeared unable (maybe even unwilling) to keep China and India on the same page insofar as this concerns Nepal. Normatively speaking, this is a wrong approach and one which is not in the long-term interest of Nepal or of the more crucial India-China-Nepal triangle.

NEPAL-CHINA RELATIONS

China and Nepal are close neighbours on the two sides of the Himalayan Mountains and have a long history of friendly ties. It is said that more than two thousand years ago, Manjushri came all the way from the Wutai Mountains in China to Nepal. He cut open the mountain with his sword and drained the water from the lake, thus creating the Kathmandu Valley. This beautiful legend gives vivid expression to the ardent desire of our two peoples for friendship. Historical records show that the friendly exchanges of China and Nepal date back to as early as the mid-7th century. At that time, China and Nepal already started exchanging emissaries. Fahien, a Chinese eminent monk in the Jin Dynasty and Huen Tsang, another Chinese eminent monk in the Tang Dynastry, came to Lumbini, birthplace of Lord Buddha, on pilgrimages. Songtsen Gompo, King of the Tubo Kingdom in the Tang Dynasty married a Nepalese princess Bhrikuti. The Nepalese artisan Arniko built a Buddhist pagoda in Lhasa in the Yuan Dynasty. The White Pagoda in Beijing's Miao Ying Temple was also built under his supervision. All these stories and historical facts show that China-Nepal traditional friendship is solidly based.

Since the establishment of diplomatic relations in 1955, the friendship and cooperation between China and Nepal has opened a new chapter. This owes much to the commitment and dedication of several generations of Chinese and Nepalese leaders. Such friendship is a great asset of our two peoples. The leaders of, both past and present, have brought about the flowering of China-Nepal friendship with their wisdom, vision and unremitting efforts. Thanks to their untiring efforts made over half a century, exchanges and cooperation between China and Nepal in political, diplomatic, economic and trade, cultural, educational and other fields have borne rich fruit. Indeed, China-Nepal relations have become a model of friendly cooperation for countries of different social systems and neighboring countries to live in friendship and harmony.

To look back the friendly history of China-Nepal relations, three obvious characteristics can be easily concluded, which have enabled China-Nepal friendship to maintain its strong momentum of growth over the years. The first is trust. The two countries never threat each other, harm each other or doubt each other; but always respect each other, believe each other and help each other. The Chinese Government and people firmly pursue the principle of non-interference in the internal affairs of other countries, have never interfered with the internal affairs of Nepal and highly respect the road of development chosen by the Nepalese people. We believe that the Nepalese Government and people have the political wisdom and capabilities to solve their own problems. On our part, we appreciate the understanding, solidarity and support that the Government and people of Nepal have given to China in its endeavor for peaceful development.

The second is equality. The Chinese Government and people firmly pursue the principle that a country is equal with others no matter how big or small it is. Following that, China has all along developed relations on the base of equality with Nepal. We consistently support Nepal in its effort to safeguard sovereignty, independence and territorial integrity. In the past 50 years, abiding by the Five Principles of Peaceful Coexistence, through equal dialogue, communication and coordination, China and Nepal have made excellent cooperation and achieved great accomplishments in bilateral political relations, regional affairs and international forums.

The third is sincerity. China treats Nepal as its closest neighbor and best friend. Although China isn't a rich country, it has provided assistance and cooperation to Nepal in all the fields within its own capacity. Over the past 50 years, with China's financial and technical assistance, more than 30 projects have been completed in Nepal. As recognized by people of all circles in Nepal, these projects have played a constructive role in the social and economic development of Nepal. The Arniko Highway, the Ring Road, stadium and the Birendra International Convention Center, assisted by China, are among the best examples. In return, the Nepalese Government and people has shown friendly sentiments to China and delivered its valuable support to Chinese people. We highly appreciate the strong support Nepal has given to us over the years on the questions of Taiwan and Tibet and other major issues related to China's sovereign rights and interests.

In recent years, the relations between China and Nepal have developed more rapidly. The top leaders exchanged visits frequently and the two countries carried out cooperation smoothly. In the political field, frequently high-level visits have greatly enhanced the mutual understanding and trust between our two countries. In the year of 2006 only, in which great changes took place in Nepal, H.E. Mr. Tang Jiaxuan, the State Councilor of China, H.E. Mr. Wu Dawei, Vice Foreign Minister, visited Nepal, expressing our strong and continuous support to Nepal despite of the changes in Nepal's politics. Likewise, Hon. Mr. K.P. Sharma Oli, Deputy Prime Minister and Minister for Foreign Affairs of Nepal, visited China, reiterating that the new Government of Nepal would insistently support China on the issue of Taiwan, Tibet and other issues of China's core interests. In January, 2007, H.E. Mr. Li Tieying, Deputy Speaker of National People's Congress of the People's Republic of China, paid a visit to Nepal, which has strengthened the exchanges and cooperation between the parliaments of the two countries.

The bilateral economic and trade relations have kept a healthy developmental momentum. According to the Chinese Customs, the total trade volume in 2006 reached US$ 268 million, with 36.5% increase over previous year. During the bilateral visits in 2006, the Chinese Government has announced to provide grant assistance of RMB120 million and concessional loan of US$ 200 million to Nepal. We are also glad to see that the people-to-people contacts between our two countries have unfolded rapidly and smoothly over the past years. In 2001, the two countries signed the Memorandum of Understanding on Tourism Cooperation, including Nepal into the list of the tourism destination for outbound Chinese travelers. Later on, the two countries signed "Air Service Agreement", according to which, Air China opened a direct air link between China and Nepal in 2004, by route of Chengdu-Lasha-Kathmandu. In addition, the China Southern Airline has also started operating air service between Guangzhou and Kathmandu since February, 2007. Likewise, the Nepal Airline is operating air service between Kathmandu and Shanghai, Kathmandu and Hongkong.

China and Nepal have also maintained sound coordination and cooperation in regional and international affairs such as peace, development, human rights and UN reform. We share the common views on many issues related to our mutual concern.

The relations between the two armies are an important component of the overall relations between China and Nepal. In the past years, the military relations and cooperation between China and Nepal have experienced continuous development. Nearly all the former Army Chiefs and Defence Secretaries of Nepal have visited China. The Defence Minister and the General Chief of Staff of China have also visited Nepal. China has rendered help and assistance to Nepal within its own capacity. The two armies have conducted good cooperation in personnel training as well. Since 1998, the Nepal Army has sent officers and soldiers to study in Chinese military universities. In the academic year of 2006/2007 in particular, 21 officers and soldiers of the Nepal Army went to China for training. China has also sent military officers to participate in the adventure trainings organized by the Nepal Army since 2002.

As looking across the globe, it is easy to come to the conclusion that peace, stability, cooperation and development are the calling of the times and the common aspiration of the mankind. Both China and Nepal face a historical opportunity to develop. By seizing this opportunity, the two neighboring countries should build on past achievements and push ahead to bring China-Nepal good-neighborliness, friendship and cooperation to a new height. No matter what changes take place in Nepal, China's friendly policy towards Nepal will remain unchanged.

In recent years, Nepal has been affected by conflicts and instability. As an immediate neighbor and close friend of Nepal, China has shown great concern. We have also tried our best to play a constructive role in urging all sides in Nepal to solve problems through dialogues and talks. To our great joy, under the endeavors of diligent, sapiential and brave Nepalese people, Nepal is now heading to a road of peace, stability, economic development and social prosperity. The Chinese Government and people respect political system and road of development chosen by Nepalese people, and sincerely hope that all constitutional forces in Nepal will set store by the fundamental interest of the country and people, and seek to appropriately settle the current difficulties and problems through dialogues, based on the maintenance of Nepal's independence, sovereignty and national integrity. The Chinese Government welcomes the progress made in the peace process. We believe that all the concerned parties in Nepal would continue to push forward the peace process, benefit the Nepalese people and make contributions to the peace, stability and development of this region.

The Chinese Government will continue to pursue a policy of friendship towards Nepal and attach great importance to developing the comprehensive and friendly relations with Nepal. We are committed to developing friendship and partnership with our neighbours, and strive to become a good neighbor, partner and friend of them. This is a solemn and long-term pledge of the Chinese Government. China will never change its friendly policy towards Nepal irrespective of changes both internationally and in our two countries.

The Chinese Government is committed to pursuing cooperation with Nepal in all areas. As developing countries, China and Nepal are both faced with the arduous tasks of economic and national development. Strengthening cooperation of mutual benefit and promoting common development are our shared aspirations and serve our mutual interests. China is ready to increase friendly exchanges with the Nepalese Government, political parties and people of all walks of life, and expand bilateral exchanges and cooperation in politics, economy, trade, culture and tourism. China will continue to support economic and social development in Nepal to the best of its capacity.

THE NEPAL CHINA ECONOMIC RELATIONSHIP

Recently, Chinese government has provided medicines and hospital equipment worth 1.4 million Nepali rupees to B.P. Koirala Memorial Cancer Hospital in Nepal. The Chinese government has been providing medicines since 1999. Even recently experts said in Kathmandu, transit economy between China and India will serve as a milestone to generate employment and boost Nepal's economy. The trade volume between China and India stands about 10 billion US dollars and the two countries plan to increase it to 30 billion US dollars within 20 years.

Nepal and China, as close and good neighbours, share a common border of over 1,400 kilometers. Nepal and China's relationship is based on the principles of equality, mutual respect and good neighborliness. We must ensure that our traditional bonds of friendship always remain. China has been a consistent partner in Nepal's development, thus, Nepal is grateful to the aid and support extended by the Chinese government for Nepal's economic development.

Officials from Nepal and China are convening for bilateral consultative meeting in Beijing on July 2. During this meeting both countries will discuss measures to boost economic cooperation and also explore new areas to strengthen bilateral ties. Among others, the two sides will for the first time discuss on the latest commitment of Nepal to develop itself as transit corridor for Indo-China trade and bridge between China and South Asia, Madhu Raman Acharya said recently.

Since the establishment of the diplomatic relations between Nepal and China in 1955, King Birendra has paid ten visits to China. China took an open-door and reform policy in 1978, the King expressed heartfelt admiration for what China has achieved. "I have been able to see for myself the impressive economic progress your country has made over the years and the current policy adopted by China has been instrumental in improving the quality of lives of its people,". Even Chinese president Jiang Zemin and King Birendra were agreed to set up a good-neighborly partnership between Nepal and China during President Jiang's state visit to Nepal in December 1996.

It was significant official visit by the head of PLA Chinese General Fu Quan You to Nepal in 2000. During his visit General also emphasized China's sensitivity regarding its own security for which Nepal's continued independence and secured sovereignty is an essential component. From the strategic point of view, Nepal is no less important for China than any of her big neighbours. China government is also convinced to fight trans-border terrorism. Nepal also will not allow any anti-Chinese activity on its territory.

China and Nepal, with different conditions, social systems and historical and cultural backgrounds, have witnessed sound and smooth progress of their bilateral relations. China-Nepalese bilateral relations, featuring equal and sincere treatment, mutual support and friendship for generations, can be an example for relations between two countries.

Nepal will be China's reliable friend. Nepal also hopes to continuously enhance people-to-people contacts and expand cooperative spheres with China. We both countries face similar development challenges and we can learn from each other to utilize trade and other economic tools to address needs of our common people. Lastly, we have now an information infrastructure in place to facilitate easy flow of business information between China and Nepal.

We shall soon set up a Chinese Business Information Centre at Kathmandu. With all these interactions, we do hope that bilateral business will be stronger. Nepal is a good investment venue, with variety of sectors to invest, such as cement, ceramics, electronics, electrical items, pharmaceuticals, fertilizer, food processing and garments,among others.

Tourism itself has emerges as a good business opportunity, indeed it is one of the fastest growing sector of economy in many countries, including in Nepal. Nepal is interested to work with Nepal in promoting bilateral and regional tourism. We do hope additional air services that may commence soon between Beijing and Kathmandu will accelerate the process of cooperation in this regard.

Beijing-Kathmandu Bus service may also positively contribute to this process. Relations between Nepal and China have been traditionally close and have reflected the links of history. Nepal continues to maintain very close and friendly relations with China, which is an important maritime neighbor. On the other side, there are many items, which can be traded between the two countries and to the mutual benefits of the two countries.

We should develop lines of common interests between the two countries. Nepal's relationship with China is unique. Since the very beginning of the establishment of diplomatic relations, China-Nepal relations were characterised by ties at the people's level. The relations have improved and the major stake in the relation lies in strengthening the border areas and in improving people-to-people contact and furthering economic relations and trade.

TIBETANS IN NEPAL: THE LOST SANCTUARY

In 2012 conflict inside Tibet has accelerated and the crackdown on Tibetans in Nepal has intensified. To date, at least 33 people have immolated themselves in public in Tibet whilst shouting for the return of the Dalai Lama. The Chinese military has predictably met all protests with brute force, imposing de facto martial law across all Tibetan regions within the People's Republic of China. China is exerting effective pressure on the new government of Baburam Bhattarai to control "anti-Chinese separatist forces in Nepal" to quote Xinhua, the official news service of the PRC.

China is now claiming suzerainty over all Tibetan Buddhist ethnic and cultural zones, which span the Himalayan Belt of Nepal, Sikkim, Bhutan, Ladakh and Arunachal Pradesh in India, as it advances its hegemonic ambitions in South and Southeast Asia with a bellicosity that could hardly be categorized as "soft power." Chinese engineers are advancing into Nepal from Tibet, building roads and monopolizing trade with a strategic advantage that no amount of western aid or international press coverage can possibly counter. Chinese security forces are well established all along the Tibet-Nepal border. Since the 2008 Lhasa Uprising, the Chinese military has sealed off most of the mountain passes linking Tibet and Nepal, which has drastically reduced the number of new escapees. Tibetans are at great risk of capture and refoulement at the Nepal-Tibet border with no international monitoring or protection and negligible media coverage.

Tibetans in Kathmandu, once a safe haven for refugees and still a nexus of Tibetan culture, religion and commerce, endure constant harassment, random search and arrest by both Nepali police and Chinese agents. Any expressions of concern for the people inside Tibet are swiftly halted and the organizers punished.

Said a Tibetan businessman born in Kathmandu: "Nepal has become a second Tibet. No one is safe anymore; we have no leadership and no voice in the government. We used to have an office managed by the Dalai Lama's exile administration and had the protection of the monarchy, but both are gone."

Nepal: The Lost Santuary

In 1959, Nepal's King Mahendra defied Chairman Mao and granted protection to refugees from Tibet. The oldest settlements in Nepal, Jawalakhel and Jorpati, were given to the Tibetans as a royal gift from the palace in 1960. Pokhara, set in a valley below the Annapurna massif, is home to four Tibetan refugee camps. The Swiss Red Cross built Tashi Peykhil in 1962 and Tashiling in 1965. The Chushi Gangdruk created the Paljorling and Jampaling Camps in 1972. There are still many small Tibetan refugee settlements along the border regions from Solokhumbu to Rewalsar.

King Birendra continued his father's policy of generous refuge for Tibetans when a second exodus began in the 1980's. Since the March 2008 uprising in Tibet, the refugee passage has dropped from about 6,000 to 8,000 escapees a year to less than 700. UNHCR continues to operate a Reception Center in Kathmandu, which provides temporary shelter, food and medical care and coordinates with the Indian embassy to process visas for the new refugees. But Nepal is not a signatory to international refugee conventions, thus there is no protection from refoulement, and no support for refugees who have lived in Nepal for 53 years.

About 13,000 Tibetan are registered as refugees with the Nepali government, but a large number of Tibetans are undocumented, thus unofficial surveys suggest that the number of Tibetans in Nepal is at more than 25,000.

For decades, Tibetans operated hotels, boutiques and restaurants, and were Nepal's first industrialists, building carpet factories that employed tens of thousands of Nepali workers and brought wealth to the Kathmandu Valley. Exiled Tibetan lamas built monasteries across Nepal, which draw pilgrims and students from across the globe and young Buddhist monks from Nepal's northern regions. The "Tibet Brand" brings tens of thousands of pilgrims and tourists to Nepal every year. Nepalis can sell Tibetan flags, tee shirts and posters, but Tibetan businessmen are threatened with extortion for hanging a photograph of HH Dalai Lama in an office or hotel lobby.

End of the Monarchy, End of Protection

After the assassination of King Birendra in 2001, the Tibetans refugees lost the protection of the palace. This complex, multi-generational refugee community still living in the old settlements is poor, marginalized, isolated, with no legal protection and no leadership.

Tibetans in Nepal have few allies to counter China's aggressive intrusions into Nepal's oversight of the Tibetan refugee populace. In February 2012, 18 Tibetan high school students staged a small protest before the United Nations headquarters in Kathmandu and were arrested and imprisoned for nearly 2 weeks. In April 2012 the BBC filmed another violent arrest of Tibetans in front of the UN offices in Kathmandu. One group scaled the walls of the UN compound and met with a UN representative, but neither the UN nor any diplomatic mission in Kathmandu has the authority to reverse Nepal's harsh new policy towards Tibetans.

The Dalai Lama's Central Tibetan Administration based in Dharamshala, India operated a legally registered Tibetan welfare office in Nepal from 1961 until 2006. The office still functions, but in a highly reduced capacity. Policies implemented by former Kalon Tripa Samdhong Rinpoche contributed to the fragmentation of the Tibetan refugee networks in Nepal, with the sale of CTA owned businesses and the termination of CTA security officials at the Reception Center and Kathmandu office. Tibetan exile government officials from India are now fearful of travelling to Nepal. The Dalai Lama has only been to Nepal once; in 1981 he made a six-hour visit to Lumbini, birthplace of the Buddha.

In October 2011, US State department officials visited the old Jawalakhel camp and were followed by 12 armed policemen at every step, and a representative of the Dalai Lama's office was arrested, without charges or warrant. He was later released after interventions from UNHCR and the US Embassy, but random raids from Nepali security forces have become routine, inciting fear and anxiety further isolating Tibetans refugees from allies and witnesses.

Since the 1990's, when the Maoist insurgency began, Nepal's Maoists have targeted Tibetan businesses with extortion and assault, forcing many to close, depriving hundreds of thousands of Nepal workers of employment, mostly in the Tibetan carpet industry, which for decades was Nepal's largest source of capital and international trade.

Officials from the US Embassy, UNHCR, the Indian Embassy and Nepali government all concur that Chinese pressure, through military exchanges, aid donations and bribery, has been highly successful in isolating and weakening the Tibetan community in Nepal. Yang Houlan, the current Chinese ambassador to Nepal, has issued several press releases stating that Nepal must be "cleansed of anti-Chinese elements". His embassy is exerting extreme pressure upon Nepal's fragile government to deny Tibetans any kind of legal residency status, to restrict all Tibetan economic and cultural activities, to the prevent Tibetan escapees from crossing the Nepal border.

This is a sharp reversal of Nepal's decades of generous humanitarian treatment of Tibetan refugees. On Nov. 20th 2011, US Ambassador to Nepal, Scott DeLisi, wrote in the Kathmandu Post: "For more than five decades the government and people of Nepal have shown tremendous generosity toward refugees, including the Tibetans who have sought refuge in Nepal and safe passage to India. The United States of America applauds Nepal's record of steadfast support, even in the face of pressure to change its policy... For the United States, humanitarian protection — not political gamesmanship — is our primary concern, and our focus will continue to be on protecting vulnerable refugees, rather than the politics of their countries of origin...Those who seek to portray our position on Tibetan refugees as anti-China fundamentally misunderstand US policy and the importance we place on upholding universal values, rights, and principles."

Chinese Inflitration of the Exile Community

The Tibetan community in Nepal is now thoroughly infiltrated with Chinese agents and spies. China maintains a highly effective espionage network of human and cyber intelligence gathering, employing Indians, Nepalis and even westerners, to collect information on Tibetans activities in exile. A large number of these agents are Tibetans from Chinese Occupied Tibet who have been trained in military academies in China and travel on Chinese passports.

Tibetans in Nepal describe being approached by such agents who offer enormous bribes in exchange for abandoning "The Dalai" and "joining us". If the bribe is refused, agents become hostile, threaten retribution and in some cases attempt kidnapping.

Said a Tibetan businessman in Boudhanath; "These Tibetan spies follow us, call us and harass us on the phone. They threaten you and they mean it. A lot of Chinese agents are shaking down local businessmen and paying the cops to harass Tibetans. It's hard to know how the Tibetans can survive in this new climate, where the Chinese are treating us like they own us. In the border regions, police are making house-to-house raids looking for Dalai Lama photos. We know of people who got so many death threats that they have fled to India."

January 2012: Wen Jiabao Visits Nepal

On Jan. 14th 2012, Chinese Premiere Wen Jiabao, made a 6-hour visit to Kathmandu. In official meetings he asked for specific details on the number and status of Tibetans in Nepal and made clear that the Tibetan community is to be repressed as a condition for Chinese investment and aid.

Wen's visit was timed to coincide with the return of 9,000 Tibetan pilgrims who entered Nepal in December 2011 en route to India, to attend the Dalai Lama's Kalachakra teaching in Bodhgaya, the site of the Buddha's enlightenment in the 6th century BC. The majority of Tibetan pilgrims travelled to Nepal on Chinese visas, by road and air, leaving their passports in Nepal and entering India overland so no Indian visa or official record would appear in their travel documents. Radio Free Asia reports that pilgrims returning to Tibet from India have been arrested, most have been sent to a detention center in Shigatse, where they are subject to beatings, torture and communist re-education, many have been "disappeared."

After Wen's visit, surveillance, harassment and intimidation of Tibetans in Nepal has visibly increased, also targeting Nepali citizens who practice Tibetan Buddhism and resemble Tibetans in dress and custom, Sherpas, Tamangs, Manangs, inciting confusion and conflict in Nepal's Buddhist communities.

There is a visible spike in anti-Tibetan media coverage in the media. *Kantipur*, Nepal's largest selling Nepali language newspaper, regularly prints anti-Tibetan editorials and diatribes. *The Kathmandu Post*,*The Himalayan* and *Republica*, the three leading English language papers, report on Tibetan events with a strong anti-Tibetan bias, frequently casting Tibetan protestors – who are small in number and never violent – as threats to national security and obstacles to China-Nepal relations. This negative reporting incites suspicion and paranoia about Tibetans in Nepal, which the fractured refugee community does not have the means to contest or alleviate.

Some Nepali writers have criticized the excessive use of force by police officers at Tibetan gatherings and express concerns that China's assault on their Tibetan neighbours is a threat to Nepal's sovereignty, but these opinion pieces are very small in number.

Said a Tibetan journalist who was born in Nepal and works in Kathmandu; "In the last year, a new attitude towards Tibetans has appeared. We are now seen as obstructing good relations with China. When people find out you are a Tibetan, they don't want to work with you, even though so many Tibetan been productive residents of Nepal for more than 50 years. Now we cannot get residency papers or exit permits, so we can't go and can't stay. We are pawns in a game; so many young people are desperate now and feel that they have no choice but to get out, even though they we born here and want to stay here."

March 10th, 2012 In Kathmandu

On March 10th, the 53rd anniversary of the Lhasa Uprising was observed throughout the Tibetan exile community in India and Nepal. Prior to the murder of King Birendra in 2001, Tibetans would gather at the great Stupa of Boudhanath, where a member of Nepal's Royal family would stand beside the Dalai Lama's representative and read aloud a statement of support in Nepali. In the late 1990's the police presence started to grow and the event frequently ended with minor scuffles, but in the last 10 years the Nepali security presence has grown so large and so lethal it far outnumbers the number of Tibetans who gather for the vigil. Many are beaten and arrested at once, and are thereafter on "watch lists" and subject to constant surveillance and harassment.

On March 10th 2012, a small gathering of Tibetans convened at Sherap Ling Monastery in Boudha. A large contingent of Nepal police stood guard outside the monastery while undercover agents moved conspicuously through the vigil. When the ceremony concluded the Tibetans fled to their homes, chased by police who entered homes and monasteries in an extremely aggressive and hostile manner, chasing monks and students with lathi sticks, threatening journalists or western observers who questioned the unwarranted use of force.

Western diplomats in Kathmandu witnessed several hundred Nepali police at the Chinese embassy in Kamalpokhari, equipped with shields, guns, handcuffs and batons, surrounding a group of 20 Tibetans. On March 14th, 2012, the 4th anniversary of the Lhasa Uprising of 2008, at least 70 Tibetans were arbitrarily arrested across Kathmandu Valley. Police also assaulted many Nepalis. Said a Nepali tour operator who happened to be passing Svayambunath Stupa, where many Tibetans live: "Police stopped our car and pulled my wife out and questioned her simply because she was wearing a maroon shawl, which is the color of a monk's robe. We saw monks being pulled off of buses, children and young men being beaten by police."

A senior Nepali official of the Home Ministry stated "China's number once interest in Nepal is the Tibetan refugees: they have detailed files on all the Tibetans in Nepal." Chinese officials insist that Dalai Lama, whom they refer to as 'The Separatist', has a large, well-financed network of agents operating in Nepal and Tibet who are a "threat to national security." Anyone who has visited the Dalai Lama's exile home in Dharamshala knows that the Tibetan refugee community is small, fragile and poor, but this propaganda is aggressively pushed by Chinese officials along with financial inducements to regard Tibetan refugees as hostile and dangerous elements.

A 28 year old Tibetan who recently escaped to Nepal said: "I was arrested walking home from the market because I don't have a residency permit, even though I've tried to get one, as a legitimate asylum seeker. The police got so violent. I was beaten with sticks on my body and the soles of my feet and called a 'Bhote Kukkur' – Tibetan dog. I couldn't walk out of the jail when they released me, I had to crawl and they kicked me and laughed."

Tibetans have virtually no freedom of movement in Kathmandu, from all quarters. In addition to the sharp increase in police aggression is a spike in gang violence directed at Tibetans, which many believe is financed by Chinese agents. Said a Tibetan exile textile merchant in Thamel, Kathmandu's tourist hub; "If we go out at night, gangs can stop our cars, take all of our money and jewelry, they also try to assault women, but we cannot report this to the police because they are doing it too."

Legal Status and Documentation

In 1998, the Nepali government stopped issuing Refugee Cards (RCs) to Tibetans born in Nepal after 1989. This third young generation of Tibetans in Nepal are today undocumented persons, they cannot obtain any valid identification papers, residency permits or travel documents, even official Nepali birth certificates are now deemed invalid.

A young Tibetan from Pokhara obtained a medical degree in Kathmandu and hoped to become a doctor, but was not permitted to practice medicine in Nepal, his birthplace, because of his ethnicity and refugee status. In 2011, Chinese agents coerced the manager of a Nabil Bank in Pokhara into firing a Tibetan woman employed by the bank for 7 years. Said a 25 year old Tibetan from Pokhara; "When you apply for a job, the first questions they ask is, are you Tibetan? Then don't come in here."

It is the poorest Tibetans living in the old, decaying camp system who are most emotionally affected by the crisis in Tibet, and most likely to participate in political demonstrations, which now incurs great risks.

On Nov 2nd 2011 Sonam Choedon, a Tibetan woman in Jawalakhel, doused herself in kerosene and attempted self immolation. She was restrained by police and taken to a clinic for burn injuries. On Nov 3rd, Sherab Tsedor, a 25-year-old Tibetan refugee living in India, set himself on fire, in front of the Chinese Embassy in the Indian capital of New Delhi.

In response to these self-immolation attempts in exile, the Nepali Ministry of Home Affairs stated that the government will soon review its policies on the Tibetan refugees that are likely to be more stringent, reports confirm. Sudhir Kumar Sah of the Home spoke to the press on November 13, 2011: "The government is in a very difficult situation since the Tibetans have begun setting themselves on fire. The government of Nepal is committed on its one China policy. We will not allow any activities that go against the interest of our neighbours. This will lead to a situation where the government may have to slash all the facilities being granted to the Tibetans residing in Nepal, such as that of their freedom to move even."

A Tibetan journalist who was born in Jawalakhel, the oldest Tibetan camp in Kathmandu, says: "We feel like we are under house arrest. We are monitored when we come and go from our homes. Our phones are tapped. We know that Chinese pressure is working, because our entire network is being pulled apart. We don't have a safe place to hold meetings anymore, like we used to. So we're not able to make plans for how to respond to this change in Nepal's policy towards Tibetans."

Escape and Refoulement

The Tibetan refugee passage is the longest and most dangerous escape route on earth: travelling on foot cross the

Himalayas. Refugees who survived the ascent from Mount Everest and eluded Chinese patrols at the Nepal border were formerly rescued by UN protection officers, but for years UNHCR has not been granted permission to operate at the border.

With the loss of international monitoring at the border, documenting cases of refoulement is extremely difficult. A young refugee named Tashi entered Nepal in mid-September 2011 with a group of five other Tibetans from his village of around the same age. The six young men each paid a guide 6000 yuan (approximately US $943) to travel from Lhasa to the Nepal border. When the group reached Nepal in mid-September, Tashi was separated from the group and the International Campaign for Tibet verified his refoulement three months after it occurred.

A group of 23 Tibetans in the border area was also detained at the same time, many of them children under the age of 10. They were taken into custody of Nepal's Department of Immigration in Kathmandu for 12 days before being handed over to the UNHCR, despite pressure from the Chinese embassy to remand the refugees to border police.

Two U.S. Congressmen, Steve Chabot and James Sensenbrenner, visited Kathmandu in late September and October and publicly stated the US support for the Tibetan refugees. On Nov. 4th, Rep. Frank Wolf (R-VA) of the US House Appropriations Committee said he would try to block funding to Nepal unless it grants exit visas to Tibetans who seek refuge in the United States. (In 2010 USAID contributed $56 million in funds in Nepal). On November 20, U.S. Ambassador Scott DeLisi's article in the Kathmandu Post was published when Nepal's Foreign Minister Narayan Kaji Shrestha visited Lhasa, Tibet, where he pledged to not allow any "anti-Chinese activities" on Nepali soil.

Pokhara

Today about 3,000 Tibetan refugees in the Pokhara camps. The camp schools are clinics are funded by the Snow Lion Foundation and European NGO's, but are cut off from the CTA based in Dharamshala.

Pokhara, once the exile headquarters of the Chushi Gandruk, is now a Chinese City. There used to be 150 Tibetan shops in the lakeside tourist district, but now there are only 12 left. Chinese businesses dominate the landscape; everywhere, hotels, restaurants, stores for Chinese tourists. In 2011, for the first time, Nepali soldiers, armed with guns and batons, stopped all celebrations of the Dalai Lama's birthday in Pokhara. (The Dalai Lama's birthday observances have been banned in Kathmandu since the 2008 Lhasa Uprising).

USAID is funding a project created by TechnoServe, in partnership with the SnowLion Foundation, to create organic farms in the Pokhara settlements. The mission statement reads: "The economic challenges faced by Tibetans living in exile in India, Nepal and Bhutan pose major constraints to sustaining settlement communities and supporting their aspirations.

The Economic Development of Tibetan Settlements (EDOTS) program is a unique opportunity to create sustainable, replicable livelihood opportunities that will reduce out-migration.

This will keep Tibetan communities together which will preserve Tibetan identity, cultural and linguistic traditions – a key objective of the Tibetan community in exile. EDOTS will demonstrate scalable models of improved organic farming and workforce development, which will result in a 10% increase in participating farmer production and revenues and 10% increase wages of people benefitting from the workforce development intervention."

But a Tibetan community leader in Pokhara says; "We get the wrong kind of aid: we don't need new houses. A house won't benefit you if you have no legal papers, when it is impossible to find a job, or put your children into a school. The Dalai Lama did so much to educate Tibetan refugee children, so we have a generation of young people who want to enter Nepali society but now they can't. We have been here for over 50 years. Our young people have no future. Re-settlement is the only option for us."

Survival in the 21st Century

Tibetans have been stateless exiles for 53 years; second to the Palestinians as the world's longest unresolved refugee crisis. The Dalai Lama is one of the world's most respected individuals, the Tibetan cause generates sympathy, but it does not translate into material support for tens of thousands of refugees scattered across the Indian subcontinent in a fragile diaspora.

The options for the Tibetan refugees in Nepal are constrained when the state of governance is fragile after a lengthy and destructive civil war wherein 15,000 citizens were killed, thousands more tortured, traumatized, driven from their homes. Nepal enters the 21st century an impoverished state of 28 million people, struggling to form a republic from an absolute monarchy. Kathmandu is choked by a toxic merger of pollution, overpopulation, chronic shortages of water, electricity and petrol.

In 2011 the Maoist government expelled two UN agencies, UNMIN and OHCHR, before they had completed their mission to investigate wartime atrocities and bring perpetrators to justice. The new constitution has yet to be drafted and ratified, thus the status of Tibetan and other refugees in Nepal remains unresolved and is likely to remain so for the foreseeable future.

Nepal, anchor of the Himalayan Belt, abode of Shiva and Buddha, the lone buffer state affixed between China and India, lurches towards an uncertain future, the age of kings eclipsed by the Communist Manifesto. In the 15 years of the insurgency, the Maoists did not bring food, schoolbooks or medicine to the rural poor. They brought combat fatigues, rifles and grenades, the torture techniques of the Khmer Rouge and the revolutionary hysteria of the Red Guards. The Maoists now rule Kathmandu, giving the People's Republic of China a foothold in South Asia.

China's expanding influence in Nepal complicates relations with India. External Affairs Minister Jaswant Singh recently spoke of the "China-Nepal nexus on the rise... there is a chilling in India-Nepal relations."

In the Cold War period China was a feared and distant presence in the Himalayan Belt. India was, and still is, Nepal's largest foreign aid donor and sole source of petrol and other essential commodities. A Treaty of Peace and Friendship, hastily enacted after India's defeat in the 1962 war – allows Indian and Nepalese citizens to travel to each other's countries without a passport or visa. Over 8 million Nepalis lives and work in India, yet in 2008 the Nepali Maoists have moved to revoke the terms of the treaty with India, while encouraging stronger ties with China. China was never a dominant presence in Nepal before the Jana Andolan movement in the early 1990's. Now China's influence in Nepal is ubiquitous; Chinese engineers are now expanding the "Friendship Highway" and developing projects along the Tibet-Nepal border. Kathmandu is filled with new organizations promoting "China-Nepal Friendship", with trade fairs, academic conferences, cultural shows and tourism.

Integration of Tibetan refugees in Nepal is increasingly untenable with the ascendancy of the Maoists and their close ties to Beijing. Resettlement would alleviate pressure on the Nepali government and rescue Tibetan refugees from danger. In 2006-7, the US government proposed re-settlement of up to 5,000 Tibetan refugees from Nepal, but the Maoist government refuses to issue exit permits for Tibetans.

In 2011 three US congressmen sent a letter to the Prime Minister Bhattarai on the status of the Tibetan refugees, which was duly noted. By raising the matter, the US government could open a new dialogue with Nepali officials about Tibetan residency papers, protection and re-settlement, which is in Nepal's interest. The US has just re-settled 80,000 Bhutanese refugees from Nepal; can the US use this as leverage to re-settle a much smaller number of Tibetans refugees?

Nepal and Tibet have a long history than spans many centuries. In the past 53 years, Nepalis have granted generous sanctuary to Tibetan refugees, and there are still strong bonds of friendship between the Nepali and Tibetan people. Let us hope that this friendship will not be yet another casualty of China's Rise. As the Tibet crisis festers and burns, the short term scenarios are bleak, but as a Tibetan lama in Kathmandu observed; "Nepalis are beginning to wonder why the Chinese demand control over their Tibetan neighbours, and many are asking, are we next?"

RECENT NEPAL-CHINA RELATIONS

China and Nepal are close neighbours on the two sides of the Himalayan Mountains and have a long history of friendly ties. It is said that more than two thousand years ago, Manjushri came all the way from the Wutai Mountains in China to Nepal. He cut open the mountain with his sword and drained the water from the lake, thus creating the Kathmandu Valley. This beautiful legend gives vivid expression to the ardent desire of our two peoples for friendship. Historical records show that the friendly exchanges of China and Nepal date back to as early as the mid-7th century. At that time, China and Nepal already started exchanging emissaries. Fahien, a Chinese eminent monk in the Jin Dynasty and Huen Tsang, another Chinese eminent monk in the Tang Dynastry, came to Lumbini, birthplace of Lord Buddha, on pilgrimages. Songtsen Gompo, King of the Tubo Kingdom in the Tang Dynasty married a Nepalese princess Bhrikuti. The Nepalese artisan Arniko built a Buddhist pagoda in Lhasa in the Yuan Dynasty. The White Pagoda in Beijing's Miao Ying Temple was also built under his supervision. All these stories and historical facts show that China-Nepal traditional friendship is solidly based.

Since the establishment of diplomatic relations in 1955, the friendship and cooperation between China and Nepal. This owes much to the commitment and dedication of several generations of Chinese and Nepalese leaders. Such friendship is a great asset of our two peoples. The leaders of, both past and present, have brought about the flowering of China-Nepal friendship with their wisdom, vision and unremitting efforts. Thanks to their untiring efforts made over half a century, exchanges and cooperation between China and Nepal in political, diplomatic, economic and trade, cultural, educational and other fields have borne rich fruit. Indeed, China-Nepal relations have become a model of friendly cooperation for countries of different social systems and neighbouring countries to live in friendship and harmony.

To look back the friendly history of China-Nepal relations, three obvious characteristics can be easily concluded, which have enabled China-Nepal friendship to maintain its strong momentum of growth over the years. The first is trust. The two countries never threat each other, harm each other or doubt each other; but always respect each other, believe each other and help each other. The Chinese Government and people firmly pursue the principle of non-interference in the internal affairs of other countries, have never interfered with the internal affairs of Nepal and highly respect the road of development chosen by the Nepalese people. We believe that the Nepalese Government and people have the political wisdom and capabilities to solve their own problems. On our part, we appreciate the understanding, solidarity and support that the Government and people of Nepal have given to China in its endeavour for peaceful development.

The second is equality. The Chinese Government and people firmly pursue the principle that a country is equal with others no matter how big or small it is. Following that, China has all along developed relations on the base of equality with Nepal. We consistently support Nepal in its effort to safeguard sovereignty, independence and territorial integrity. In the past 50 years, abiding by the Five Principles of Peaceful Coexistence, through equal dialogue, communication and coordination, China and Nepal have made excellent cooperation and achieved great accomplishments in bilateral political relations, regional affairs and international forums.

The third is sincerity. China treats Nepal as its closest neighbour and best friend. Although China isn't a rich country, it has provided assistance and cooperation to Nepal in all the fields within its own capacity. Over the past 50 years, with China's financial and technical assistance, more than 30 projects have been completed in Nepal. As recognized by people of all circles in Nepal, these projects have played a constructive role in the social and economic development of Nepal. The Arniko Highway, the Ring Road, stadium and the Birendra International Convention Centre, assisted by China, are among the best examples. In return, the Nepalese Government and people has shown friendly sentiments to China and delivered its valuable support to Chinese people. We highly appreciate the strong support Nepal has given to us over the years on the questions of Taiwan and Tibet and other major issues related to China's sovereign rights and interests.

In recent years, the relations between China and Nepal have developed more rapidly. The top leaders exchanged visits frequently and the two countries carried out cooperation smoothly. In the political field, frequently high-level visits have greatly enhanced the mutual understanding and trust between our two countries. In the year of 2006 only, in which great changes took place in Nepal, H.E. Mr. Tang Jiaxuan, the State Councilor of China, H.E. Mr. Wu Dawei, Vice Foreign Minister, visited Nepal, expressing our strong and continuous support to Nepal despite of the changes in Nepal's politics. Likewise, Hon. Mr. K.P. Sharma Oli, Deputy Prime Minister and Minister for Foreign Affairs of Nepal, visited China, reiterating that the new Government of Nepal would insistently support China on the issue of Taiwan, Tibet and other issues of China's core interests. In January, 2007, H.E. Mr. Li Tieying, Deputy Speaker of National People's Congress of the People's Republic of China, paid a visit to Nepal, which has strengthened the exchanges and cooperation between the parliaments of the two countries.

The bilateral economic and trade relations have kept a healthy developmental momentum. According to the Chinese Customs, the total trade volume in 2006 reached US$ 268 million, with 36.5% increase over previous year. During the bilateral visits in 2006, the Chinese Government has announced to provide grant assistance of RMB120 million and concessional loan of US$ 200 million to Nepal.

We are also glad to see that the people-to-people contacts between our two countries have unfolded rapidly and smoothly over the past years. In 2001, the two countries signed the Memorandum of Understanding on Tourism Cooperation, including Nepal into the list of the tourism destination for outbound Chinese travelers. Later on, the two countries signed

"Air Service Agreement", according to which, Air China opened a direct air link between China and Nepal in 2004, by route of Chengdu-Lasha-Kathmandu. In addition, the China Southern Airline has also started operating air service between Guangzhou and Kathmandu since February, 2007. Likewise, the Nepal Airline is operating air service between Kathmandu and Shanghai, Kathmandu and Hongkong.

China and Nepal have also maintained sound coordination and cooperation in regional and international affairs such as peace, development, human rights and UN reform. We share the common views on many issues related to our mutual concern. The relations between the two armies are an important component of the overall relations between China and Nepal. In the past years, the military relations and cooperation between China and Nepal have experienced continuous development. Nearly all the former Army Chiefs and Defence Secretaries of Nepal have visited China.

The Defence Minister and the General Chief of Staff of China have also visited Nepal. China has rendered help and assistance to Nepal within its own capacity. The two armies have conducted good cooperation in personnel training as well. Since 1998, the Nepal Army has sent officers and soldiers to study in Chinese military universities. In the academic year of 2006/2007 in particular, 21 officers and soldiers of the Nepal Army went to China for training. China has also sent military officers to participate in the adventure trainings organized by the Nepal Army since 2002.

As looking across the globe, it is easy to come to the conclusion that peace, stability, cooperation and development are the calling of the times and the common aspiration of the mankind. Both China and Nepal face a historical opportunity to develop. By seizing this opportunity, the two neighbouring countries should build on past achievements and push ahead to bring China-Nepal good-neighborliness, friendship and cooperation to a new height. No matter what changes take place in Nepal, China's friendly policy towards Nepal will remain unchanged.

In recent years, Nepal has been affected by conflicts and instability. As an immediate neighbour and close friend of Nepal, China has shown great concern. We have also tried our best to play a constructive role in urging all sides in Nepal to solve problems through dialogues and talks. To our great joy, under the endeavors of diligent, sapiential and brave Nepalese people, Nepal is now heading to a road of peace, stability, economic development and social prosperity. The Chinese Government and people respect political system and road of development chosen by Nepalese people, and sincerely hope that all constitutional forces in Nepal will set store by the fundamental interest of the country and people, and seek to appropriately settle the current difficulties and problems through dialogues, based on the maintenance of Nepal's independence, sovereignty and national integrity. The Chinese Government welcomes the progress made in the peace process. We believe that all the concerned parties in Nepal would continue to push forward the peace process, benefit the Nepalese people and make contributions to the peace, stability and development of this region.

The Chinese Government will continue to pursue a policy of friendship towards Nepal and attach great importance to developing the comprehensive and friendly relations with Nepal. We are committed to developing friendship and partnership with our neighbours, and strive to become a good neighbour, partner and friend of them. This is a solemn and long-term pledge of the Chinese Government. China will never change its friendly policy towards Nepal irrespective of changes both internationally and in our two countries.

The Chinese Government is committed to pursuing cooperation with Nepal in all areas. As developing countries, China and Nepal are both faced with the arduous tasks of economic and national development. Strengthening cooperation of mutual benefit and promoting common development are our shared aspirations and serve our mutual interests. China is ready to increase friendly exchanges with the Nepalese Government, political parties and people of all walks of life, and expand bilateral exchanges and cooperation in politics, economy, trade, culture and tourism. China will continue to support economic and social development in Nepal to the best of its capacity.

POLITICS OF NEPAL

The politics of Nepal function within a framework of a republic with a multi-party system. Currently, the positions of President (head of state) and Prime Minister (head of government) are occupied by Ram Baran Yadav and Madhav Kumar Nepal, respectively. Executive power is exercised by the Prime Minister and his cabinet, while legislative power is vested in the Constituent Assembly. Until May 28, 2008, Nepal was a constitutional monarchy. On that date, the constitution was altered by the Constituent Assembly to make the country a republic.

POLITICAL CONDITIONS

1990–1996: Parliamentary Monarchy

Until 1990, Nepal was an absolute monarchy running under the executive control of the king. Faced with a people's movement against the absolute monarchy, King Birendra, in 1990, agreed to large-scale political reforms by creating a parliamentary monarchy with the king as the head of state and a prime minister as the head of the government. Nepal's legislature was bicameral consisting of a House of Representatives and a National Council. The House of Representatives consisted of 205 members directly elected by the people. The National Council had 60 members, 10 nominated by the king, 35 elected by the House of Representatives and the remaining 15 elected by an electoral college made up of chairs of villages and towns. The legislature had a five-year term, but was dissolved by the king before its term could end. All Nepalese citizens 18 years and older became eligible to vote.

The executive comprised the King and the Council of Ministers (the Cabinet). The leader of the coalition or party securing the maximum seats in an election was appointed as the Prime Minister. The Cabinet was appointed by the king on the recommendation of the Prime Minister. Governments in Nepal have tended to be highly unstable; no government has survived for more than two years since 1991, either through internal collapse or parliamentary dissolution by the monarch.

In the first free and fair elections in Nepal in 1991, the Nepali Congress was victorious. The 1994 election defeat of the Nepali Congress Party by the Communist Party of Nepal (Unified Marxist-Leninist) (CPN(UML)) made Nepal the first communist-led monarchy in Asia, with Man Mohan Adhikary prime minister. In mid-1994, parliament was dissolved due to dissension within the Nepali Congress Party. The subsequent general election, held 15 November 1994, gave no party a majority and led to several years of unstable coalition governments. As of the May 1999 general elections, the Nepali Congress Party once again headed a majority government. There have been three Nepali Congress Party Prime Ministers since the 1999 elections: K.P. Bhattarai (31 May 1999–17 March 2000); Girija Prasad Koirala (20 March 2000–19 July 2001); and Sher Bahadur Deuba (23 July 2001–2003). The final distribution of seats in Parliament gave the Nepali Congress 113; the CPN(UML) 69; the RPP 11; the RJM 5; the NSP 5; the Workers and Peasants Party 1; and the United People's Front 1. Nepali Congress Party has divided to Nepali Congress Party led by G. P. Koirala and Nepali Congress (Democratic) led by Sher Bahadur Deuba. Amongst the elected MPs, 39 MPs belong to Nepali Congress (Democratic). Former Prime Minister and Influential Leader Krishna Prasad Bhattarai has expressed his support for Nepali Congress (Democratic). Both Congress parties regard Krishna Prasad Bhattarai as their main leader.

King Gyanendra discharged Sher Bahadur Deuba and on 4 June 2003 appointed Surya Bahadur Thapa as Prime Minister.

1996: Maoist Insurgency

In February 1996, the Communist Party of Nepal (Maoist) began a violent insurgency in more than 50 of the country's 75 districts. About 11,000 police, civilians, and insurgents have been killed in the conflict since 1996. In July 2001 Prime Minister Deuba announced a cease-fire, which the Maoists pledged to observe, as part of a government effort to seek a negotiated solution to the conflict. Although Maoist-instigated intimidation and extortion continue, the killings have largely subsided since the cease-fire was announced. The government and Maoists held talks in August and September 2001.

Political parties agreed in 1991 that the monarchy would remain to enhance political stability and provide an important symbol of national identity for the culturally diverse Nepali people. The King exercises limited powers, including the right to declare a state of emergency in the event of war or armed revolt, with the advice and consent of the Council of Ministers and the Prime Minister. According to the constitution, the King's declaration of a state of emergency must be approved by a two-thirds majority of the lower house of the Parliament.

2001: Royal Massacre

On June 1, 2001, Crown Prince Dipendra was officially reported to have shot and killed his father, King Birendra; his mother, Queen Aishwarya; his brother; his sister, his father's younger brother, Prince Dhirendra; and several aunts, before turning the gun on himself. Although he never regained consciousness before dying, Crown Prince Dipendra was nonetheless the king under the law of Nepalese royal succession. After his death two days later, the late King's surviving brother Gyanendra was proclaimed king.

2005–2007: Suspension of Parliament and Loktantra Andolan

On 1 February 2005 King Gyanendra suspended the Parliament, appointed a government led by himself, and enforced martial law. The King argued that civil politicians were unfit to handle the Maoist insurgency. Telephone lines were cut and several high-profile political leaders were detained. Other opposition leaders fled to India and regrouped there. A broad coalition called the Seven Party Alliance (SPA) was formed in opposition to the royal takeover, encompassing the seven parliamentary parties who held about 90% of the seats in the old, dissolved parliament. The UN-OHCHR, in response to events in Nepal, set up a monitoring program in 2005 to assess and observe the human rights situation there.

On 22 November 2005, the Seven Party Alliance (SPA) of parliamentary parties and the Communist Party of Nepal (Maoist) agreed on a historic and unprecedented 12-point memorandum of understanding (MOU) for peace and democracy. Nepalese from various walks of life and the international community regarded the MOU as an appropriate political response to the crisis that was developing in Nepal.

Against the backdrop of the historical sufferings of the Nepalese people and the enormous human cost of the last ten years of violent conflict, the MOU, which proposes a peaceful transition through an elected constituent assembly, created an acceptable formula for a united movement for democracy. As per the 12-point MOU, the SPA called for a protest movement, and the Communist Party of Nepal (Maoist) supported it. This led to a countrywide uprising that started in April 2006. All political forces including civil society and professional organizations actively galvanized the people. This resulted in massive and spontaneous demonstrations and rallies held across Nepal against King Gyanendra's autocratic rule.

The people's participation was so broad, momentous and pervasive that the king feared being overthrown. On 21 April 2006, King Gyanendra declared that "power would be returned to the people". This had little effect on the people, who continued to occupy the streets of Kathmandu and other towns, openly defying the daytime curfew. Finally King Gyanendra announced the reinstatement the House of Representatives, thereby conceding one of the major demands of the SPA, at midnight on 24 April 2006. Following this action the coalition of political forces decided to call off the protests.

Twenty-one people died and thousands were injured during the 19 days of protests. On 19 May 2006, the parliament assumed total legislative power and gave executive power to the

Government of Nepal (previously known as His Majesty's Government). Names of many institutions (including the army) were stripped of the "royal" adjective and the Raj Parishad (a council of the King's advisers) was abolished, with his duties assigned to the Parliament itself. The activities of the King became subject to parliamentary scrutiny and the King's properties were subjected to taxation. Moreover, Nepal was declared a secular state abrogating the previous status of a Hindu Kingdom. However, most of the changes have, as yet, not been implemented. On 19 July 2006, the prime minister, G. P. Koirala, sent a letter to the United Nations announcing the intention of the Nepalese government to hold elections to a constituent assembly by April 2007.

December 2007 to May 2008: Abolition of the Monarchy

On 23 December 2007, an agreement was made for the monarchy to be abolished and the country to become a federal republic with the Prime Minister becoming head of state. Defying political pundits, who had predicted it to be trounced in the April 2008 elections, the Communist Party of Nepal (Maoist) became the largest party amidst a general atmosphere of fear and intimidation from all sides. A federal republic was established in May 2008, with only four members of the 601-seat Constituent Assembly voting against the change, which ended 240 years of royal rule in Nepal. The government announced a public holiday for three days, (May 28—May 30), to celebrate the country becoming a federal republic.

Current (2008 onwards)

Major parties such as the Unified Communist Party of Nepal (Maoist), Communist Party of Nepal (Unified Marxist-Leninist) and the Nepali Congress agreed to write a constitution that replaces the interim one within the time limit of 2 years. However, incooperative and "selfish" behaviour of the political parties has been cited as the major cause behind the derailing of the peace process. The Maoists, as the largest party of the country, took power right after the elections were held and named Pushpa Kamal Dahal or Prachanda as the Prime Minister of the country. CPN UML also joined this government but the Nepali Congress took part of the main opposition. People soon saw that the country's situation deteriorated and political turmoils were in store. Prachanda soon fell into a dispute with the then army chief Rookmangud Katwal and decided to sack him. But the President Ram Baran Yadav as the supreme head of military power in the country revoked this decision and gave the army chief additional time in office. An angry Prachanda and his party quit the government, majorly citing this reason and decided to be the main opposition to the government headed by CPN UML and co-partner Nepali Congress afterwards.

Madhav Kumar Nepal was named the Prime Minister. The Maoists have been to this date demanding superiority of civilian supremacy to army supremacy. This created turmoils in the country and showed vividly that development was a dream far away and the political leaders were just wrangling for power. The Maoists have been forcing closures or commonly known as *bandhs* in the country and have also declared autonomous states for almost all the ethnic groups in the country, seen as a part of revenge against the action that foiled their decision to sack the army chief. Political leaders are discussing plans to end this turmoil, but none of the talks have been successful. Rising inflation, economic downturn, poverty, insecurity and uncertainty are the major problems. Many analysts opine that this freedom has brought anarchy to the country. Many don't even believe the political parties will be successful on writing a constitution.

6

China the Emerging Global Authority from a Nepalese Perspective

About two hundred years ago Napoleon Bonaparte evaluated China saying 'Let China sleep, for when she wakes, she will shake the world.' Indeed China has converted the quotation in practice. China has emerged as world power particularly the economically power. Being neighbor, Nepal and China share the common boarder of over 1000 km. We have long and cordial historic relation between our two countries. Nepal can greatly be benefited from Chinese prosperity and incredible economic growth.

China has a long the past. Before 221, Zhou dynasty is the longest dynasty in China history. During the period, great spiritual Saint Lord Confucius had impressed in old China. And then, the unification of China occurred in 221 B.C. by the Emperor Qin Shi Huang-Ti who destroyed the Zhou dynasty and proclaimed himself as China's first emperor. He captured the state power and destroyed and burned all the China's historical sources, materials, inscriptions and temples. The King Qin Shi Huang-Ti had expanded Chinese territory to Mongolia in the north and annexed many places. He constructed the Great wall (approximately 6,000 kilometers long) for the security purpose. He is immortal in his acts not only in China but also all around the world. Emperor Qin Shi Huang destroyed all the historical evidences, but the philosophy of Saint Confucius 25 hundred years old still exists today in China. Confusions philosophy is the light of China. Time creates people and people create history. A man is 'nature' while the history is 'manual'. Time creates individuals that can give creative thought and such individuals become immortal in the world.

China in fact is big country with large economic production and domestic expenditure. In order to maintain the ratio of development through the country, political regions are allocated as per need of the country. In modern China, there are 34 geo-political divisions, classified as 23 provinces, 4 municipalities, 5 autonomous regions, and 2 special administrative regions. Since its foundation in 1949, the People's Republic of China has considered Taiwan to be its 23rd province. However, the Chinese government has never controlled Taiwan. Four major metropolitans namely Beijing, Tianjin, Shanghai and Chongqing Municipalities are directly under the Chinese government, with status equal to that of the provinces. In practice, their political status is higher than common provinces and centers of economic activities. Besides two autonomous and self-governing Special Administrative Regions- Hong Kong and Macau Special Administrative Regions are sub national subject and are directly under the Central People's Government. Except in foreign policy and military defence, special administrative regions are fully independent. There are five autonomous regions namely Inner Mongolia, Guangxi Zhuang, Tibet, Ningxia Hui and Xinjiang Uyghur. The autonomous regions enjoy their legislative rights and leadership is appointed from respective minority ethnic group.

China knowledgeable critical stages for many centuries. The great leader of China, Mao Ze Dong made his country recognized by the rest of the world fighting against imperial powers. Modifying (improving) the same policy, another leader Deng Xiaoping brought changes in Chinese communism. Even after the death of Deng Xiaoping, his Chinese policy was continued and China emerged as a global economic power. China, not only in the field of trade and business, but also became able to develop science and technology. Moreover China is heading towards integrated and multilateral development. Adopting the path of open policy, China has stood against imperialism in the globe. Beijing Review of Dec-2012 rightly describes - "The drastic increase of the existing poverty gauge shows that the Chinese government is pragmatic about the difficulties and challenges in faces in poverty reduction. China's poverty reduction drives in unique in history. No other nations in history have ever been able to bring so many people out of poverty in such a short time. China's success is lifting millions of people out of poverty is unprecedented. Currently, poverty reduction not only means providing adequate food and clothing for those in need, it also means letting them live with dignity".

Though the Communist party of China (CPC) with more than 66 million members is the country's sole political party in power, but there are also eight other political parties too. China is run through communism principle and is a communist nation. This is true. But, in put into practice China is more inclined to capitalist ventures through economic reforms. China's energy is now mostly concentrated on increasing its products to sell to the global market, and make Chinese citizens independent. Chinese leader Deng Xiaoping said- 'Poverty is not socialism, to be rich is glorious.' The leader Deng put forward the concept of building socialism with Chinese characteristics 31 years ago. Recently Communist Party of China, has appointed Xi Jinping as General Secretary and China's President since March 2013. President Xi Jinping succeeded President Hu Jintao. The new President has taken the high priorities on corruption, inequality and the environment. President Xi said- people cannot deny what was done before the reform and opening up based on what happened after it and vice versa. We should seek the truth from the facts and tell apart what is important and what is not.' The president Xi Jinping, has said that he will fight for the great renaissance of the Chinese nation.

China has overtake Japan as a world's second largest economy. It is accepted that Chinese economy will overtake the US economy almost by 2030. Because, to deliver cheap labor and cheap land of factories that would product with big brands a small prices. The characters between the sociologists and capitalists indicate the case of differences. Several economic forecasts suggest that China's GDP will overtake that of the U.S. in the coming decades. This fact, along with the recent economic downturn in the U.S., may be influencing U.S. perceptions of Chinese strength.

Due to the Nepalese princess Brikuti who married with the King of China- the famous Shronchan Gompo, speeded the Buddhism and the craftsman Araniko who built numerous famous Buddhist statues in China and Tibet. From the time of Shronchan Gompo, Buddhism became gradually popular in China. In ancient time, Manjushree, came to Nepal from greater ancient China and made the Katmandu Valley habitable by draining out of the water as a lake in Kathmandu Valley, and started a new civilization. Prof. Dr.Triratna Manandhar writes- 'in fifth century A.D. Faxan, a Buddhist monk and scholar from China visited Kapilvastu and Lumbini. His visit was followed by the visit of Nepali Buddhist scholar Buddhabhadra, to China, Faxian and Buddhabhadra collaborated to translating some of the Buddhist Sanskrit texts into Chinese which staying at monastery in China.

In the seventh century A.D. Xuan-Zang visited Lumbini, Kapilvastu and Kathmandu Vally, and left a short description of Nepal, which gives a short glimpse of Mahayana and Therabad Budhism in Nepal during ancient period. Sino-Nepali relations revived in the 13th Century when Kublai Khan invited a team of artists from Nepal to erect a golden Stupa. A Nepali team led by Arniko visited China and constructed golden pagoda-styled monasteries in Tibet and China to the satisfaction of the Chinese Emperor. Arniko was given a high post in China, and after his death, his sons continued to work in China. Nepal Kings and Prime minister were decorated by Chinese titles. Rana Bahadur Shah got the Chinese title of 'Ertini Wang' and Bahadur Shah- 'Dhung'. Jang Bahadur received a new Chinese title- Thong Ling Pimma Ko Kang Shang.' Then, we are maintaining the cordial relation between Nepal and China.

We Nepalese populace have been offending by knowing the conspiracies policy of America. Nepal is landlocked country between two big neighbours– India and China. China always maintained friendly relation with Nepal and extended cooperation on various fields. The President Xi Jinping has already expressed his intention to develop strategic relation with Nepal with the objective of amassing development potentials and contributing to uplifting the life of the people in the region. But Nepal had been influenced by Chinese good conduct- while that of Britain was the Rule of Might. Such behavior has reflected in reality of Nepal, India and China. In fact 'Nepal is a Yam between two rocks.' The quotation of the founder of modern Nepal PN Shah is still relevant. Hence, Nepal is politically neutral. America and UN should understand the compulsion of Nepal. We Nepalese people are neither pro-China and anti-India nor pro-India and anti-China. Due to our nearest neighborhood, we have the sense of cordiality to maintain the balanced relation. Nepal shouldn't be battle field. From the very beginning of history Nepal and China have been regarding their sovereignty each other. Nepal always respects the Chinese integrity and security. No doubt, Nepal supports- 'One China policy'. Nepal shares Chinese border with Tibet which of course is an integral part of China. Therefore Nepal is strategic partner with China in case of Tibet as well. We do not support Tibet be free.

CHALLENGES AND RANGE FOR CHINA-NEPAL RELATIONS

Sino-Nepali diplomatic ties duly re-established 53 years ago on 1 August, 1955 are poised for new challenges and opportunities. The time these ties were re-established was no less challenging either. Challenges at that time basically pertained to conducting international affairs independently and in the sovereign manner. But the prevailing Cold War sought to expand aggressive designs and spheres of influence in the name of transferring ideology and establishing security bloc.

Relatively weak and small nations who were asserting independence to a fuller extent were more vulnerable to the

Cold War machinations. China's rise as a "People's Republic" and its immediate weak and small neighbours including Nepal and other countries with different social systems provided a major incentive to the Cold War powers and their allies to reach out to China's these neighbours in whatever expedient ways. In that context it was not easy for Nepal to move ahead in a planned way in re-establishing ties with China.

Reflecting over those times, Chinese Premier Zhou Enlai said in his speech on September 30, 1950, "China shall never tolerate any foreign invasion nor shall watch it taking place in any neighboring country with folded arms." Withstanding the challenges emanating from foreign aggressive designs and interference, China and Nepal were able to base the bilateral ties on the Five Principles of Peaceful Coexistence, including the principles of peaceful co-existence and non-interference in each other's internal matters.

Any matter which was prejudicial to China's territorial integrity such as status of Tibet or for that matter its "independence" were never raised during the re-establishment of bilateral ties as Nepal throughout in history - recent or past - never recognized Tibet as an independent state. All treaties and agreements pertaining to Nepal's ties with Tibet were signed between the competent authorities of China and Nepal. Ample evidences to this historical fact are Sino-Nepali Treaty of 1792, Sino-Nepali Treaty of Thapathali of 1856 and the 1956 Agreement between China and Nepal on the maintenance of friendship and trade and transport between Tibet region of China and Nepal. The 1956 Agreement replaced the 1856 Treaty.

State leaders who contributed to developing stable Sino-Nepali ties were Nepali kings Mahendra (1955-1972) and Birendra (1972-2001), and prime ministers Tanka Prasad Acharya (1956-1957) and B.P. Koirala (1959-1960). G.P. Koirala, who occupied the seat of premiership for the most part of the Nepali multi-party politics from 1990 to 2008, happened to be more intricately circumscribed by political expediency. Nevertheless, the fact remains that in the said period and in the backdrop of China's West China Development Strategy, it was he who was courageous enough to sign six cooperation agreements, including the second road link between the two countries in 2001 with visiting Chinese Premier Zhu Rongji. From the Chinese side, Chairman Mao Zedong, Premier Zhou Enlai, Vice-premier Deng Xiaoping, Vice-premier Huang Hua and President Jiang Zemin not only nurtured China's Nepal ties with a personal touch but often evaluated it highly as a model of state-to-state relations.

The bilateral ties suffered a deep shock in June, 2001 when the entire family of King Birendra was annihilated in a Royal Palace massacre in Kathmandu. In hindsight, the condemnable massacre brought to the fore a new Cold War already in the making in the region.

It is a "Cold War" because covert, tacit and subversive games are still its basic operational character. The old Cold War camp which could not deter the successful restoration of bilateral ties between Nepal and China in 1950s seems to have been at work to regroup itself in the new form with the comparative differences in abilities listed above. This camp deliberately plays down independence, national interest and security of the weak and small nations not belonging to the camp in the name of the new Cold War consideration. This camp seemed to be shaken by unconfirmed reports that King Birendra was negotiating hand in glove with the anti-government force or the Communist Party of Nepal-Maoist (CPN-M). The CPN-M had since 1996 been waging a "people's war" for "equitable" changes and reforms in Nepal's domestic and international policies.

Whereas the CPN-M got started primarily as a home-grown outfit, the West projected it as a China - supported group. And to do so was in their new Cold War interest. China from the beginning denied any link and support to CPN-M. Mistaken scholarship in the West buttressed coloration of the CPN-M in the new Cold War interest. The CPN-M, a mistaken identity in certain circles aside, continued ascending in state political power through a multi-party republican program agreed in New Delhi in November, 2005. This agreement is noteworthy but no less noteworthy is the fact that along with the CPN-M's ascendancy, forces of aggression and interference have also started making their marks in Nepali politics in an accelerated speed.

Consequent to the agreement, the CPN-M continuously scored political gains. Wrong reading of history and misrepresentation for divisive political interest however seem to have unwittingly inspired the groups of indigenous people in Nepal and its southern neighborhood to assert their cultural roots, political identity and economic rights.

Groups of various indigenous people in Nepal who have always been a foundation of the Nepali nation and economy suffered long in the hands of powerful landed aristocracy of predominantly external origins. Conscious people in the Nepal understand well that imposition of a divisible political superstructure in the name of state restructuring primarily serves foreign motives.

The story does not end here. A separatist group in the name of the "Tibetan refugees" in Nepal in close collaboration with the "Tibetan government-in-exile" in India started violating and undermining Nepal's sovereignty and territorial integrity with daily demonstrations. Though this group's planned anti-China demonstration at this time clearly speaks of its immediate intention of giving a bad name to China vis—vis the Beijing Olympic Games, a closer look at the same time informs that these demonstrations in the longer term inherently target Nepal's sovereignty and territorial integrity in Kathmandu, the seat of Nepal's central authority.

History is witness to the fact that whenever China and Nepal narrowly defined their national interest, each suffered by the machinations of the aggressive and interfering forces. So it happened, for example, in 1814-16 when Nepal alone had to fight the invading Britain, and, Tibet did not receive help from Nepal when British India engineered armed expedition to Tibet in 1904. Now climbing down the Mount Qomolangma and, proactively addressing foreign aggression and interference against national integrity and harmonious development, China and Nepal need to promote a comprehensive framework of cultural diplomacy. Contents of this diplomacy should be entrepreneurially strategic, and the guiding principles should be mutual trust and co-existence characterized by courage and devoid of any appeasement. Chinese people have a saying, "Ivory can not grow on a jackal's mouth."

CHINA AGAINST ANY STATE INTERFERING IN SINO-NEPALESE TIES

The three day visit to Nepal late this March by general Chen Bingde, chief of (PLA), was important, but apparently slipped under the radar due to India's preoccupation with another important domestic issue. The visit achieved some first-ever success. It was the first visit to Nepal by a Chinese army chief in a decade. It was the first time that China's PLA signed a military aid agreement directly with the Nepal army, ignoring the request of Nepal's ministry of defence that the agreement should be signed with it. And, importantly, it was the first time that a Chinese PLA chief asserted on Nepalese soil that China would not tolerate a third country coming in the way of friendship between Nepal and China.

The last declaration, which is code for India's alleged interference, reinforces cautionary remarks by a senior Party leader in 2008 and again in 2009. In November 2008, Liu Hongcai, vice-minister of the Chinese Communist Party's (CCP) International Liaison Department, which is responsible for the CCP's relations with foreign countries, stated that 'China will not tolerate any meddling from any other country in the internal affairs of Nepal—our traditional and ancient neighbour'. Three months later he declared 'we oppose any move to interfere in the internal affairs of Nepal by any force'. The 15-member Chinese military delegation included: Qiu Guohong, China's ambassador to Nepal; Wang Jianping, commander of the Chinese People's Armed Police Force (PAPF); Yang Jinshan, commander of the PLA's Tibet Military District; Qian Lihua, director-general of the foreign affairs office of China's ministry of national defence; Zhang Yanling, director of the Health Department of the General Logistics Department of the PLA; and Wang Jin, deputy director of the First Department (Operations) of the PLA's General Staff Department (GSD). Inclusion of the commanders of the PAPF and Tibet Military District reflects the importance accorded to issues relating to border security and cementing of military ties.

An significant indication of the growing warmth in China-Nepal relations was the highest-ever military aid extended by China to Nepal of US$19.8 million. It includes medical equipment for the Military Hospital in Kathmandu, engineering equipment including heavy construction vehicles, and logistics for rescue operations. General Chen Bingde, who arrived by special aircraft, was given a warm welcome and received separately by Nepal's president Dr Ram Baran Yadav, prime minister Jhala Nath Khanal and defence minister Bishnu Poudel. He had extensive talks with his Nepalese counterpart, general Chhatra Man Singh Gurung.

General Chen Bingde prefaced all discussions by emphasising that good Sino-Nepal relations are essential for regional peace and stability. The issue of the almost 20,000 Tibetans resident in Nepal was a central topic. To president Rambaran Yadav and prime minister Jhalanath Khanal, he expressed concern that the European Union (EU) might 'instigate' the Tibetans and extracted assurances that Nepali territory would not be permitted to be used against China. Talks with the Nepal army chief were more candid with the Chinese general reportedly voicing China's resentment with the EU, US and India for 'instigating the Tibetans' or interfering excessively in Nepal's internal affairs. Coincidentally, the Chinese PLA Chief's visit materialised soon after Kathmandu declined to allow Tibetans settled in Nepal to vote for a new 'prime minister', or 'Kalon Tripa', of the Tibetan 'government-in-exile' this March. Last October, the Nepalese government had disallowed voting in internal elections of the Tibetan organisation, Chu Shi Gang Druk. This appointment, which at once raises the PLA's profile in Sino-Nepal relations, comes in the backdrop of Beijing's persistent efforts to expand influence in Nepal. The trend accelerated with the advent of Maoists, and especially Prachanda's government, in Nepalese politics. China is already trying to create belts of influence by unilaterally disbursing old-age pensions in Nepal's poorer northern border areas and establishing a string of Chinese Study Centres along Nepal's borders with India.

Once finished, extension of the Lhasa-Xigaze railway to Kathmandu will exponentially expand China's influence. It will facilitate transportation of huge volumes of goods and supplies to Nepal, thereby bringing Nepal closer to dependence on China. India's special trade and transit treaty with Nepal will additionally permit Chinese goods to flow into India on extremely concessional terms. New Delhi needs to warn Kathmandu that its relationship with China is now unacceptably poised to cross the 'red line'.

THE CHINESE DEGENERATE WORKERS' STATE

By Spring 1949, the PLA had reconquered China North of the Yangzi river. After the collapse of the KMT armies in Manchuria in late 1948, most KMT-held territory and towns were surrendered without any fighting. Fu Tso-yi, for example, surrendered Peking in January 1949 as soon as the PLA advanced towards the city, indeed, he joined them in the march South.

In April 1949, after the expiry of a last deadline for Nationalist surrender, the PLA crossed the Yangzi and entered South China. They met little resistance and disarmed some two million KMT troops in a period of six months. In September, the Political Consultative Conference met in Peking and established a central government headed by Mao Zedong, leader of the CCP, Zhu De, a principal commander of the PLA, Soong Ching-ling (the widow of Sun Yat-sen and sister in law of Chiang Kai-shek), Li Jishen, leader of the Revolutionary Committee of the KMT (and the butcher of the Canton Commune in 1927) and Zhang Lan, President of the Democratic League.

The CCP had achieved its aim of establishing a popular front coalition government. Mao Zedong had outlined the policy that such a government would follow in 1945: "The task of our New

Democratic system is to promote the free development of a private capitalist economy that benefits instead of controlling the peoples' livelihood, and to protect all honestly acquired private property."

This was the policy which was followed between 1949 and 1952, which meant both defending capitalism and containing and if necessary repressing the demands of the workers and peasants. When in 1952 the CCP decisively struck out at the bourgeoisie, expropriating their property, it was a moment not of the CCP's choosin. It was a vital defensive measure forced on the Stalinists by the onslaught of US imperialism. As Mao was to declare in 1957 "socialism": "came to our country too suddenly."

The economic life of China at the time of the accession to power of this government was only one step away from complete paralysis. The collapse of the central administration, soaring inflation and the displacement of millions of people from the areas of military operations were accompanied by floods and droughts that affected 20 million acres and threatened 40 million people with starvation. Coal production stood at 50 per cent of its previous highest point, iron and steel were down by 80 per cent, cotton goods down by 25 per cent, grain 25 per cent, raw cotton 48 per cent and livestock 16 per cent.

To make matters yet worse the railway network was out of operation with 50 per cent of the track destroyed and most of the maritime fleet was in Hong Kong, Taiwan or Singapore. The first priority of the People's Government was expressed in the Common Programme of October 1949: "A policy that is concerned with private and public interests, that benefits the bosses and the workers, that encourages mutual aid between our country and foreign countries in order to develop production and bring prosperity to the economy."

In other words, the existing framework of capitalist property relations was to be maintained. The policy of tolerance and encouragement extended to the "national" capitalists was not extended to the "bureaucratic" capitalists. Their possessions were immediately nationalised, giving the state control of nearly one-third of all industrial production. While the state had majority holdings in heavy industry (70 per cent of coal, 90 per cent of steel and 78 per cent of electricity) heavy industry was historically chronically underdeveloped in relation to light industry, much of which was often dependent on imported materials. It was in light industry that the "national" capitalists now dominated along with the distribution and transport networks. This group owned two-thirds of all industrial capital in 1949.

The modern sector of the economy was, however, a small percentage of the economy as a whole. In 1945 it had been calculated at between 10 and 15 per cent. Largely because of its years of control in the "liberated zones" the CCP/PLA already had within it a relative experienced administrative cadre. However, with the partial exception of those who had been in Manchuria this cadre lacked experience of urban and industrial administration. This lack was partly made up by the entry into the CCP of ex-officials of the KMT regime and educated elements of the middle classes in the cities. At the time of liberation, a sample of 6,000 cadres had the following composition: 2,500 middle class, 1,150 ex-KMT officials, 400 liberal professionals, 150 members of the privileged classes, 140 from the working class. Workers made up a mere 2 per cent of party members in 1949.27 With a membership of this sort it was possible for the CCP-dominated government to take state capitalist economic measures such as nationalisation and statification, primarily aimed at the universally hated "bureaucratic" capitalists, so long as this remained within the general framework of capitalist property relations.

In March 1949, the state formed six major trading corporations for the distribution and procurement of Food, Textiles, Salt, Coal, Construction materials and "miscellaneous" goods. In addition, a network of state owned retail outlets was established. These two measures, coupled with the introduction of a new currency, a sliding-scale of wages linked to the monetary value of essential foods, an enforced loan at 5 per cent interest from capitalists and the state distribution of goods that had been hoarded by the KMT and its supporters, allowed a rapid improvement in the living conditions of the masses and brought inflation under control. By mid-1951 it was down to 20 per cent and prices were essentially stable in 1952.

That, despite this statification of essentials, the popular front government was anxious not to scare the "national" bourgeoisie into fleeing, can be seen from the assurances given them by Chen Yun the Chairman of the Financial and Economic Commission, in August 1950, "... industrial investments undertaken for a long time by the national capitalists, if they remain progressive in character, will be useful to the state and the people." The Agrarian Reform of June 1950 shows the same clear intention of maintaining friendly relations with the capitalists in order to maintain production. Article 4, dealing with whose lands could or could not be expropriated, said:

"Industry and commerce shall be protected from infringement, industrial and commercial enterprises operated by landlords, and the land and other properties used by the landlords directly for the operation of industrial and commercial enterprises, shall not be confiscated."

The new land reform was only applicable in the south where, as we have noted, the ties between landlords and the urban bourgeoisie were stronger than in the north. In addition to the strictures on landlords' lands, it was also expressly forbidden to confiscate all the "surplus" lands of the wealthiest peasants and that of the "richer middle peasants" was to be left alone entirely. Mao explained why at the third session of the Central Committee, 6 June 1950: "... our policy towards the rich peasants ought to be changed. Their excess land must no longer be confiscated, but their life must be preserved to speed up the restoration of production in rural areas."

Despite these limitations imposed by the state, the land reform did involve a massive transfer of land in South China, some 7 million acres out of a Chinese total of 17 million. On average all individuals over sixteen held one-third of an acre after the reform. As in the country generally, so in the cities the chief priority of the new government was to re-establish order Far from utilising the entry of the Liberation Army to ensure a proletarian takeover of the towns and industrial plant, Un Biao, commander of the Fourth Army, issued the following proclamation in January 1949:

"The people are asked to maintain order and to continue their present occupations. KMT officials or police personnel of provincial, city, county or other level of governmental unit district, town, village, or Bao Jia personnel are enjoined to stay at their posts".

In addition, whilst granting statutory rights to workers' organisations the People's Government showed in its Labour Law of 1950 that its interest lay solely in regularising the labour-capital relationship, not in abolishing it. With regard to disputes, for example, it laid down the following procedures: "the first step in procedure for settling labour disputes shall be consultation between the parties the second step shall be mediation between the parties by the Labour Bureau [a state department-Eds] and the third step shall be arbitration by the arbitration committee established by the Labour Bureau."

The nature of the unions set up by the government, and modelled on those of the Soviet Union, can be judged from the fact that one of the Vice Chairmen of the All China Federation of Trade Unions was Chu Xuefan, previously the head of the yellow unions of the KMT, the Association of Labour. In addition, the Minister of Labour, U Lisan was simultaneously vice-president of the ACFTU. The Chairman of this body made perfectly clear what the priorities of the government were: "The immediate and sectional interests of the working class must be subordinated to the long term and over all interests of the state led by the working class."

That "subordination" was to be taken absolutely literally was shown by Un Biao when he sent his troops against the workers of the Sun Sun Textile plant in Shanghai who had occupied their plant to prevent its removal to Manchuria, under the government's policy of thinning out industry. Ten workers were killed or wounded in the clash. While capitalist representatives shared the government with the CCP, between 1949 and 1951 and the policy of that government was clearly to defend capitalism, the repressive apparatus of the state-the police, army, secret police etc., remained firmly in the hands of the Stalinists.

This special form of dual power already witnessed in Eastern Europe and Yugoslavia, continued to exist until it was resolved decisively against the capitalists. The popular front period played an important role for the Chinese Stalinists in demobilising the aroused workers and peasants. At the time when capitalism was at its weakest and the mobilisations of the workers and peasants at their strongest, the CCP acted to limit those mobilisations and to restrain them within the limits of capitalist property relations. The dangers of this policy of maintaining and strengthening the capitalists swiftly became apparent. The utopian goal of the Stalinists a stable New Democracy where capitalists and Stalinists worked in harmony was never a possibility. The onslaught of American imperialism in the Korean war produced a growing threat of capitalist counter-revolution inside China amongst sections of the remaining bourgeoisie. America and Chiang Kai Shek were ready to act as their heavily armed allies.

This forced the CCP towards the close of 1951 to move swiftly to resolve the situation of dual power in its favour through a bureaucratic, anti-capitalist workers' government. As in the other Stalinist social overturns this necessitated striking out at both the capitalists and suppressing the last remnants of the independent workers' movement.

The immediate cause of the change of policy and, eventually, the nature, of the government, was the outbreak of the Korean war in June 1950. As American armies (supposedly UN) advanced towards the Yalu River (the border between Manchuria and Korea) under the rabid anti-communist, MacArthur, the People's Government was forced to change its policy both internationally and domestically.

The initial victories of the PLA under Peng Dehuai, which forced the US back beyond the 38th parallel, were met by Washington with the rearmament of Chiang Kai-shek and the delivery of considerable economic aid to Taiwan. The US Seventh Fleet took up station between Taiwan and the mainland, thereby forcing the Chinese to divert troops from Korea to the coastal province of Fujian. In addition a total economic blockade of China was instituted. The New York Times, 5 April 1951, reported that, "MacArthur favours a Nationalist second front on the Chinese mainland and is convinced that the fate of Europe will be decided in the war against communism in Asia." Now, under both economic and military pressure from imperialism and fully aware of the potential alliance between foreign, Taiwan based and domestic capital, the CCP took steps to mobilise the masses against the "national" capitalists. In the countryside, the Agrarian Reform was accompanied by the building of the People's Tribunals, organised by the Party cadres with the purpose of applying a degree of terror and intimidation to the landlords. Although the campaign was limited to the terms of the Agrarian Reform, the wave of executions, fines and expropriations both broke the class power of the landlords and served to bind the peasantry yet closer to the regime.

At the same time the control of the CCP ensured that this did not go beyond its own predetermined limitations. Indeed, so bureaucratic was the procedure for ratifying redistribution of land that, in Canton province it still had not been completed by December 1952. A parallel movement was set in train in the cities for similar purposes. The so called "three anti's" campaign, introduced alongside the "five anti's" campaign at the end of 1951, was aimed at CCP and government functionaries. The masses of members who had been recruited to the CCP on the basis of its popular front programme, were now considered unreliable a massive purge took place in the party, involving the expulsion of over one million members (a fifth of the party) between 1951 and 1952. It was also in this period that the Stalinists struck out against the left. Chinese Trotskyists, many members of the 'nternationalist Workers Party had been active leading strikes in Canton and Shanghai. They had suffered repression before 1952 at the hands of the CCP, but at the end of that year a nation wide raid by the secret police completely decimated the Chinese Trotskyists two or three hundred were thrown into gaol. Leading members Cheng Ch'ao-Un and eleven others were only released 27 years later in June 1979. The "Five anti's" campaign which ran parallel with the "three" was aimed at weakening and intimidating the bourgeoisie. Mass meetings were held throughout the country to whip up feelings against the capitalists. Businesses were investigated for fraud and corruption. In the first six months of 1952 nearly half a million businesses were inspected and over three quarters found guilty of infractions.

Many were heavily fined, contributing $850m to state coffers. Those who could not pay were nationalised instead. By these bureaucratic methods, albeit backed up by mass mobilisations and denunciation sessions, the CCP-led government, a bureaucratic anti- capitalist workers' government came to control 64 per cent of wholesale trade and 42 per cent of retail trade by mid 1952. Initially, this led to a fall in production as the bourgeoisie retaliated by closing down plants. Between January and February 1952, at the height of the campaign, production fell by 34 per cent and the state was obliged to slow down the campaign.

Once again Chen Yun offered reassurance: "Private factories will, according to concrete conditions, be guaranteed a profit of around 10, 20 or up to 30 per cent on their capital." Once again private capital survived in China, but it was now severely curtailed in its freedom, state control of orders placed with private industry, for example, was a powerful weapon for ensuring that the capitalists did not step out of line. This respite was short lived however and in 1953 at a government convened National Congress of Industry and Commerce the remaining capitalists were told that the first aim of the government was to have a fully socialist economy in which private industry would have no place.

After 1951 primarily under pressure from imperialism, the popular front government was transformed into a bureaucratic, anti-capitalist workers' government which removed the foundations of the class rule of the capitalists, "not by decree but by relentless, high-pressure gradualism". In this way it ensured that its prime enemy, the independently organised revolutionary working class, remained firmly excluded from political power within China. Because the fundamental bastion of the bourgeois state its bodies of armed men had already been smashed, the CCP was able to carry out the military-bureaucratic overthrow of the Chinese bourgeoisie relatively peacefully.

It was against a background of economic blockade by the West, majority state control of heavy industry and effective control of trade in the modern sector that the government of the People's Republic moved against the essential foundations of capitalism with the introduction of planning in 1953. At first this took the form of annual plans for 1953 and 1954, these were then incorporated into, and used as a basis for, the First Five Year Plan 1953-57. This was not published until late 1955.

The introduction of planning in 1953 on the clear basis of subordinating the operation of the law of value, marks the establishment of a degenerate workers' state in China. The plan was modelled on the Five Year Plans of the Soviet Union. Planners exhorted plant managers to take careful heed of the "advanced experience" of the Soviet system. The ability of the plan to even begin the industrialisation of China was, in a large measure, due to the aid provided by the USSR. Since 1950 China had been in receipt of an annual $300m loan from the Soviet Union. In March 1953 this was added to by a commercial agreement with the USSR, supplying China with many of the materials necessary for industrial expansion.

The plan revealed the dynamic lodged within the post capitalist property forms, and, at the same time, the way in which the bureaucracy acts as a fetter on the full realisation of this dynamic. The bureaucracy claimed that 1953 saw a 13 per cent increase in industrial output over the 1952 level, while in 1954 output rose a further 17 per cent higher than the total for 1953.

However, the exclusion of the masses from political control of the plan meant that these advances were undermined by the bureaucracy's tendency to plan blind. In 1955, when the collection of statistical data took place on a national scale, the figures often disguised the problems of the plan. In 1956 these surfaced. On March 18th 1956 the People's Daily was forced to admit that only just over 50 per cent of the capital construction programme had been fulfilled. Shortages, particularly in construction materials, began to block the fulfilment of targets. Inflationary pressures mounted and the bureaucracy was forced to reduce its targets in heavy industry.

As usual with bureaucratic plans the fulfilment of targets did not mean that the goods produced were of a high quality. The tyranny of the "target" in fact meant that workers often took little care with their products, and ended up producing shoddy goods, but at a faster rate! These features of bureaucratic planning have been apparent in the Chinese economy since 1953. They are an inevitable product of a regime under which the working class is excluded from political power. In China the economic power of the bourgeoisie was destroyed, bureaucratically, through induced bankruptcies and, after 1955, by state purchases of majority shareholdings. In 1956 the modern sector of the Chinese economy was virtually 100 per cent nationalised, and the bourgeoisie as a class was eliminated. But perched at the top of this workers' state was a Stalinist bureaucracy, ruling over the working class.

7

Nepal – China Closeness: What India Loses?

India and Nepal are not only connected due to the proximity of land, but it is the cultural affinity that binds the two nations. The common linguistic and ethnic identities, Hindu religious practices, similar festivals, affinity of food, resemblance of dresses, and the overall way of thinking, all make inseparable ties between India and Nepal.

Added to this range of similarities and affinities, is the presence of many prominent Nepali political leaders that have their ancestors or relatives in India. Some view this as a domination created by well thought moves of the Indian government since Independence; while others regard it as historical civilizational inter-linkages. No matter with what lens one looks at it, the relationship between India and Nepal is an age-old deeply inter-connected relationship. Yet, a recent visit to Nepal will make Indians feel strangers in a foreign land. It will come as no surprise that most of the Nepali businessmen now prefer to speak Chinese rather than Hindi, and prefer Chinese tourists over Indian. Why such a change? Will this closeness of Nepal with China impact India-Nepal relations? What if Chinese government strongly influences Nepali government? Is Chinese government using soft power tactics to strategically link Nepal with China? These are the most haunted apprehensions of the Indian government and are not without any basis.

At a recent class organized by HNB Garhwal University on India-China Relations, Prof. Lok Raj Boral, Executive Chairman of the Nepal Centre for Contemporary Studies, stated that "Nepal is developing ties with China, but this has no contradiction with Nepal's relations with India. It is purely based on a win-win situation for all sides as Nepal is just exploring economic opportunities with China". Do economic opportunities refer to the goods China is dumping in neighbouring states? Or does it refer to the military assistance, which China is overwhelmingly offering to Nepal in order to counter the role of any regional power to be active in the soil of Nepal, a direct counter-measure against India.

Flash back of the past will take historians to dwell into the border conflicts that resulted in Nepal-Tibet-China war (1789-1792) over territorial dispute. Further advancement in time will give even grimmer picture of Nepal-Tibetan war of 1855 that was concluded in 1856 with the Treaty of Thapathali with the special status of China as a mediator. Thereafter, by the early 19th century, Nepal broke all relations with China. Can such hostile relations shake the foundation of two thousand year old ties between India and Nepal? Not really, unless we see the developments of Nepal-China relations in the present times and reassess the grounds on which the current relations are established.

Nepal and China resumed diplomatic relations in the mid 1950s. The basis of signing the Treaty of Peace and Friendship in 1960 was Nepal's recognition of Tibet as a part of China and a resolution to the long-standing border problem. Thereafter, China has constantly spread its sphere of influence on the Himalayan Kingdom by expanding greater economic linkages and extending substantial military assistance to Nepal.

In the 1970s, when King Birendra of Nepal proposed Nepal as a "zone of peace" between India and China, India did not show keen interest, while China was quite supportive. These and many such issues created a rift in Nepal-India ties; while at the same time China has been pro-active to support and aid Nepal.

Although Nepal and India have an open border and free mobility of populace across borders; it is China that is increasingly working to take over India's position of the largest trading partner of Nepal. In 2011-2012, India-Nepal trade was USD 3 billion and the total volume of trade between Nepal and China amounted to USD 1.2 billion. To enhance these ties, China has offered zero-tariff treatment to 60 per cent products of Nepal. Simultaneously, there is added emphasis on boosting cultural exchanges. There are now almost 19 China Study Centres (CSC) and Confucius Institutes in Nepal to promote Chinese language and culture. The aim now is to have a comprehensive cooperation that serves mutual development and prosperity with the promotion of trade and tourism, joint border management, development of hydropower projects, building infrastructure for greater connectivity, and bring in overall socio-economic growth of Nepal.

For Nepal, China serves as a possible supplier of goods and assistance that it badly needs in order to recover its economy. Almost half the population of Nepal is unemployed and more than half is illiterate. At the same time, more than 30 per cent of the people in Nepal live in abject poverty. To deal with its internal problems, Nepal surely has serious business to engage with China. However, China also has deeper motives than just business cooperation. The Tibetan community in Nepal is a serious concern for the Chinese authorities. In particular, the clandestine operations that have its roots in Nepal pose greater challenges for the unity of China's southern periphery. In April 2008, China could use its influence on Nepalese administration to crackdown on Tibetan activities. Hence, it is not wrong to posit that China's business ties are redefining the power equations with that of Nepal.

China's open political policy in Nepal remains to exploit the resources of Nepal and take advantage of Indian market. Hence, it has recently completed 22-km road in central Nepal connecting its southern plains with Kyirong, county of Tibet, making the shortest motorable overland route between China and India. Besides, it has been active to engage itself in the Nepal-China-

India trilateral meeting for enhancing trilateral cooperation, which was held in January this year. One of the major focuses of the meeting was energy projects based on trans-country power trade agreement, which allows free trade of electricity among Nepal, China, and India and through a regional grid connected to all the countries.

While China's relations with Nepal grow, resentment against India is on the rise. Nepali sentiments that India has expansionist tendencies are gaining ground. In particular, the Chinese economic clout over Nepal is giving space for open antagonistic view against India.

On January 9, 2013, at the inaugural session of the 6th General Assembly of the Nepal Communist Party (Maoist) in Kathmandu, Chairman Mohan Baidya Kiran stated, "China respects Nepal's sovereignty unconditionally, while India has set an evil eye... there exists several unequal treaties between the two countries." Such concerns were also for the first time openly expressed by the Indian side at the end of last year when Pranay Sahay, Director General of Armed Border Force Sashastra Seema Bal after an India-Nepal border meet told the press that the Chinese activities in the southern part of Nepal have increased. Nepal is also increasingly become concerned over the trade deficit it has with India, which has surged to 33.7 per cent. The unsettled India-Nepal border remains as a thorn in India-Nepal relations. Yet, Nepal wants to maintain a tricky balance between the unequal rising powers in its neighbourhood.

It is of urgent need that India relooks its policy options and cooperative ties with Nepal. Although, there is no immediate threat to India's relations with Nepal, but a cautious approach and reassessment of this relationship is the need of the hour. A benign factor that can work to India's advantage is the decline in China's economy, which demoralises China to remain as a constant supplier of monetary aid to Nepal. If India cashes on this opportunity to rework its relationship with Nepal, it has greater choices in terms of its proximity and close affinity with the Nepalese.

INDIA, CHINA AND NEPAL: AN PROMISING TRILATERAL RELATION IN THE 21ST CENTURY

India-nepal Relations

Turning to India-Nepal relations, India is Nepal's biggest trading partner and also the largest foreign investor. India is also home to an estimated 5-6 million people from Nepal who live and work in India. They can freely reside, purchase property and work not only in the private sector but in the Government of India and in State governments. There are Nepali citizens in the Indian army at every level - from generals, brigadiers and colonels to soldiers. It is the historical, cultural and civilizational affinity between the two countries and an open border that makes all this possible.

Economic development today is all about connectivity and energy. It is for this reason that India is building over 1400 kms of roads in Nepal and constructing five rail lines connecting Nepal with the Indian railway network for the rapid movement of goods and people. Even in the area of hydropower India and Nepal are complementary. India presents a vast ready market for hydropower for Nepal. With only run-of-the-river projects, in the summer when there is peak demand in India, there would be surplus in Nepal to export and in winter when Nepal is unable to generate much electricity as water levels in rivers go down, she can use whatever is generated to meet domestic demand and import any shortfall. Already in India, power trading between regions is a thriving business. Even with only 4% of India's electricity being traded, the turnover in power trading is Indian Rs 30,000 crores. Such power trading has the potential to make Nepal the richest country in South Asia.

Finally, for any country, peace, stability and prosperity of its neigbhours is of utmost concern. There is an old Chinese saying that it never rains on your neighbour without you getting your feet wet. India is committed to assist Nepal in any way it desires to build a peaceful, stable and prosperous Nepal.

For India, China and Nepal, Geography has made us neighbours. History has made us friends and Economics has made us partners. Those who are joined by geography, history, and economics cannot but work together for their common benefit.

India-china Relations

In many ways, the last twenty years or so have seen India and China rediscovering each other. At the political level, there is unprecedented dialogue between the leaders of the two countries at the highest levels. Our leaders meet either bilaterally or on margins of international and regional summits at least two to three times a year. This has resulted in building trust and confidence between the two sides. Both India and China aver that there is enough space in the world for both countries to grow. We have agreed to describe our relationship as a "Strategic and Cooperative Partnership for Peace and Prosperity". Earlier this year, President Hu Jintao on a visit to India proposed five points on how to raise this strategic partnership to an even higher level. Prime Minister Dr. Manmohan Singh then described the relationship as "one of the most important bilateral relationships of the 21st Century".

The number of bilateral mechanisms we have instituted together are too numerous to mention. We have recently instituted a Strategic and Economic Dialogue, we have a defence dialogue, our armies carry out joint exercises and our navies are doing the same with close cooperation in anti-piracy in the Indian Ocean.

We have close coordination and cooperation on burning international issues such as on climate change, and in the G-20, we have cooperated well in giving developing nations more say in the global financial governance architecture.

Nor is this relationship limited to governments. In 2010, I had the privilege of helping to organize a Festival of India in China spread over eight months and covering the length and breadth of the country involving many dozens of performances and hundreds of artistes. A similar festival was organized by China in India. Visits of school children and youth are organized from both sides every year. Indian television dramas are dubbed or subtitled in Chinese and have proven to be immensely popular. During my visits to provinces in China, many people have told me how popular and addictive they are.

On the other hand, the Central Board of Secondary Education of India has only last month signed an agreement with the Confucius Institute Headquarters to introduce Chinese as a foreign language for middle school students in CBSE schools in India starting with 500 schools and gradually extending to all 11,500.

But in no other area is the growth of our relationship as spectacular as that in the field of economics. Nearly 20 years ago when I was a young First Secretary in Beijing, our bilateral trade was 438 million US dollars. By 2000 this had grown slightly to just about 3 billion US dollars. In a decade since then, this grown to 74 billion US dollars. To put this figure into perspective, the bilateral trade between India and China is four times Nepal's entire GDP. And we are targeting bilateral trade of US$ 100 million by 2015.

Today, China is India's largest trading partner in the world and India is China's seventh largest export destination. And nor is this relationship limited to only trade. There are presently 723 Indian projects in China with well known names like Infosys, TCS, APTECH, Wipro, Mahindra and Mahindra, Dr. Reddy's, Suzlon Energy, Reliance Industries and many others all active in China. As many as 10 Indian banks have operations in China.

Similarly more than 100 Chinese companies have operations in India ranging from automobiles, energy, machinery, telecom to steel. A company like Huawei has located its international R&D center in Bangalore that employees over 2000 Indian IT professional. Till December last year, the total contractual investment of projects being implemented by Chinese companies in India was US $ 55 billion covering such sectors as energy, aluminium and steel.

These economic relations have blossomed as they are backed by a host of bilateral agreements including BIPPA signed in 2006 and Double Taxation Avoidance Agreement signed in 1994.

NEPAL: THE CHINA CARD?

South Asian politicians, traders and intellectuals call it The China Card. In the geopolitical game, it has been drawn as an attempt to counterbalance the overwhelming influence of India on Nepal. It has been played for decades, particularly since King Mahendra established diplomatic relations in 1955 and signed the border treaty with China in 1961. His son Birendra strengthened the northern ties, visited the People's Republic ten times, and purchased arms from Beijing.

Keshav Mishra recalls the two times when India imposed an economic blockade on Nepal. The first time was in 1962, to which China's foreign minister, Marshal Chen Yi, retorted: "In case any foreign army makes a foolhardy attempt to attack Nepal, China will side with the Nepalese people."

The second time was in 1989 (partly in response to Birendra importing arms from China), to which Chinese premier Li Peng articulated in a press interview: "China understands the current situation concerning Nepal. We consider it unjustified for a neighboring country of Nepal to impose a blockade against the kingdom because the direct victims of this blockade are the Nepalese people. China supplied goods to Nepal through the Tibet Autonomous Region (TAR) during the blockade.

This chapter speaks of Sino-Nepalese relations, showing an age- old connection despite the world's highest mountain range between them.

We look at the principles of foreign policy from both sides of the relationship, and the interests that stand behind them. Investment, cooperation, trade, aid, exchanges and security concerns form the basis of the friendly and pragmatic affiliation. The last section looks at the effects of Sino-Indian relations on Nepal and on the Himalayan region as a whole. Throughout the chapter, the reflection points to the conclusion that China would benefit from an explicit nomination of Nepal as a Zone of Peace, based on the assumption that it was and therefore is supportive of the idea.

Earliest Relations

The first recorded official relations between Nepal and China date back to the middle of the fifth century BCE. Monks, scholars, philosophers, artists, traders and adventurers travelled back and forth, exchanging news, gifts, inventions and commercial opportunities. Arniko, a Nepalese architect and artist, supervised the construction of the White Pagoda in 1278 during the Yuan Dynasty. Arniko's Pagoda in Beijing became a standard of architecture in China, a style that traveled further east to Korea and Japan. It still stands in Beijing today. (The Arniko Highway connects Kathmandu with the Tibetan border and continues on to Lhasa. The road runs first along the Sun Kosi or "Golden River," then the Bhote Kosi or "Tibet River." It was built through China's assistance in the 1960s, after the Sino-Indian war. Many Chinese philosophers and learned Buddhist monks travelled the Silk Route seeking intellectual and spiritual exchange with other scholars in the Ganges plains, South India and Sri Lanka. Huen Tsang (603-664 A.D.), in particular, left records about his visit to Nepal.

Nepal's China Policy after the creation of the Nepali State (18th-20th Centuries): The 18th century saw the creation of Nepal as a "modern state," with the founder Prithvi Narayan Shah and his successor expanding territory to further frontiers known as "Greater Nepal." Nepalese adventurism was then everywhere, including Tibet. The Chinese intervened in favour of Tibet and defeated the Nepalese armies, consequently forcing unto Nepal the Sino-Nepalese Treaty of Betrabati in 1792 that established tribute-paying missions to the emperor every five years (until 1908). This repetitive act was symbolic of Chinese political and cultural supremacy in the region. However, this would not be the end of Sino-Nepalese conflicts (over Tibet).

During the Anglo-Nepalese War of 1814-16, Nepal asked China for military assistance but was refused. With the superiority of the British military, this implicitly meant that China surrendered its influence in Nepal to the expanding British powers. The British East India Company granted Nepal its independence against exclusive economic ties.

When Nepal once again invaded Tibet in 1854, China intervened like the previous time. The Treaty of Thapathali was concluded in March 1856, explicitly recognizing China's significant position in the region, forcing Nepal to give a yearly tribute (until 1953) and committing Nepal to help Tibet in the event of foreign aggression. However, towards the end of the 19th century, Nepal aligned itself with the British Raj in India, contributing to armies that suppressed Indian nationalistic rebellions and supporting their invasion of Tibet.

In 1904, the British military marched to Lhasa. Their motivation was the fear that Russia was extending its influence into Tibet by providing military aid to the Tibetan government (this later proved to be unfounded). As the British troops invaded Tibet, Nepal rejected Tibet's request for help. Kathmandu did not want to jeopardize its good relations with the British.

The Anglo-Chinese Convention of 1906 recognized Chinese sovereignty over the region. However, when China sought to claim Tibet in 1910, Nepal sided with Tibet and Britain. Nepal then broke relations with China after Tibet drove the Chinese forces out in 1911, in the wake of the Chinese Revolution (the Xinhai Revolution of 1911 which led Emperor Puyi to abdicate). China then concentrated on its revolutions, civil wars, invasions, famines, the Second World War spreading onto its territory and the ultimate creation of the Communist People's Republic. Until 1949, Tibet remained independent from all such events and their influence.

Nepal's China Policy in the Second Half of the 20th Century

Nepal's China policy is best understood in relation to events linked with India: two years after the end of the Second World War, India gained its independence and the British Raj left the subcontinent. The separation of its Muslim population into a two-part Pakistan (East and West) occurred in an atmosphere of mistrust that turned into hatred. The exchanges of population between Pakistan and India took place with utmost brutality. Three wars between them and countless skirmishes, particularly in the northwest (Kashmir), have kept a heightened state of conflict in the region for over 60 years, a recent consequence of which was the Mumbai bombing in November 2008.

As explained, India stepped into the dominion over Nepal as previously exercised by the British Raj, directing de facto most of its political and economic development. With the perception of being surrounded by real or potential foes, the security of India depended on its ability to outwardly and inwardly control its neighbours. In the early 1950s, Indian military missions included the provision of training for Nepali troops and the posting of Indian military personnel along the northern border (in 1951, also in response to China annexing Tibet; this long-term military mission did not withdraw until 1969).

Arthur Stahnke gives a comprehensive account of the Sino-Indian political relations and the prevailing regional circumstances that led to the 1962 war between them. This war was the culmination of antagonistic sentiments that had grown between them over the last seven years. There was the border issue, with claims of territory unacceptable to either side, and there was the Tibetan issue, whereby India sympathized with the Dalai Lama, his government in exile and Tibetans in general. The communist and the democratic ideologies were contrary and their respective agendas to exercise leadership in the developing world stood in competition. China also wanted to stop the perceived Soviet-US-India encirclement at the time. Pakistan, aware of the Sino-Indian enmity and irrespective of its own pro-western direction, approached Beijing for closer ties. Ayub Khan suggested in 1960 to settle the demarcation between Pakistan-held Kashmir and China, thereby dismissing any possible misunderstanding (implying that the cause for trouble could now only come from India).

After independence, India had inherited Britain's occupation of parts of Chinese territories. Furthermore, it advanced northward by pushing its borderline to the McMahon Line in 1953. This was equivalent to an occupation of 90,000 sq km of Chinese territories. In 1959, India claimed the Aksai Chin areas, which counted 33,000 sq km (in the Xinjiang Uygur Autonomous

Region of China). Diplomatic letters between Chinese PM Zhou Enlai (under Mao Tzetong) and Indian PM Nehru between 1959 and 1960 could not resolve the border situation in Aksai Chin. Nor was it resolved by a visit by Zhou Enlai to Delhi in April 1960. China's insistence over its territorial rights to Aksai Chin and India's forward policy of sending troops into the frontier brought the confrontations to a head. Furthermore, border disputes also included an area in the extreme northeast of India, at the Himalayan border, then called North East Frontier Agency (before it was renamed Arunachal Pradesh)-a territorial claim also made by China in then South Tibet.

The Sino-Indian war started in June 1962 between the People's Liberation Army of China and the Armed Forces of India. The actual engagement was a Chinese attack on an Indian patrol north of the McMahon Line. The conflict widened to include the region of Aksai Chin which the PRC regarded as a part of China (a strategic link, via the China National Highway or route G2 19, between the Chinese-administered territories of Tibet and Xinjiang). In less than six weeks of bloody fighting, the Chinese had driven Indian forces back behind Chinese claim lines. The war ended when the Chinese secured the disputed area and unilaterally declared a ceasefire on 20 November 1962. Following the ceasefire, China kept most of its claim in Aksai Chin but gave India virtually all of India's claim in the North Fast Frontier Agency-about 70% of the disputed land.

In the 1960s, therefore, Nepal was anxious to keep on good terms with both neighbours. During the Sino-Indian conflict of 1962, it reasserted its neutrality and warned that it would not submit to aggression from any state. Although the warning was directed at China, Nepal continued to support China's application for membership in the United Nations.

In view of the border conflicts, China had made a preliminary border settlement with Nepal which provided clarity in recognition of its sovereignty. Nepal affirmed this good foreign policy time and again as it gradually sought to get closer to Beijing, playing the China card. An explicit friendship with China, besides being wise neighborly behavior, was part of the attempt to decrease dependency on India. While seeking to maintain equal friendship with both, Nepal also hoped that competition between them (regarding investments in Nepal) would enhance its own economic development. Economic opportunities with China, however, started seriously at the turn of the new millennium, and most particularly since the end of the People's War.

During a visit to China in August 1979, King Birendra, in his speech at the banquet in his honor, explained: "Nepal's foreign policy is founded on her desire to safeguard her independence and sovereignty and the related quest for peace. Our commitment to the institutionalization of peace in Nepal and our appreciation of your support for the objective is as strong as ever." Birendra was referring to China's positive response to the king's proposal of the Zone of Peace.

In 2004, as Manmohan Singh became Prime Minister of India and headed a United Progressive Alliance (UPA) government, the External Affairs Minister, Natwar Singh, went soon after his debut to Nepal. Besides the key questions of economic cooperation and dealing with the Maoist insurgency, the minister stated that Sino-Indian relations were improving and asked if Nepal would provide a transit route for their trade. There seemed to be no more "zero-sum game between Nepal, India and China."

CHINA IS ALWAYS CORDIAL FOR NEPAL : BUT WHY INDIA INTERVENES?

Nepal, China and India are permanent nations adjoining each other. The southern neighbor- India was liberated from the status of colony of the British Empire in 1947. The northern neighbor- China was overtaken by a communist regime two years after in 1949. Both of the nations have huge expanse of territory. Nepal lies between these two giant nations. Although Nepal is small in size but it was never colonized by any Empire. Unlike India and China, Nepal was never ruled by a foreign government. It was successful in saving its dignity from imperialist nations. After independence, under the leadership of Jawaharlal Nehru-the PM, India followed the path to build a new constitution through the Constituent Assembly (CA) as united federal states. After the CA India and Pakistan separated whereas, in China the Chinese Communist Party (CCP) under the leadership of Mao Ze Dong moved ahead progressively.

On the one side, Nepal has faced a communist regime while on the other a republic system. Nepal had to preserve its dignity and move ahead between such two nations. Nepal did not want to support either the communists or the Indian democracy; nor did it want to oppose any. The quality of Nepal, by adopting a neutral position was desirous of maintaining a harmonious relation between these two nations. But after India became independent its leaders conspired to draw Nepal under its umbrella.'Nepal is a yam between two boulders'- the message of the great King Unifier Prithbinarayan Shah is still relevant. China never troubled Nepal ever since communism was established in China. Although Nepal has ties with India-geographically and culturally since the Muslim rule, it is a matter of worriless that Nepal always faced threat from India. In that context, Nepalese scholar diplomat Keshar Bahadur KC said- 'If there was no China, Nepal would have ceased to exist.'

In the context of Nepal, China and India family member the former PM Kirtinidhi Bista opines on Nepal, China and Indian relation- 'The symbiotic relationship that exists between India, Nepal and China can neither be belittled nor neglected or disturbed if regional stability in South Asia is to be maintained. Nepal's national interests are integrally linked to the prospect of lasting peace and stability in South Asia. For this reason alone Nepal must always be vigilant, proactive where necessary, and try to maintain the delicate balance in its relations with the two emerging regional powers of Asia. For Nepal there is no alternative to including its next-door neighbours as common partners in its development efforts while keeping the door open for other countries interested in the region's peace and stability. For the world-at-large, too, it will have to pay dearly if any attempt. Nepal is linked by its sacred soil with India and China, as well as by rivers flowing from China through Nepal to India.

These factors, more than anything else, establish the ground for unbreakable relationship among the three. This cordial relationship has to continue for the benefit of the vast South Asian region as well as China. Nepal, for her part, has been making modest efforts within her means to consolidate and strengthen the compact that exists between the unequal partners of Asia. Fully realizing the fact that Nepal's rich natural resources and its development not only benefits the country, but also others countries in the region, King Birendra had proposed the development of Nepali hydropower for the benefit of the South Asian region.

The proposal that was floated at the tenth Colombo Plan Consultative Conference held in Kathmandu in 1978. Any country looking to secure a bright future has to first mind its business and that is where its national interests come into play. In this connection Nepal has to face a tough challenge of not only safeguarding its national interest but also creating a stable and peaceful situation favorable for the all-round development of the country, in close cooperation with her fast-developing neighbours in India and China.' But, India could not understand the reality of Nepalese prestige. In 1950 India and Nepal reached a Delhi agreement through which India had a design to capture Nepal. India wanted a new constitution in Nepal through a CA. When Nepal and China entered bilateral relations in 1956 India became hesitant. As anti-India sentiment was increasing and due to the interest shown by the communist China in Nepal, then, India canceled the necessity of CA in Nepal.

India, in fear of China, totally abandoned its scheme of capturing Nepal and the idea of a constitution through CA. And then, In 1958 King Mahendra formed a commission through which he declared a constitution for the country. In the same year on basis of this constitution a parliamentary election was held. After the election Nepali Congress (NC) came to form the government in the leadership of the PM B.P. Koirala. After the formation of NC Govt. India began to conspire in various ways to influence the NC led government. India wanted to take advantage of its friendship with NC leader BP Koirala. India continued to intervene in Nepal's internal matters. India succeeded in taking control over some Nepal's rivers.

Chinese leader Mao deliberate the fact that Nepal and China could remain secure only in the presence of royal institution in Nepal. So he looked to enhance the understanding with King Mahendra. That became the headache for India. There was no game of conspiracy behind promotion of Nepal's harmonious relation with China. Nepal does not want to move against the interest of India or China. Nepal only wants to maintain a good relation with both of the powerful neighbours. But India has never wanted to understand this fact. The Indian rulers have time and again harassed Nepal due to which Nepal is ever suspicious of its southern neighbor. Although there is consistent visits from Indian nationals to Nepal and vice versa; although Nepalese and Indian people maintain a cultural bond and relation, the Indian rulers have always wanted to misuse this harmonious understanding. Due to this fact, Nepalese people, in spite of difficult geographical connection with China, despite unfamiliarity of language and other traditional norms, have trusted China. China too has never taken interest in Nepal in negative prospective. Nepal will never bargain off its sovereignty to India on grounds of its relation pertaining to religion, culture and geography or any other. Nepal adores nothing more than its sovereign existence.

In 1960 King Mahendra took over the authority against the Indian intervention and conspiracy. In the real sense, it was not against the interest of Nepali Congress. And introduced the Panchayat system after which India drew back. There was no any negative aspect in regards Nepal-India relation from 1960 to 1978. But, there started the conspiracies that in 1973 the Indian intelligence agency 'RAW' supported the hijacking of an airplane and in July the same year backed the act of arson at Singha Durbar. China had shown interest in Nepal's security in relation to these acts. A Chinese Professor at Hunan University Wang-Chung published a book 'Nepal's National Defensive Strategy and Nepal-China Relation' and divulged many facts. He wrote that in June, 1973 Congress activists hijacked a Nepal Airlines' passenger plane and forced it to land in India. The book also delved on facts relating to the fire at the Nepal government's central Secretariat at Singh- Durbar in July and then the attempt to kill the King in March, 1974 (the bombing at Janakpur).

Prof. Wang-Chung writes-'On 23, June 1975 the Indian Prime Minister Indira Gandhi declared emergency in entire India, in which, a ban was issued on the political activities of Nepali Congress leader BP Koirala and the party activists in exile in India. After that BP Koirala returned to Nepal with the policy of national reconciliation to join the hands with the King. BP was convinced that the security of Nepal lay in the reconciliation between him and the King and that Nepal could never benefit from India. However, after the death of BP, there was no reconciliation between NC and the monarchy. And then India had another opportunity to play.

The Indians did not like King Birendra for his independent and self-sustaining foreign policy. So it is not unusual to suspect a black hand of Indian intelligence agency in the royal palace massacre that took place on 1 June 2001. He further writes-'When China provided economic support to Nepal, India did not allow China to get involved in Nepal's Terai region. India fears Chinese involvement in Terai region could make China spread communist ideology in India.' It is not necessary to add anything more here after mentioning what a Chinese intellect has explicitly written about black Indian conspiracy. It is a matter of investigation to find out who was responsible for the arson at Singha Durbar. When a Chinese intellect has pointed out that it was an Indian conspiracy we too are bound to accept it as true when we look at the dirty game played by India. Yes!

If there is fire in a house the populace of that house know less about it than their neighbours. Neighbours first see the smoke coming out of the fire. Such is the case of Nepal in relation to Indian intervention, arson at Singha Durbar and the royal palace massacre. After Rajiv Gandhi came to power the Indian policy became more discriminate towards Nepal. In 1988 India went on to issue a blockade of Nepal on an irrelevant reason of commerce transit. For the same reason it fuelled the NC and the leftist parties in support of an uprising. To avoid the prospect of foreign intervention King Birendra with great understanding reinstated democracy in 1990. In the democratic setup the misunderstanding between the ruling party and the opposition, corruption from the ruling side and Indian intervention increased. Under Indian direction the factories made under Chinese support as Harisidhi Brick-Tile Factory, Bansbari Leather Shoe Factory, Gaindakot Paper Factory among 12 other factories in profit were sold at a worthless price.

The then ruler took huge sum of commission to carry out this dirty act of India. As the scale of injustice soared India backed the Maoists' rebellion in the hills that terrorized Nepal. Many innocent people, policemen and army personnel were killed and infrastructure worth billions destroyed. Such acts of destruction carried out intentionally made Nepal unstable. India had designated the Maoists' as terrorists but they supported the same terrorists to destroy Nepal. Then after, in 2005, India mediated pact between the Maoists', NC and UML in the name of 12-point understanding. And, the uprising began by the paid workers of Maoist and Christians including the threatened villagers with aggressive. Then the King handed over the state to the political parties after the uprising-2006. The uprising came to a halt in agreement with the monarch and after the party leaders deceived the agreement by the hints of RAW and CIA. At the backing of India and western nations Nepal was declared secular and republic. These are the causes of current crisis.

With the statement of the royal institution in Nepal, India and China both are in difficulty in security point of view. In absence of the royal institution India fears that China may intervene in Nepal to establish Communism in Nepal and India. In absence of monarchy in Nepal Chinese fear is of the danger of America and its CIA European nations' and Indian agency's activities in name of human rights that will be used in the name of Free Tibet to disintegrate China.

So, China in order to avoid a security lapse is showing more interest in Nepal. It is looking to participate in activities of Nepal with economic support and development schemes. The ensuing tussle between China and India is creating a very difficult scenario for Nepal. It is true that Nepalese forever will remain in suspicion and fear of the economic and other support lent by India. Nepalese are always skeptical whenever their Prime Minister goes on an official Indian visit. They fear if the PM would handover Nepal's rivers, natural resources, Nepal foreign and security policy to India. Despite the extent of cultural bond and contact between the Indian and Nepalese people the black deeds of Indian rulers has always posed a security threat to Nepal.

In this context, a scholar Dr. Ramesh Dhungel writes- 'It is notable that the very exercise of Nepal as an independent country was made possible only because of geographical situation of the region by Prithbinarayan Shaha alongside the committed, dedicated and trusted ministers and generals belonging to the various origins. Very surprisingly, Nepal was able to stand its ground as an independent, unique and powerful multi-ethnics state situated in the lap of the Himalayas, even in such a vulnerable situation where such extreme colonial encroachment in South Asia was rife. People of different ethnic backgrounds seemed to have united under the umbrella of the newly emergent Nepal. In many cases, a practical policy, offering dependent states to smaller friendly principalities was adopted by the king of Nepal.' So, to remove all the confusion, there must be reinstatement of the Nepalese monarchy and in the presence of the King, there should be a joint conference between Nepal, India and China to reach a concrete decision which these three nations can adopt permanently as diplomatic strategy.

CHINA IN NEPAL: INDIA-CHINA NEED TO WORK TOGETHER

Nirupama Rao, the Foreign Secretary of India is slated to visit Nepal from January 18, 2011. She is expected to access the halted peace process in Nepal and discuss bilateral and other issues of common concern with the caretaker Nepalese Prime Minister, senior government officials and the leader of opposition

Maoist Party, Pushpa Kamal Dahel Prachanda. She would also attempt to pull out the jittery relations from the quagmire, which further nose dived in October 2010 in the aftermath of Unified Maoists' Party cadres hurling several pairs of shoes at the Indian ambassador to Nepal, Rakesh Sood. China would be watching each and every word of the Indian diplomat while in Nepal, as it is considered as the main weight behind the Maoists.

In order to get a better sympathetic of the present contours of the increasing footprints of the Chinese in Nepal and their implications to India, it is pertinent to go back to the historical background of this triangle at least in the 19th and 20th centuries, for the events that unfolded during this time has changed the entire geo-political situation in these three countries, and the legacy, both the colonial in India and imperial in China continues to haunt us even today. In the early 18th century, Nepal was under the rule of various chieftains, whose governance and culture was highly influenced by Tibet. During 1760s Gurkhas conquered these chieftain states, and emerged so strong that they threatened the surrounding kingdoms including Tibet. Their expansion resulted in overrunning many Tibetan territories in 1788. The Gurkha action against Tibet, which was a tributary state (*fushu guo* stated in Chinese historical documents) of China, enraged the Chinese emperor Qianlong (1736-1795) so much that he dispatched forces against Nepal in 1791-92, and reduced Nepal to the status of yet another vassal in China's periphery. Nepal was forced to send tribute to China once in every five years.

When expanded to the south, the Gurkhas met a deadlier foe, the British. The confrontation culminated in the Anglo-Nepalese War of 1814-1816. Nepal being a tributary of China, requested for help but in vein. The main reason why China refrained from help was its tiny stature, distance from China and dislike for the Gurkhas. Quoting Chinese historical records, Lu Zhaoyi of the Chinese Academy of Social Sciences and the author of *British India and China's South-western Border: 1774-1911*(Chinese edition 1996) records that the Qing government considered "Gurkhas as bullies and insatiably avaricious, and held them responsible for fomenting trouble and instability in the south-western frontier" When Nepal threatened to throw its allegiance to the British, China got irked and rebuked Nepal: "if you throw your allegiance to the British, then you would not be entitled to send tributes to the Celestial Empire...As regards dealing with the tribes outside our frontiers, the Celestial Empire will not extend militarily assistance to any of the warring side [referring to the Nepalese invasion of Sikkim]. The Celestial Empire is least bothered if your country concludes peace or goes to war with the British, approach or eventually throws your allegiance to the British"

Nepal had no option but to conclude the 1815 Treaty of Sugauli with the British on latter's terms. Nepal had to cede Kumaon, Garwal and some Tarai areas to the British, besides being reduced to a British protectorate. However, Nepal was allowed to send tribute missions to China. The last mission it sent to China was in the year 1908. Between 1854 and 1856, Nepal fought yet another border war with Tibet. The 1856 peace treaty with Tibet heavily weighted in favour of Nepal. The treaty however, agreed to pay their respect as before to the Chinese emperor. The Tibetan agreed to pay sum of 10,000 rupees annually to the Gurkha government. Nepal also offered military protection to Tibet in the event it is invaded by other states, and acquired extraterritorial and trading rights in Lhasa.

By mid 19th century Ranas captured the political power in Nepal and forged good ties with the British. During the early 20th Century, in recognition of the contribution of Nepal during World War I, the "treaty of perpetual peace and friendship,' which recognised the independent status of Nepal and upgraded the British resident to an envoy was signed in Kathmandu on 21 December, 1923. It was the 1923 treaty that used to govern the Anglo-Nepalese relations prior to the Indian independence; the treaty was replaced with the 'India and Nepal Treaty of Peace and Friendship' concluded on July 31, 1950. Even though the treaty allows the free movement of people and goods between India and Nepal, however, continued to interlock Nepalese economic and security interests with those of India owing to the

China factor. In recent years, the treaty has generated a lot of heat in various quarters in Nepal and has been very unpopular, for it is believed that the treaty impinges upon the sovereignty of Nepal.

China's Wellbeing in Nepal

India-Nepal relations during King Tribhuvan's time were excellent; however, after his death in 1955, his son King Mahendra amidst the deteriorating Sino-Indian relations dismissed the Nepali Congress Government in 1960. The move was considered by India as undemocratic and essentially anti-India. Amidst deteriorating relations with India, China seized the opportunity, and went on to develop "special relations" with Nepal. China accused India of 'expansionism' and 'hegemonism.' In 1960, China and Nepal signed a peace and friendship treaty and also the border agreement, and commenced the construction of Kathmandu-Tibet highway a year later. China's another interest in Nepal was to flush out the Tibetan guerrillas who were operating from Mustang Area of Nepal with the help of CIA. The joint Nepalese-People Liberation Army (PLA) operations against the Tibetan insurgents/refugees in the area in the 1960s are well known. However, Shakya, a Tibetan scholar posits that King Mahendra was still sympathetic towards the Tibetans. In 1969 the Crown Prince, Birendra even met the new leader, Gyatho Wangdu in Mustamg camp. After the death of Mahendra in 1972, Birendra continued the equidistance policy of his father. He became the first foreign dignitary to visit Tibet in 1976. Two years later Deng Xiaoping visited Nepal, and consolidated the cultivation of "special relations" with Nepal.

With the improvement in India-China relations during the 1970s, and given the close socio-economic and geographical proximity of Nepal with India, China probably saw the futility of excessive courting of Nepal during the 1980s. This was evident when India imposed economic sanctions and closed 13 of the 15 transit points on India-Nepal border in 1989. India was annoyed, when it learnt that Nepal was purchasing arms and ammunition from China. China attempted to salvage Nepal by transporting some goods for some time, but could not subside the increasing social unrest and cost of goods in Nepal. Moreover, with the change of political command and initiation of economic liberalization, China itself talked less of 'hegemonism' and 'expansionism.' During Zhao Ziyang's 1981 visit to Nepal, though Chinese supported the Nepalese proposal of turning Nepal into a Zone of Peace, but talked about promoting cooperation among developing countries. China herself adopted a policy of equidistance towards Nepal and India. In November 1989, during his visit to Nepal, Li Peng expressed China's inability to extend substantial support, advising the Nepalese leaders to peacefully resolve their differences with India.

China's 'Excessive' court of Nepal and India's Apprehension

It was perhaps for its international image that China denounced Maoists insurgency in Nepal during the monarchy. It repeatedly stated that Mao's China had nothing to do with the Maoists in Nepal and India; instead the latter were misusing the name of their helmsman. However, when Maoists formed the government and Pushap Kamal Dahel Prachanda was sworn in as Prime Minister, the first country he visited was China. He was 'invited' to attend the closing ceremony of Olympic Games in 2008. It must be reminded that after the successfully concluding the Olympics and showcasing its economic miracle to the world, China adopted an increasingly aggressive and assertive posture internationally, which not only has affected China's international standing but also its relations with the neighbouring countries. Prachanda's visit lasted for five days and the special bonding between the Maoists and China was exposed. There are people who argue that China is not only courting the Nepalese Maoists, but also rendering political as well material support to the Indian Maoist whose ultimate aim is to overthrow the parliamentary democracy through an armed struggle. The sheer political capital of the Maoists, and the anti-China Tibetan protests in March 2008 in various parts of Tibet including Sichuan, underscored the importance of Nepal to China, for Nepal has a sizeable Tibetan community, 20,000 according to one of the representatives of the Dalai Lama. In fact, all Tibetans those who escape Tibet, had to register at the office of UNHCR in Nepal before entering India. It was perhaps in the history of Nepal that brute force was used by the Maoist supported Nepalese government to suppress the anti-China protests.

It has been seen that with the deterioration of India-Nepal relations, Nepal has sought a countervailing force in China. We have mentioned of 1989 episode; in 2005 China further supplied arms to King Gyanendra; in the same year Nepal voiced for the inclusion of China into SAARC irrespective of the fact that India had expressed its reservations; in September 2008, China invited Nepalese Defence Minister Ram Bahadur Thapa as an observer to the military exercise 'Warrior 2008', and during his meeting with China's Defence Minister Liang Guanglie, China announced a military aid package of USD 1.3 million to Nepal. In December 2008, Lieutenant General Ma Xiaotan of the PLA pledged USD 2.6 million in non-lethal military aid to Nepal during his Nepal visit. It could be discerned that there is a close bonhomie between the two sides.

Conversely, in 2007 when India sent non-lethal military assistance to Nepal, it created a furore with the Maoists lodging vigorous protests and accusing New Delhi of trying to sabotage the peace process. Politically, even as Prachanda called for the revision of 1950 Treaty, Nepal accepted the draft of a 'Peace and Friendship Treaty' submitted and proposed by Hu Zhengyue, Assistant Chinese Foreign Affairs Minister during his Nepal visit in April 2009. It may also be mentioned that Nepal is reluctant to sign the Extradition Treaty proposed by India in 2008, thus ignoring India's concerns over terrorists having links in Nepal.

Besides deepen political and military ties, scores of China Study Centres (CNC) across Nepal has also generated lot of apprehensions in India even though Upendra Gautam, the general Secretary of the CNCs Nepal tried to allay the Indian fears by pronouncing that the Centres have been established "with a view to promoting and further strengthening friendly ties between Nepal and China at the people to people level, and firmly upholds the principle of Panchasheel in inter-state relations." Another apprehension of the Indian government in Nepal is the reconstruction of the Nepal-China highway by China. The highway was built in 1958 and opened to traffic in 1965. It starts from Lhasa, capital of Tibet Autonomous Region and ends in Katmandu, capital of Nepal with a total length of 900 kilometres. Of the total length only 100 kilometres is in Nepal. The renovation is expected to consume a whopping 800 million RMB (about 100 million USD), and is likely to be completed in 2010. This would be another milestone for China after the completion of Qinghai-Tibet railway. China predicts rapid border trade development with neighboring countries, especially in South Asia and sees these projects as extremely important landway channels to communicate with South Asia. Besides, China has also handed over the Zhangmu-Kathmandu optical fibre cable project to Nepal in 2008. China is also helping Nepal in the construction of the Melamchi Water Supply Project. The Project is supposed to improve the health and well-being of the people in Kathmandu Valley by alleviating the critical water stress in the region, where 1 million urban dwellers receive piped water for only two hours every two days. The project is budgeted at 294.4 million USD and is expected to be completed by 2014. It is believed that China has invested millions of dollars in Nepal's hydroelectricity projects.

The Way in Front

It is obvious that there is a flurry of diplomatic as well as economic activities between China and Nepal. In 2009 alone, an unprecedented 38 Chinese delegations visited Nepal. With the deterioration in India-China relations, China not only courted Nepal but also other countries in India's vicinity. Moreover, with China's increasing economic muscle, its political, economic and diplomatic assertiveness is also increasing. Of late its engagement with Nepal and other countries surrounding us has been multi-dimensional and designed to diminish the Indian influence in South Asia in both short and long run. Why China has been able to change the perceptions of the people in the subcontinent favourable to China calls for introspection, and requires corrective and immediate measures, for India cannot afford to take our historical and cultural ties with Nepal and other countries for granted.

China is aware of the fact that it would be almost impossible to shift the cultural influence of India in Nepal to its favour. Therefore, New Delhi's approach should be if Nepal wishes to renegotiate the 1950 treaty and delink our national security interests with it, so be it. If it wants close the present open border with India, we should be happy, as we have increasingly declared the border as a 'hotbed of ISI intrigue.' Meanwhile India needs to proactively engage and integrate these nations into our economic development, show magnanimity in various disputes and increase out footprints in these countries. This is the policy India not only needs to initiate with its immediate neighbours but also within the fringes of our own borders.

Given China's military and other quasi-military projects in Nepal, Sri Lanka, Bangladesh, Myanmar and Pakistan, it is amply clear that China has consistently followed the strategy of pinning India to the subcontinent, and has used our differences with countries in our vicinity to their own advantage with a lethal statecraft. However, the question we must ask ourselves is that do we have the capabilities to undertake the projects the Chinese companies are taking in our vicinity, or is it because of the sloppiness of our government as well as private sector to avail such opportunities in our neighbourhood? As far as China's infrastructural development projects in our vicinity are concerned, these may generate multiplier effects and pave way for trade and commerce for Indian companies as well. However, China also must be careful in inciting anti-India rhetoric in these countries and also domestically, for this may prove the 'string of pearls' thesis of containing India true, and force India to move closer to the United States as well other countries and regions that are antagonistic to China. Therefore, India and China need to work closely in their shared neighbourhood on the issues of security, including the maritime security as most of the Shipping Lines of Communication run through the Indian Ocean.

8

Be Supposed to India Worry about the Dragon in Nepal?

Bharat has to compete with two major enemies – the Christian-imperialist-West axis; Jihadi terrorism; and an inimical entity, China, whose great power ambitions pose a threat to her security. All three forces are asuric, and are not listed in any special order of priority. As a Hindutva-vadin, the present writer is concerned with all three, though this article is concerned with the menace faced from the Dragon. In this connection, the writer has found the articles by defence analyst B. Raman, former secretary, Cabinet Secretariat, and currently associated with the Chennai Institute for Chinese Studies, particularly helpful.

The Nepal Maoists are at present split into various factions and are no longer the unified force they were during the insurrection, 1996-2006. B. Raman has examined various aspects of the Chinese presence in Nepal and how this impacts on India. The Chinese enjoyed a certain privileged relationship with the Nepalese kings who did a balancing and clever act between India and China. Until the Maoists came to power in the coalition government in 2006, after a ten year insurrection, China had distanced itself from the Maoists and even helped the king to fight the insurrection. So did India, until it appeared that King Gyanendra was playing a double game. But now the Chinese are using the Nepalese Maoists to further their own aims in the region.

As the world knows, China is an unabashedly capitalist country. The noble aim of Karl Marx: from each according to his ability, to each according to his needs, was never practiced in Maoist China. Today, China is in league with the world's capitalist powers. What is Beijing's agenda in Nepal where it now has a significant presence through the exercise of soft power - aid to Nepal, hydroelectric projects, exchange of students, subsidising trips to China etc?

China has three goals in Nepal: to use the Nepalese Maoists to oppress and quell Tibetan revolts against Chinese domination; to downgrade India which stands in the way of its great power ambitions in south Asia and its domination of Tibet; and to build its own economic clout by exploiting the natural resources of Nepal. While the West is also fishing in troubled waters in Nepal, that is not yet an imminent threat to India. And issues such as the presence of genetically modified crops by Western corporations such as Monsanto are being taken up by the relevant NGOs (as well they should).

India must center clearly on the first two questions. Tibet has always been a home of Buddhism outside India. While Buddhism in the Far East, in Vietnam and Japan, has been eclipsed by conversions to Christianity, Tibetans continue to follow their traditional religion, a mix of the native Bon and Buddhism from India. In that sense the Dalai Lama is a dharmic leader, and whatever the reasons for the Western powers' support of his cause, Hindus of India have a religious/spiritual reason to oppose Beijing's policy in Tibet. The selection by China of the Panchen Lama did not go well with the people and the Chinese leadership fears that if and when the Dalai Lama passes on there will be disturbances. Hence their use of Nepalese Maoists to keep the Tibetans in line.

Indic scholars create it abundantly clear that the Chinese are simultaneously pragmatic and ambitious in their relations with the world and especially their neighbour India. Raman has pointed out that while they may not repeat the adventurism of 1962 since they have a lot more to lose now than then, an aerial attack cannot be ruled out. Their pragmatism tells them not to waste time, money and resources in fresh battle with India, but their ambitions cannot always be held in check. A nuclear attack is also not on the cards. However, they engage in what is called 'salami slicing', the slow incremental advance, as in Arunachal Pradesh. Their early and ongoing military and logistical support to Pakistan is not altruistic, but to keep India off balance. Should war break out, India will have to fight on two fronts. Hence, while a cautious and limited economic engagement with the Dragon is well advised (such as business enterprises by noted giants like Tata) it should be kept well under control. The recent scandal involving telecommunications is a case in point. China cannot be allowed to have input into India's telecommunications. Trade in goods and other services can be encouraged up to a point, but not to the extent that it is allowed to flood the market with cheap goods and drive Indian small and medium entrepreneurs out of business.

In Nepal, India's soft power is slowly declining because of the steady beat of anti-India propaganda. Many Indian companies are finding it difficult because of the hostility being fanned against them. At the same time, China is vigorously promoting its own projects in Nepal, which are not only profitable to it, but demonstrate the use of soft power. Unlike in Tibet, this is working for them. The highway, the railway line etc. are also effective support for their military designs against India. In such a context, India must not only safeguard its territory using military defence and diplomacy, its enterprises and its economy, but also its Hindu ethos. This last call cannot be neglected because no civilisation folds up purely from external causes and attacks. The strength of Bharatiya civilisation for several millennia has always been and will continue to be its enduring dharmic ethos as upheld by the ordinary citizen and the traditional acharyas and mathams.

Elements in the middle class however, can be lured by the attractions of a false communistic propaganda. The effect of this propaganda is two-fold: the illusion that some millenarian style (revolutionary) action is the solution to the problems of society, hence the refusal to engage in a careful modest approach to social reform. The devilish actions of the Naxalites are well known; many of its leaders were middle class ideologues.

There is a story that Maoist Kishanji who used to train potential revolutionaries by hardening them to bloodshed by the routine slaughter of helpless animals and slogans such as power lies in the barrel of a gun. There is misleading propaganda that state power has to be seized and dismantled to achieve social goals. In India, there is mindless violence against individual policemen such as beheading. In Nepal, the numbers of civilians killed runs into thousands, and the retaliation by the Nepalese state is said to be equal. The direct link of the Nepalese Maoists to Indian insurgents is well known, so also China's clandestine support via this route.

These practices are borrowed directly from the Maoist dictionary from across the border. To the extent that Beijing keeps up its propaganda in Nepal and elsewhere, it acts as a magnet to immature and unsteady minds elsewhere. The fact that the Nepalese Maoists have given up all thoughts of world revolution is not the issue; they have. What has persisted, hovering over their psyches, are the diabolical philosophies that they learned from Maoism. The asuric forces across the border must be resolutely rejected. Under no circumstance should they be glorified. Hindus should worry about the Dragon while setting their own house in order so that diabolical influences cannot make inroads. The question then is not only should Hindus worry about the Dragon in Nepal, but also in what sense they should so worry.

FAULT LINES IN INDO-NEPAL RELATIONS

India has formally named a new ambassador to Nepal. Mr. Jayant Prasad, son of Prof Bimal Prasad, who had served as the Indian ambassador to Nepal from 1991-1995 and whose tenure was regarded as engaging and effective, takes over from Mr. Rakesh Sood. It has certainly been an inheritance of loss taking over reins from Mr. Sood whose tenure was marred with controversies. The outgoing Indian ambassador was often accused of arrogant diplomacy, a notorious case in point being

Mr. Pushpa Kamal Dahal's outburst against Mr. Sood's obtrusive meddling into Nepali affairs and unwanted arm-twisting of the government leading to the former's resignation as the prime minister.

While the South Block's damage control mode might reap some dividend, the fault lines of Indian diplomacy in Nepal go deeper. Without doubt, India is the elephant in the room in South Asia and the asymmetries in geography, economy, and political clout between India and its neighbours often frames India's very own 'Melian dialogue' in the region — " the strong do what they can and the weak suffer as they must." Even in 'realist' terms, what India often forgets is that it needs Nepal for its geostrategic engagement, domestic security and its emerging market just as Nepal needs India for its investments, imports/exports and access to sea.

Historically, despite – or rather because of – the geographical and cultural affinity, both sides have often had serious issues with each other. Ingrained in the Nepali public memory is a history of unequal treaties (1950 Treaty of Peace and Friendship), resource exploitation, an economic blockade, international vetoes and incessant political meddling. Similarly, India has complained about Nepal's insensitivity to concerns about Indian security coming from China as well as the Maoists. India is locked up with China in a battle for stakes in new Asia and world order, and it feels China is using sources in Nepal to threaten Indian security. With Maoists, the confrontation is both ideological and political given the closeness of the Maoists in Nepal with the radical left in India. Naxalism, with its reach in one-third of Indian districts, at the moment is India's biggest internal security worry. India also grudges Nepal's insistence on being an equal partner rather than pushing for a "special relation" (unlike Bhutan) with India. A rising anti-India sentiment in Nepal also worries policymakers in India.

FAULT LINES IN INDO-NEPAL DIPLOMATIC MECHANISM

The Indo-Nepal diplomatic mechanism is yet to mature to be called a "special relation". Several factors account for the stunted scope of the relation, while some are domestically generated concerns that are still being bargained, the others are exogenous India's behavior historically concerning Nepal has been one of seeking dominance without responsibility. Indian engagement with Nepal has been fraught with unplanned designs, covert and contradictory operations, injecting – often, muscling in – India favored policies and players, and rejection of newer political realities in Nepal. The moral and material support to the Maoists (as revealed by the Siliguri meeting in August 2001) and then contradictory a month later in September 2001 labeling the Maoists as terrorists and simultaneously stepping up military assistance to the Nepali Army demonstrates the ad hoc nature of Indian foreign policy toward Nepal. On the one hand, India has repeatedly insisted that it supports a logical conclusion of the Nepali peace process; on the other hand, however, it has subverted the process by actively lobbying for UNMIN's exit. Neither has it shown any inclination to help tangibly – both in terms of ideas and resources – to lead toward the conclusion of the peace process. At best, it shows a thorough confusion in India's Nepal policy, and at worst a conscious design to sabotage the process. Reservations against the Maoists based on the paradigm that India is "uncooperative" to Nepal shows Indian reluctance to accept that there are now new important players in Nepal who have the legitimacy from the people at large.

In cultivating cultural and ancestral ties with Nepali people, India has strangely confined itself to the Madhes region. Madhesis comprise 40 percent of Nepali population and share a deeply entrenched relation with India often cited as roti-beti relation. The Madhesis, given the open border and shared culture, are already informal ambassadors of Indian culture in Nepal. However, by only worrying about the concerns of the Madhesis, India ignores the other 60 percent of population in the mountains and upper hills, which is openly critical of Indian policies in Nepal. Connecting with these masses is critical to assuring a positive public opinion toward India. Engaging the challenger has been a primary norm of diplomacy, which India seems to have overridden.

Indian engagement in Nepal is guided by two sole questions: How can Nepal be useful for us? And, are we matching up with/ against Nepal-China bilateral? Wariness of Chinese interaction and reach into Nepal has been a persistent Indian worry. In light of these two dominant questions, Nepal's gains and developmental goals have usually been relegated to a backdrop.

China-Nepal relationship is relatively new, the two are geographically separated by the Himalayas and thus ethnically-culturally much dissimilar, and their mutual interactions are not as intense as Nepal's with India. The public opinion in Nepal is largely in favour of China, but partly, among other things, that is a positive spin-off of this geo-historical seclusion and relative novelty of the relationship. Not surprisingly, Indian government has been crying foul on every Chinese investment in Nepal from the $19.9 million dollars to the Nepal Army to the construction of the Lhasa to Khasa railway.

What the Indian diplomats fail to realize is that you burn your fingers only when you touch fire. As long as Indian covert veto refrains Nepal from engaging politically with China, the public opinion toward China would remain positive and work counter-productively for India. A perceptive student of regional history would point out that it was the annexation of Tibet that propelled Bhutan to turn to India and become a protectorate of India. History, of course, repeats itself only as tragedy; however, this example has a certain import. Excessive Chinese diplomacy is naturally going to raise alarms in Nepal. Only with deep sustained interactions, differences between Nepal and China could be brought to fore. Recently, the 12-minute tape where an alleged Chinese diplomat offered $6.9 million to bribe 50 Nepali legislators for help in forming a Maoist-led government that would favour China did hamper public opinion toward China.

The last argument may not have been convincing for Indian foreign policy pundits, but from Nepal's perspective and for long-term Indian interests, it is only worth highlighting that monopolizing foreign influence while often challenging Nepal's sovereignty would always be counter-productive for India. With its geo strategic importance, Nepal will and should try to attain maximum leverage from China, India and the rest of the international community. India has been reluctant and has rejected any third country influence in Nepal, which is Nepal's foreign policy right and an issue of Nepal's sovereignty. A diversified foreign policy is a right as well as necessity for Nepal. India's concerns about China may still be genuinely cast in terms of threat to its own security, but it has also vocally raised concerns about the growing influence of US-UK in Nepal. This is no more the language of a concerned neighbor worried for its own security but a coercive hegemon vigorously demanding submission to its dictates.

Regionalism is often the answer to overarching bilateral problems as proved by the Franco-German mortar in the European Union experiment. In South Asia, regionalism has been reduced to bilateral engagement of individual countries with India. A successful regional mechanism could ensure better prospects for bilateral and multilateral relations. With enhanced regional instruments, mutual worries of both the sides would have been taken care of. SAARC is often termed as "a slow boat to nowhere". A fresh reinvigorated alternative mechanism for furtherance of SAARC would be apt not only for Indo-Nepal bilateral ties but would answer Indian security and economic concerns in light of India's rocky neighborhood.

Economically, India is the largest investor in Nepal amounting to 45 percent of the total foreign investment in Nepal. Despite the FDI flow, political uncertainty has restricted the exploration of upper threshold in terms of Indian investment. However, since large Indian investments have always been viewed skeptically; helping Nepal strengthen its supply side capacity in goods with comparative advantage could be an ideal long-term economic investment that could leverage political gain.

The ambitions of foreign relations are often limited by lack of alternatives especially with regards to one's neighbours. As the Indians themselves often like to say (with regards to Pakistan) – one can choose your friends but not your neighbours. Thus India and Nepal both need to revise their terms of engagement. The anti-India rhetoric that usually guarantees political dividend cannot thrive for long. Rationality of geopolitical realities, economic dependence, and cultural affinities need to be prioritized to craft a mutually benefitting bilateral relationship based on rational policy of neutrality in foreign affairs.

India needs to rethink on its used and abused strategy of political meddling, trampling of sovereignty in some instances, and concerns only on India's gain because offensive diplomacy might distance Nepal to other developmental partners instead. The comparison of Nepal to a Hindu wife, tied to a single man for life, might not hold true given the growing interest and investment possibilities and aid in Nepal. In another vein (rather a suggestive indulgence), Ambassador Prasad would be greatly equipped if he has read his own father's magnum-opus Origins of Indian Foreign Policy rather well. There is no other book in Indian foreign policy literature that narrates the realism of idealism in Indian Foreign policy better.

Nepal Caught between China and India

A recent recording making the rounds in Nepal featured a Maoist party leader speaking to a man with a Chinese accent. During the 12-minute tape, the Chinese voice offers $6.9 million to bribe 50 Nepali legislators for help in forming a Maoist-led government that would favour China over India.

Whether the tape is genuine, whether the voice is really that of a Chinese official and whether India's intelligence wing released it as part of a propaganda exercise haven't been established.

But the tape reinforced a long-standing view in Nepal: The strategically located, landlocked nation of 30 million people is a playground for its two giant neighbours. A "delicate yam between two boulders" is the way King Prithvi Narayan Shah summed it up as far back as the 18th century.

Early this month, after 17 attempts to name a prime minister, reflecting Nepal's political paralysis, Jhalnath Khanal was picked for the post. Among the many challenges facing the new leader is balancing relations with the two neighbours.

"My government will deepen and strengthen the relationship with both" India and China, Khanal said shortly after his election.. "I haven't decided yet" which country to visit first.

For much of its history, Nepal has been heavily influenced by India. Four million Nepalese work in India. And a long, porous border, shared religious traditions and a common history under the British Empire have bound the two.

Contact with China was long impeded by the 30,000-foot Himalayan peaks to the north.

But an ascending Middle Kingdom is changing the equation, making India anxious.

"I see Delhi as both confused and nervous," said Bhekh B. Thapa, Nepal's former foreign minister.

China's footprints are widely evident.

Beijing is building a $1.9-billion railroad from the city of Lhasa to the Tibet-Nepal border that may eventually reach Katmandu. Chinese trade, aid and infrastructure projects are pouring in.

"Now China is the goose with the golden eggs," said Kesang Tseten, a Katmandu-based documentary filmmaker.

Nepali politicians traveling to Beijing are tripping over one another as China funds Nepali police training, border control, roads, even garbage trucks.

"The new China is flexing its muscles in line with its economic might," said Kanak Mani Dixit, Katmandu-based editor of Himal Southasian magazine. "It's also trying to rattle India."

India has traditionally viewed Nepal as a buffer against China, with which it lost a war in 1962. Last month, India arrested three Chinese for allegedly sneaking into India and taking pictures of strategic installations. Beijing denies that they are spies.

One key barometer of China's growing clout here is Katmandu's treatment of exile Tibetans, who number about

20,000 in Nepal. After unrest spread across the Tibetan plateau in March 2008, Beijing leaned heavily on Nepal's Tibet policy.

The number of Tibetan refugees crossing into Nepal from China after 2008 fell to about 500 annually from 3,000 a year, as China provided money, equipment and training to Nepal to tighten the border, analysts said. In a leaked U.S. cable released by WikiLeaks in December, an unnamed source said China paid bounties to Nepali border guards who handed Tibetans over to China.

"The pressure has become very hard on the Nepal government," said Trinlay Gyatso, the Dalai Lama's de facto representative in Nepal. "There's no reason Nepal should be a puppet. It's a sovereign nation."

In February, three ballot boxes used for Tibetan community elections were seized by police in riot gear, the International Campaign for Tibet reported. This followed a similar confiscation in October as Tibetan exiles here were voting for the self-proclaimed Tibetan government-in-exile based in Dharamsala, India, an exercise exiles said had taken place here 14 times since 1960 without incident.

In June, three Tibetans were arrested, transported by helicopter to the Chinese frontier and handed over to Chinese border officials, the same activist group reported. Two landed in Chinese jails.

The fate of seven other refugees arrested by Nepal authorities in October and nine detained last month isn't known.

Last week U.S. Undersecretary of State Maria Otero expressed concern to Khanal over the problems faced by Tibetan refugees in Nepal. The prime minister reportedly responded that Nepal would deal with the issue in line with the views of its immediate neighbours, China and India.

India has long enjoyed a significant voice in Nepal's politics. New Delhi was instrumental in brokering a 12-point agreement in 2005 under which the Maoists eventually put down their guns, ending a 10-year civil war.

But some say India's voice has become more strident and highhanded of late, perhaps in reaction to China's growing influence.

NEPAL: CAUGHT BETWEEN CHINA AND INDIA

Chinese Prime Minister Wen Jiabao, left, and Nepal's Prime Minister Madhav Kumar Nepal inspect the Chinese People's Liberation Army honor guards during a welcome ceremony at the Great Hall of the People in Beijing

Nepal may be most well-known for its majestic Himalayan peaks, but much of the country is a vast stretch of plains, the terai, which have long been underdeveloped and largely ignored by the two powers on either side. No longer. India has just launched a plan to spend $361 million over the next several years on roads and rail links in the terai, announcing the grants just before Nepali President Ram Baran Yadav made his Feb. 15 official visit to New Delhi. China, meanwhile, recently increased its annual aid to Nepal by 50% to about $22 million.

The money is certainly welcome in Nepal, which has the lowest per capita income in South Asia. But the jockeying for influence between China and India may be undermining Nepal's fragile democracy, as the country's 24 political parties trade charges of being pawns of one or the other. Even a tiny royalist party, supporters of Nepal's deposed King Gyanendra, have gotten into the act, staging a rally in Kathmandu on Feb. 22 that shut down the capital for a day. Meanwhile, the parties are debating complex constitutional issues, including a proposed federal system of 14 ethnicity-based states. Nepal's interim constitution will expire on May 28, and if its politicians cannot agree on a new one by then, the constituent assembly will be dissolved, new elections will be called and, many observers fear, the country will enter a period of deep uncertainty. Says Nihar Nayak, a researcher with the New Delhi–based Institute for Defence Studies and Analyses: "They are moving toward a political crisis."

India, for its part, maintains that it has always had a "very deep and vast relationship" with Nepal based on its shared cultural ties. Both countries have a majority Hindu population, and they share millions of cross-border migrant workers. But the character of that relationship has changed. India used to engage Nepal only at the highest levels, in meetings between bureaucrats, ministers and — until Gyanendra stepped down in 2008 — representatives of the King. That has changed dramatically over the last few years, since Nepal's Maoists came to power in a 2006 peace agreement that ended the monarchy, halted a decade-long insurgency and set the country on the road to democracy. The Maoist leader Pushpa Kamal Dahal, known as Prachanda, has cultivated close diplomatic ties with China. In the meantime, India's government changed too: the ruling Congress Party severed its parliamentary alliance with the leftist parties in 2008, resulting in the closing of a key channel of communication to Nepal.

Recent security concerns, however, have given India new reasons to reassert itself in Nepal by investing in infrastructure as well as more troops on the border. Security experts say that that jihadist groups in the region exploit the porous border between India and Nepal, and they worry that India's Maoist insurgency may do the same. "That is their biggest concern," says Nayak.

China's main interest in Nepal has always been led by its concerns over Tibet, which has been ruled by China since 1950. Beijing's involvement with Nepal grew much more intense after the March 2008 ethnic Tibetan uprising against Chinese rule, which deeply embarrassed the Beijing government on the eve of its expensive Olympic Games. There are an estimated 20,000 Tibetans living in Nepal but, with China pushing Nepal to tighten its border with Tibet, the number of new refugees reaching Nepal has dropped to about 500 from an annual figure of around 2,500. But it too has increased its focus on economic ties — trade between China and Nepal has quadrupled since 2003. This week, China said it would restart the tourist bus route between the Tibetan capital Lhasa and Nepal's capital Kathmandu. It had suspended the service in 2006. The clear jostling for influence is making Nepal's tricky politics even trickier. By far the most difficult issue left unresolved since the

2006 peace talks is the integration of the former Maoist guerrilla fighters into Nepal's army, a conflict that led to Prachanda's resignation as Prime Minister last year. India's military academies have historically been the training ground for Nepal's top officers — the Nepali army chief graduated from the Indian Military Academy in Dehradun — so the Maoists have long claimed, most famously in a fiery speech by Prachanda in December, that India backs the Nepal army and wants to restore the monarchy. Ironically, the influence of India is the one point on which the former King and the Maoist former Prime Minister agree. When Gyanendra was on the throne, he too chafed at any hint of excessive Indian influence. It may be an inevitable dilemma for a small country squeezed between two giants — and one that Nepal has less than three months to resolve.

WHY NEPAL HATES INDIA?

The Nepalese Maoists aligned with Bharati Maoists which control 40% of Bharati territory—no wonder you guys are jittery. Worry about you own Northern borders and the MaCmohan Line–wasn't that a relic of colonialism also.

The artificially created buffer state which was manufactured by the British taking territory from Pakistan,Tajikistan and Uzbekistan–is going to merge itself with Pakistan.

On the one side, Nepal has faced a communist regime while on the other a republic system. Nepal had to preserve its dignity and move ahead between such two nations. Nepal did not want to support either the communists or the Indian democracy; nor did it want to oppose any. The quality of Nepal, by adopting a neutral position was desirous of maintaining a harmonious relation between these two nations. But after India became independent its leaders conspired to draw Nepal under its umbrella.

'Nepal is a yam between two boulders'- the message of the great King Unifier Prithbinarayan Shah is still relevant. China never troubled Nepal ever since communism was established in China. Although Nepal has ties with India-geographically and culturally since the Muslim rule, it is a matter of worriless that Nepal always faced threat from India. In that context, Nepalese scholar diplomat Keshar Bahadur KC said- 'If there was no China, Nepal would have ceased to exist.'

A Symbiotic Relationship

In the context of Nepal, China and India relation the former PM Kirtinidhi Bista opines on Nepal, China and Indian relation- 'The symbiotic relationship that exists between India, Nepal and China can neither be belittled nor neglected or disturbed if regional stability in South Asia is to be maintained. Nepal's national interests are integrally linked to the prospect of lasting peace and stability in South Asia.

For this reason alone Nepal must always be vigilant, proactive where necessary, and try to maintain the delicate balance in its relations with the two emerging regional powers of Asia. For Nepal there is no alternative to including its next-door neighbours as common partners in its development efforts while keeping the door open for other countries interested in the region's peace and stability. For the world-at-large, too, it will have to pay dearly if any attempt.

Unbreakable Relationship

Nepal is linked by its sacred soil with India and China, as well as by rivers flowing from China through Nepal to India. These factors, more than anything else, establish the ground for unbreakable relationship among the three. This cordial relationship has to continue for the benefit of the vast South Asian region as well as China.

Nepal, for her part, has been making modest efforts within her means to consolidate and strengthen the compact that exists between the unequal partners of Asia. Fully realizing the fact that Nepal's rich natural resources and its development not only benefits the country, but also others countries in the region, King Birendra had proposed the development of Nepali hydropower for the benefit of the South Asian region. The proposal that was floated at the tenth Colombo Plan Consultative

Conference held in Kathmandu in 1978. Any country looking to secure a bright future has to first mind its business and that is where its national interests come into play. In this connection Nepal has to face a tough challenge of not only safeguarding its national interest but also creating a stable and peaceful situation favorable for the all-round development of the country, in close cooperation with her fast-developing neighbours in India and China.' But, India could not understand the reality of Nepalese prestige.

India in Fear of China

In 1950 India and Nepal reached a Delhi agreement through which India had a design to capture Nepal. India wanted a new constitution in Nepal through a CA. When Nepal and China entered bilateral relations in 1956 India became hesitant. As anti-India sentiment was increasing and due to the interest shown by the communist China in Nepal, then, India canceled the necessity of CA in Nepal.

India, in fear of China, completely abandoned its scheme of capturing Nepal and the idea of a constitution through CA. And then, In 1958 King Mahendra formed a commission through which he declared a constitution for the country. In the same year on basis of this constitution a parliamentary election was held. After the election Nepali Congress (NC) came to form the government in the leadership of the PM B.P. Koirala. After the formation of NC Govt. India began to conspire in various ways to influence the NC led government.

India wanted to take advantage of its friendship with NC leader BP Koirala. India continued to intervene in Nepal's internal matters. India succeeded in taking control over some Nepal's rivers.

Enhancing Understanding With King Mahendra

Chinese leader Mao studied the fact that Nepal and China could remain secure only in the presence of royal institution in Nepal. So he looked to enhance the understanding with King Mahendra. That became the headache for India. There was no game of conspiracy behind promotion of Nepal's harmonious relation with China. Nepal does not want to move against the interest of India or China. Nepal only wants to maintain a good relation with both of the powerful neighbours. But India has never wanted to understand this fact. The Indian rulers have time and again harassed Nepal due to which Nepal is ever suspicious of its southern neighbor.

Although there is consistent visits from Indian nationals to Nepal and vice versa; although Nepalese and Indian people maintain a cultural bond and relation, the Indian rulers have always wanted to misuse this harmonious understanding. Due to this fact, Nepalese people, in spite of difficult geographical connection with China, despite unfamiliarity of language and other traditional norms, have trusted China. China too has never taken interest in Nepal in negative prospective. Nepal will never bargain off its sovereignty to India on grounds of its relation pertaining to religion, culture and geography or any other. Nepal adores nothing more than its sovereign existence.

CHINA SHOWS INTEREST IN NEPAL'S SECURITY

In 1960 King Mahendra took over the power against the Indian intervention and conspiracy. In the real sense, it was not against the interest of Nepali Congress. And introduced the Panchayat system after which India drew back. There was no any negative aspect in regards Nepal-India relation from 1960 to 1978. But, there started the conspiracies that in 1973 the Indian intelligence agency 'RAW' supported the hijacking of an airplane and in July the same year backed the act of arson at Singha Durbar.

China had shown interest in Nepal's security in relation to these acts. A Chinese Professor at Hunan University Wang-Chung published a book 'Nepal's National Defensive Strategy and Nepal-China Relation' and divulged many facts. He wrote that in June, 1973 Congress activists hijacked a Nepal Airlines' passenger plane and forced it to land in India. The book also delved on facts relating to the fire at the Nepal government's central Secretariat at Singh- Durbar in July and then the attempt to kill the King in March, 1974 (the bombing at Janakpur).

Prof. Wang-Chung writes-'On 23, June 1975 the Indian Prime Minister Indira Gandhi declared emergency in entire India, in which, a ban was issued on the political activities of Nepali Congress leader BP Koirala and the party activists in exile in India. After that BP Koirala returned to Nepal with the policy of national reconciliation to join the hands with the King. BP was convinced that the security of Nepal lay in the reconciliation between him and the King and that Nepal could never benefit from India. However, after the death of BP, there was no reconciliation between NC and the monarchy. And then India had another opportunity to play.

The Indians did not like King Birendra for his independent and self-sustaining foreign policy. So it is not unusual to suspect a black hand of Indian intelligence agency in the royal palace massacre that took place on 1 June 2001. He further writes- 'When China provided economic support to Nepal, India did not allow China to get involved in Nepal's Terai region. India fears Chinese involvement in Terai region could make China spread communist ideology in India.'

Chinese Intellect Points out an Indian Scheme

It is not necessary to add anything more here after mentioning what a Chinese intellect has explicitly written about black Indian conspiracy. It is a matter of investigation to find out who was responsible for the arson at Singha Durbar. When a Chinese intellect has pointed out that it was an Indian conspiracy we too are bound to accept it as true when we look at the dirty game played by India. Yes!

If there is fire in a house the people of that house know less about it than their neighbours. Neighbours first see the smoke coming out of the fire. Such is the case of Nepal in relation to Indian intervention, arson at Singha Durbar and the royal palace massacre. After Rajiv Gandhi came to power the Indian policy became more discriminate towards Nepal. In 1988 India went on to issue a blockade of Nepal on an irrelevant reason of commerce transit. For the same reason it fuelled the NC and the leftist parties in support of an uprising.

To avoid the prospect of foreign intervention King Birendra with great understanding reinstated democracy in 1990. In the democratic setup the misunderstanding between the ruling party and the opposition, corruption from the ruling side and Indian intervention increased. Under Indian direction the factories made under Chinese support as Harisidhi Brick-Tile Factory, Bansbari Leather Shoe Factory, Gaindakot Paper Factory among 12 other factories in profit were sold at a worthless price.

Nepal Unstable due to Maoists' Revolt

The then ruler took huge sum of commission to carry out this dirty act of India. As the scale of injustice soared India backed the Maoists' rebellion in the hills that terrorized Nepal. Many innocent people, policemen and army personnel were killed and infrastructure worth billions destroyed. Such acts of destruction carried out intentionally made Nepal unstable.

India had designated the Maoists' as terrorists but they supported the same terrorists to destroy Nepal. Then after, in 2005, India mediated pact between the Maoists', NC and UML in the name of 12-point understanding.

And, the uprising began by the paid workers of Maoist and Christians including the threatened villagers with aggressive. Then the King handed over the state to the political parties after the uprising-2006. The uprising came to a halt in agreement with the monarch and after the party leaders deceived the agreement by the hints of RAW and CIA. At the backing of India and western nations Nepal was declared secular and republic. These are the causes of current crisis.

With the deposition of the royal institution in Nepal, India and China both are in difficulty in security point of view. In absence of the royal institution India fears that China may intervene in Nepal to establish Communism in Nepal and India. In absence of monarchy in Nepal Chinese fear is of the danger of America and its CIA European nations' and Indian agency's activities in name of human rights that will be used in the name of Free Tibet to disintegrate China.

CHINA AND INDIA CREATING VERY DIFFICULT SITUATION FOR NEPAL

So, China in order to avoid a security lapse is showing more interest in Nepal. It is looking to participate in activities of Nepal with economic support and development schemes. The ensuing tussle between China and India is creating a very difficult scenario for Nepal. It is true that Nepalese forever will remain in suspicion and fear of the economic and other support lent by India. Nepalese are always skeptical whenever their Prime Minister goes on an official Indian visit. They fear if the PM would handover Nepal's rivers, natural resources, Nepal foreign and security policy to India. Despite the extent of cultural bond and contact between the Indian and Nepalese people the black deeds of Indian rulers has always posed a security threat to Nepal. 'It is notable that the very exercise of Nepal as an independent country was made possible only because of geographical situation of the region by Prithbinarayan Shaha alongside the committed, dedicated and trusted ministers and generals belonging to the various origins. Very surprisingly, Nepal was able to stand its ground as an independent, unique and powerful multi-ethnics state situated in the lap of the Himalayas, even in such a vulnerable situation where such extreme colonial encroachment in South Asia was rife.

Joint Conference between Nepal, India and China

People of different ethnic backgrounds seemed to have united under the umbrella of the newly emergent Nepal. In many cases, a practical policy, offering dependent states to smaller friendly principalities was adopted by the king of Nepal.' So, to remove all the confusion, there must be reinstatement of the Nepalese monarchy and in the presence of the King, there should be a joint conference between Nepal, India and China to reach a concrete decision which these three nations can adopt permanently as diplomatic strategy.

NEPAL-INDIA RELATIONS: QUAKE HITS KATHMANDU

Frustration among India's so-called Nepal experts over Nepal's increasing proximity with China was there for all to see at a mysteriously organized seminar held at Hotel Yak & Yeti December 3, 2011, wherein the distinguished Indian participants repetitively clarified that India's relations with Nepal will not depend on the state of Nepal-China relations.

Interestingly, one of the seminar organizers was the Ministry of External Affairs of India, MEA. The banner read like this. A reputed Chinese columnist Li Hongmei in a fresh article penned for the Chinese official news agency, Xinhua, had claimed that India's concerns over China's rise is nothing but India's "inferiority complex" and"loud jealousy".

The timing of the seminar sponsored by India's Ministry of External Affairs, Federation of Indian Chambers of Commerce and Industries (FICCI), Federation of Nepalese Chambers of Commerce and Industries and Society of Economic Journalists of Nepal (SEJON), was such that it took place at a time when the government of Nepal is preparing for the forthcoming state visit of Chinese Prime Minister Wen Jiabao to Nepal.

The Chinese Prime Minister is arriving Nepal shortly. Sukh Deo (S.D) Muni- the honorable *guru* of Nepal's Prime Minister Baburam who had come all the way from his newly found home in Singapore went so aggressive that he even challenged Nepal to produce at least 10% of the total electricity demand of the country on its own.

This speaks of Muni's uneasiness which is also a challenge to Nepali businessmen. "If Nepal is suspicious towards India, Nepal should look toward other countries to harness its water resources. India will happily buy electricity from Nepal".

Analysts can easily understand Muni's inner pains in saying so. Muni and Nepal's foreign relations expert Mr. Jayaraj Acharya presented their working papers at the session chaired by another Jawahar Lal Nehru University Graduate, Hari Sharma. Sharma currently serves the presidential secretariat.

He is a great admirer of India's Finance Minister Pranab Mukherjee.

"India will not object even if Nepal cooperated with the US or China to produce electricity. Nepal can anytime even close down the industries established with Indian investments. It will make no difference to India," claimed Muni. Visibly Muni looked angry when he made the statement. Who cares! Yet calm down Professor or else such an aggressive statements may up your Blood Pressure. Muni however, claimed that in the last three years India has corrected its policy towards Nepal. He did not elaborate where the Indian establishment had made mistakes in the past.

Yet, by implication it does tell that India indeed deviated from its Nepal policy and now is in a mood to correct the political aberrations. The price though has been paid already. Bolt from the blue, Acharya-a staunch Nepali Congress supporter declared that Nepal's Monarchy ended primarily because of its failure to practice a 'balanced foreign policy'.

Perhaps Acharya was pointing towards the then Monarch's visionary decision to invite China as an observer in the India dominated SAARC framework which may have pained the made diplomat. "The monarchy may have gone but the visionary steps taken then by King Gyanendra to invite China in SAARC, and finally he succeeded, has considerably narrowed down India's hegemony in South Asia", analysts beg to differ with intelligent Acharya and add, "With Nepali Monarchy gone, China came to its senses that Nepal cannot be left to the mercy of whimsical Indian establishment that values its relations with the Westerners more than the regional stability."

China too must have felt the brunt of the absence of Nepali monarchy. The Chinese annoyance is visible. Widely unpopular India's Former Ambassador to Nepal who was elevated to the post of India's foreign Secretary upon completion of his Nepal assignment, Shyam Saran escaped from the seminar. Perhaps he did not want to see Professor Lok Raj Baral who had recently made some dangerous comments against Shyam Saran.

Analysts hope that Mr. Saran may drop in Kathmandu several times in the near future for obvious reasons. With Saran gone from Nepal, steps in Shiva Shankar Mukherjee from India who also contributed significantly to deteriorate the already strained relations between the two countries. Mukherjee was present at the seminar. Mukherjee was followed by Rakesh Sood as Ambassador to Nepal. I served the Nepal mission for three years and a half, said Mukherjee and added, I did not find Nepal playing China card against India during my stay.

When Mukherjee was in Nepal, the Nepali Congress President Girija Prasad Koirala was the prime minister. No surprise there was 'no China card' during his Nepal sojourn. Obviously, only the players of the Indian Card ruled Nepal then. But hasn't India groomed Nepal PM Bhattarai played the China card by inviting first the Chinese Prime Minister to Kathmandu?

Mukherjee was responding to a query posed by a participant that whenever Nepal's Prime Ministers take steps to enhance its relations with China, India derails the government (implied out of revenge). Ambassador Mukherjee who is currently associated with FICCI said, "India always prioritizes desires of the Nepali population. It was a Nepali decision to accept the republican order, India took it positively. Chinese investment in Nepal is no worry to India."

Are you sure Mr. Mukherjee? "I do not think that India had the capacity to uproot monarchy and bring Prachanda in power. If that was true then India would have shaken the entire world."

Analysts wish to remind Ambassador Mukherjee to recall as to what sorts of filthy languages he had then used against the then sovereign Nepal Monarch, good or bad, while appearing in Nepali Television Channels. Just recall, for example, your Kantipur interview. Mukherjee also requested that Nepal should not consider itself land or India locked country. "Nepal is open towards India. It is time to move forward", Mukherjee advised.

What a cruel joke! Having said that the Nepali population is yet to forget India imposed sixteen months long economic blockade on Nepal, March 23, 1989, that ended with regime change in Nepal. Then India had blamed Nepal for inclining towards China.

Comparatively the sober (compared to his three predecessors) serving Indian Ambassador Jayant Prasad claimed that Indian investors are planning to invest USD 15 Billion in Nepal's water resources. The investment will significantly reduce the prevailing 'dangerous trade deficit' Nepal has with India.

INDIA AND CHINA: DEFINING UNDEFINED RELATIONS IN A DEFINED CENTURY

Officially, both Indian and Chinese authorities have admitted on last Monday that they have agreed to pull their forces back to the earlier positions held before the standoff. In a declaration India's foreign ministry spokesperson, Syed Akbaruddin said, "The governments of India and China have agreed to restore status quo ante along the Line of Actual Control (LAC) in the Western Sector of the India-China boundary as it existed prior to 15 April, 2013."

In a similar statement, issued on the same date, spokesperson of Chinese foreign Ministry Hua Chunying stated, "China and India have reached an agreement on resolving the incident in the western section of the border. The frontier forces of the two countries have terminated the standoff at the Tiannan River Valley area".

According to Times of India, though the government of India maintained that no concession was offered to the Chinese to end the Laddakh faceoff, Indian forces appear to have agreed to demolish the army's bunkers in Chumar – close to the line of actual control (LAC). However,both the India and China have denied giving any details of the deal.

According to Indian and International media, Chinese troops stationed 19 kilometers inside the area that India claims as its northern border, withdrew on Sunday. The incident that was standing as a major obstacle against the proposed visit of Indian minister of External affairs Salman Khursid on May 9-10 aimed to make preparations for the China's Prime Minister Li Keqiang's visit to India as his first foreign visit later this month.

At a time when the ongoing charges of corruption against the Indian government and its high ranking officials has already eroded the credibility of the world's largest democracy followed by its political disarray that has paralyzed the government, the border problem created much discomfiture to New Delhi. The news was also most embarrassing for the government when the country was soaked in grief and fury after Sarabjit Singh, an Indian convicted of spying by a Pakistani court and was serving prison terms for the last 22 years in Pakistani Jail, had died on May 2 following fatal injuries inflicted on his head. Singh had suffered a brutal attack inside the Lahore jail by the Pakistani inmates that Indian side accuses as a conspiracy.

Amid the intense sense of grief and humiliation the news of the accused Chinese incursion into the Daulat Beg Oldi sector in eastern Laddakh where some 50 Chinese soldiers had tented with some high altitude guard dogs. A PLA raised signpost that read "You are in Chinese side please go back", had deeply assaulted the Indian psyche. The accused Chinese incursion that took place on April 15 was not reported to the public by Indian government until April 26. The Indian government beside its intensive diplomatic initiatives had ordered the Indo Tibetan Border Police (ITBP) to face the Chinese troops stationed at the height of some 5000 meters.

According to New York Times, even leaders like Mulayam Singh Yadav – the senior leader of the government coalition, made harsh comments on the government saying that it was "cowardly, incompetent, and good for nothing. Quoting Arun Jaitley – a leading opposition politician, The New York Times reported, "You may have some security options, you may have some diplomatic options, but being clueless is not an option".

However, Indian Prime Minister Manmohan Singh termed it as "a localized problem", and showing restraints and confidence said, "We do believe it can be solved. We have a plan. We do not want to accentuate the situation."

On the other hand as reported by the Global Times, China's defence ministry refuted any such reports about Chinese border troops and military helicopters intruding across the line of actual control. Instead, Yang Yujun, the spokesperson for the Chinese Defence Ministry had claimed, "Currently, border troops from China and India are maintaining communications through the existing mechanism. Chinese border troops have strictly observed relevant agreements between China and India and have been working to safeguard border peace and tranquility." the online edition of People's Daily in its editorial warned its government not to indulge India's bad habits, and lies of the Indian news media.

According to Times of India China had repeatedly asked the Indian Army to stop infrastructure build-up and construction of bunkers in the Fukche and Chumar regions of Laddakh, and dismantle the observation post located there as the pre-condition for withdrawing its troops.

The bunker built at a point of highly – strategic significance and Chumar observation post had become a matter of concern for Chinese army as it overlooks Karakoram highway and can detect any troop movement there. The faceoff site was also just about 40-km south of the strategic Karakoram Pass, which is at the tri-junction of China-Pakistan-India borders facilitating to monitor the Siachen Glacier-Saltoro Ridge to the west and the Indian observation post in the Chumar sector to the east. The noted Indian daily further analyzed that India was worried about the deep Chinese intrusion in the Depsang Bulge area, a tabletop plateau, since it threatened to cut its access to around 750 sq. km. area in the region.

Rajat Pandit in Times of India has even reported that the Chinese had earlier even tried to immobilize the surveillance cameras positioned at the Chumar post by cutting wires there. In June last year, Indian troops had also intercepted two Chinese personnel on mules across the Chumar post.

It is a serious matter to note that the two largest powers of Asia, have yet to demarcate their borderline and had fought a brief border war 50 years ago in 1962. Since then although China had returned to its earlier positions in India's Arunachal Pradesh –covering some 90,000 square kilometer, that China claims as its territory. Similarly, China is accused of holding some 38,000 square kilometers of the territories in Aksai Chin plateau in the Laddakg region of the western Himalayas. India also maintains that Pakistan has also ceded some of the Kashmiri territories occupied by Pakistan since 1948.

Undefined Relations in a Defined Century

Even so numerous years after their modern entity, when major global powers like India and China have failed to live within a demarcated border, it is hard to get assured of the global peace and stability. Even China has chosen to issue different visas for the natives of Jammu- Kashmir and Arunachal Pradesh claiming them as disputed territories. Even China has often objected the visits of Indian Prime Ministers and Presidents to Arunachal.

Two other nuclear powered countries- India and Pakistan are yet to reconcile with the territory of Jammu and Kashmir province under their control. On the other hand, China's closest relation with Pakistan, heavy armaments Pakistani army by the Chinese and deep distrusts and animosities between India and Pakistan has transformed the region as the most vulnerable one. Beijing's growing military might, huge budgetary allocations to its defence spending that is three times bigger than India's, have created deep suspicion in Indian psyche. Besides, China's growing influence in India's neighboring countries has in some way, scarred India.

Obviously, China needs a modern army and defence technology to defend the economic interest of the world's most populous state and protect its huge land mass and naval routes that work as an artery of world's second largest economy. Naturally, its defence expenditure is likely to scale up to the size of its economy to meet challenges it foresees ahead. Nevertheless, every here and there – its ongoing disputes with countries like Japan, South Korea, Philippines, Vietnam, and

India over some territories in land and seas, has entrapped China to develop and recognized as a respected global power.

A World Bank study says that China has lifted 500 million people out of poverty in the last 30 years. This kind of success could not have been achieved by the humanity in its long history. During the same period, its GDP growth averaged 10 percent a year. But, this is only a part of the story. With its cheap products from garment to electronics goods, China has eased the life of millions and millions people all over the world. It has become a household name in every part of the globe.

A knowledge society based on ICT development would have become almost impossible without market domination of cheap modern electronic gadgets from mobile phones to computer and internet router that are made or assembled in China. With its huge manufacturing capacity its cheap products from garment to electronic gadgets, machines and tools China has helped low income people of many poor countries and maintain peace and order there.

Power has its own scope, dimension and language. It is manifested in many ways. When a power speaks even in modest terms, it can be understood or explained differently. A simple gesture to express some basic concerns might be taken as an assertive rhetoric and behavior. A major world power like China is expected to make deep impact study of its every speech, pronouncement and official statements that its leaders make in China and abroad.

Moreover, how long will China continue to dispute with its neighbours over some outlying patches of land and will continue to pay its price. If China abandons its claim over them or reaches a negotiated settlement in favour of its small neighbours and win their confidence, it will be taken as China's magnanimity and it may compensate China manifold. But, a South Korea, Vietnam or Japan, if does the same, it will be considered as a sell out to a bullying power. Obviously, they can never dare it. Instead, a new Cold War situation or trouble spots will emerge in China's surroundings and ultimately the long-term interest of billion plus people will be questioned. Same is the case with India. India has gained impressive growth record in the last two decades after it decided to liberalize its economy. Although for India's comparatively weak and debilitated efforts to liberalize its economy – Indian private sector even with minimal policy support has succeeded tremendously. Gurucharan Das has aptly termed this situation as "India grows at night while the government sleeps". China's state enterprises and India's private sector have created a new global history. They have many things to share and learn from each other. Bilateral trade between India and China jumped from $5 billion in 2002 to nearly $76 billion in 2012, and it is estimated to reach more than $100 billion by 2015.

Problem lies with political relations between India and China- that in the beginning of their modern existence was remarkably cordial. Take one example – when China annexed Tibet, Indian Prime Minister, Jawaharlal Nehru was the second prominent world leader after Joseph Stalin – who supported it in unequivocal terms and without any condition. Amid stronger criticism even within his own party, Nehru not only extended his political support but his acknowledgement was even stronger on moral grounds. Speaking at Indian Parliament In May 1954, he reiterated Indian position and said that they have recognized the China's sovereignty over Tibet from the beginning. Giving reference to some criticism against the Indian recognition he said, "... Apart from that fact, I am not aware of any time during the last hundred years when Chinese sovereignty or if you like suzerainty was challenged by any outside country and all during this period whether China was weak or strong and whatever the Government of China was, China always maintained this claim to the sovereignty..". Nehru not only laid his government's unconditional support to Chinese sovereignty over Tibet but also compelled Nepal to do the same and abandon some of its rights over Tibet that Nepal had been enjoying under a treaty between Nepal and Tibet.

However, China invaded India in 1962 and India suffered a humiliating defeat. It was a terrible shock to Nehru. Many interpret that he was badly shaken, was worn out of the courage and confidence to lead his country and this was considered as the cause of his premature death two years later. Even after 50 years of that war, both India and China are yet to find a modality to define their relations and maintain a peaceful neighborhood.

The Prospect of Indo-China Relations and Nepal

In his book – Monsoon, acclaimed strategic analyst Robert D. Kaplan has described about a trilingual stone tablet erected by a Chinese admiral Zheng in Sri Lanka in 1410. The tablet unearthed 500 years later near Galle was inscribed in Chinese, Persian and Tamil language that invoked the blessings of the Hindu deities for a peaceful world built on trade. Chinese trading ships even in those days sailed from China to Sri Lanka (formerly Ceylon) and to Persia and Ethiopia. Later, although the situation developed differently, it signifies China's focus on peace and trade development for centuries.

The financial, political, and military powers that China has attained these days are based on trade that it describes as their peaceful rise. Apparently, no other people need peace more urgently than traders do – whether individual, group or nation. Similarly, nothing others than war or warlike situations impede trade. Chinese probably know it far better than any other country.

A widely read Indian strategic analyst C. Rajamohan in his recent book – Samudra Manthan, has admitted that both India and China followed disastrous experimentations in finding a possible "third way" between the economic and political model of the East and the West in the beginning of 1950s. That left both their economy pathetically stagnated. After they pursued new policy directives, their economy began to soar and again to quote Rajamohan "China's two way trade stood at around $ 3.5 trillion (2011 estimate). The combined value of India's merchandise exports and imports was around $ 750 billion in 2011".

With greater success, greater challenges emerge. The countries that have yet to demarcate their border for more than half a Century, cannot assure the global community that they can be trusted for their commitment for a peaceful and rule based global order of the 21st Century.

The pull and push issue in global geo-politics may create uncertainties around them – detrimental to their long-term national interests. When both India and China exhibited enormous courage and confidence in liberalizing their economy that time, it was an impossible task to their context but urgently needed to save their country from ruin. However, it was much riskier and could create untoward consequences that could also wreck the country in a different way. But, sticking to their traditional economic policy could soon become their inevitable suicidal game and were therefore prepared to choose a new and historic path of national pride and honor.

They dared and accepted the risk and a new China and India is there among us. It changed the course of global order – a new destiny to the countries worldwide. Similarly, If India and China can demonstrate similar courage and confidence in resolving their border disputes; it will bring multiple benefits in tremendous scale – to both their countries and to the larger interests of the global community.

In this regard, the nature of the state accounts. Shashi Tharoor in his newly published book – Pax Indica, has given a fine example how things work in India and China. Within a period of 15 years, China was able to build the world's largest hydro electricity facility with a reservoir that was 660 kilometer long and 186-meter high. The dam can produce some 22,500-mega watt electricity. Tharoor further elaborated that while the reservoir of the Three Gorges Dam displaced 2 million people in China, there was no fuss. However when India embarked on the Narmada Dam project to generate some 1450 mega watt electricity, irrigate some 18,000 square kilometer areas in draught prone region and provide drinking water to millions, it had to spent 30 long years while fighting activist groups and court battle.

Sticking to their present border positions for another five decades or more and shying to demonstrate foresightedness, courage, and confidence, India and China will only be jeopardizing the larger interest of their future generations. Impending global challenges from food and water shortages to climate change and nuclear terrorism – affecting the millions of people in their country and worldwide, they are needed to stand for an immediate but bold and unified position.

Therefore, China with its apparently more stable political order and confidence might initiate in developing a border package deal that accepts the present Line of Actual Control (LAC) along the borderline. This will also help India and Pakistan to reach on a similar deal – a fundamental to build trust and bring prosperity in the region.

C. Rajamohan's article published in Indian Express on May 7, 2013, has explained how Nepal's Maoist leader Pushpkamal Dahal "Prachand" in his recent visit to China and India reflected a significant political evolution of the Maoist worldview in Nepal in relation to their policy towards India. May be Prachanda's proposal of trilateralism was inopportune due to the tension brewing out of border standoff between India and China. May be that can be taken as a shortsighted political strategy from a leader with a mercurial temperament, he might lose patience, competency and courage to lead this idea for long. May be he has played some multiple but secret cards during his recent visit to China and India to advance his petty political interests.

However, his bid that a weak and poverty stricken Nepal cannot address the security concerns of its two big neighbours carries much meaning and weight. Only a vibrating Nepalese economy that ensures jobs to thousands of unemployed youths and address the ethnic tension among people that is causing growing anarchy, instability terrorism taking new shape every day, can address long-term security interests of its both neighbours. Sandwiched between two global powers Nepal neither can ignore security concerns of both India and China nor does it have any options except maintaining good relations with both of them but what if a weak, fragile, and poverty-stricken country fails to honor their concerns?

Indubitably, the scarcity among masses and thousands of youths lacking both jobs and hopes for life if fall prey to a new kind of terrorism – a weak, instable and unpopular ruling class in any name and shape with any amount of delayed international support, can control them. It only means – a new Afghanistan between India and China. Therefore, as suggested by Rajamohan, New Delhi could consider four practical ways to further trilateral economic cooperation with Kathmandu and Beijing that includes encouraging Indian and Chinese companies to run joint venture for the development of Nepal's massive hydropower potentials – that serves the power hungry markets of both Nepal and India. Similarly, a sound networks of east-west and north –south transportation corridors in Nepal will not only integrate Nepal, it will help to connect to the markets of western China and northern India.

C. Rajamohan has further mentioned his remaining two proposals – the one opening up its territory for a two-way transit trade between India and China – while offering duty free access to Nepali products in their markets. The last proposal that Rajamohan suggests is Indian participation to a Chinese consortium to build excellent facilities in Lumbini that could integrate the entire Buddhist Circuit in Nepal and India and contribute economic growth of the poorest regions of both countries.

It demands greater visionary zeal and courage in parts of India and China, but a functional and vibrating trilateralism as Prachand proposed cannot be isolated from the overall geo-political and economic relations between India and China. However, there must be some starting point and trilateralism as forwarded by Prachand and the corresponding four proposals suggested by C. Rajamohan are big ideas for these two big Asian countries that can not only ensure peace and stability of Nepal, but will serve larger interests of both India and China.

INDIA FALLING BEHIND CHINA DIPLOMACY

India has always been a local superpower, being by far the largest country within South Asia, and is, in fact, the only one in the group that borders every other South Asian country except Afghanistan, which shares a border with Pakistan. But India's economic performance was stunted by years of state control of the kind now prevalent in Iran. Over the past 15 years, however, economic growth has been strong, enabling the country to have a much greater diplomatic reach than at any time since the 1950s when India briefly emerged as the leader of those countries that were being de-colonized by the European powers. Given this situation, it ought to have been the case that New Delhi would be preeminent in its own backyard. Instead, over the past two decades, India has lost the status of being the lead player in any South Asian country barring Bhutan, a country with which it still has a treaty relationship. In almost the entire region, China has overtaken India in that intangible quality - influence - especially in Nepal and Sri Lanka, while Beijing's existing alliances with Pakistan and Bangladesh are growing stronger.

This is not due to a lack of quality within India's diplomatic service. Instead, the Indian Foreign Service (IFS) has produced a modern corps of skilled diplomats, many experts in different regions of the world, and eager to do more to advance their country's interests. The wall they face is the ambivalence that has become second nature to the country's top policy makers, both within the political crust as well as the administrative backup. Phrases such as "going all the way" and "going for the kill" are inelegant. Yet they represent a reality that is that sometimes a country has to formulate and then determinedly implement a clear policy to be carried out till success is achieved.

In South Asia, such a quality was recently displayed by President Percy Mahinda Rajapaksa of Sri Lanka. He succeeded in wiping out the terrorist group known as the Liberation Tigers of Tamil Eelam (LTTE) where, over the past three decades, all his predecessors had failed. Unlike them, President Rajapaksa did not heed (well-meaning but disastrous) advice to slow down his offensive or agree to a cease-fire, the latter being a device that the LTTE used since 1987 to gain time to recover after having lost the initiative in the field. Once the LTTE recovered its strength, the ceasefire would be abandoned. This point was repeatedly made by Rajapaksa to the peacemakers who clustered around him, especially in the final months of the brief, brutal war against the LTTE that began with his coming to office in 2005.

Once India, because of political considerations such as the need to avoid alienating the country's sizable Tamil population, refused to give the Sri Lankan army equipment, Rajapaksa turned to Pakistan and China. Both countries opened their warehouses to him, and so built up immense capital both within Sri Lanka's Sinhala most importantity as well as the country's policy establishment. Rajapaksa showed none of the half-heartedness that has characterized so much of Indian policy and, as a result, emerged a winner. In the case of India, the desire to win brownie points with key international players (by heeding their sometimes incorrect advice) as well as an aversion to risk ensured that much of Indian diplomacy was too watered down to be effective. This is especially the case in its immediate neighbourhood.

This on-again, off-again excellence can be seen in Indian diplomatic policy towards Pakistan especially in regard to the long-term pattern of instituting confidence building measures (CBM) being followed - usually after a mass terror attack - with strong rhetoric and a withdrawal of contact. The reality is that in the case of Pakistan, conventional war may have ceased to be an option. This is because the Pakistan army has itself lost control of many of the jihadis that it has trained, equipped and funded for so long.

Instead of reducing the risk of a terror attack, going after the Pakistan military would inflame a large segment of the Pakistani population thus making them susceptible to recruitment in the ongoing jihad against India. Given that situation, it may have been preferable for Indian policymakers to publicly resort to a conventional war except in the case of a conflict started by Pakistan, an unlikely possibility. The military option would work only if (a) the Pakistan army controls the jihadi networks and (b) is comprehensively defeated in battle. Neither condition exists.

A "No War" declaration by India would remove the Pakistani military establishment's most frequently used excuse to station more than 60 percent of its army along the India border, even as the force is engaged in a life-and-death struggle with the Pakistan Taliban. Instead, even though New Delhi has no intention of going to war, the prospect of one is deliberately kept open especially after terror strikes such as Mumbai 11/26-28. Thus, the benefits of India's "No War" declaration are denied, while the other side is aware that the mock-aggressive posture is a bluff and hence will not change its behaviour as a result of the threat.

A glaring example of how promoting the idea that India would go to war over Pakistani provocations has hurt New Delhi can be seen in the 2002 standoff with Pakistan in the mountains separating the two. Ostensibly to scare the international community into putting pressure on Pakistan to call off its Kashmir jihad, the then-Vajpayee government mobilized two Indian army strike corps on the border, keeping them and their support units on a hair-trigger alert for the greater part of the year. Aware that the Indians were bluffing, the Pakistan government refused to budge from its policy of helping jihadists active in Kashmir. The long Indian army mobilization created a perception of regional instability that affected India's status as a safe investment destination even as it exhausted the elite army units on the front line. Given the information that India would not attack, the 2002 mobilization came at a horrendous cost and no benefit. In a system where posturing comes easily to the higher levels of the Indian policy establishment, Prime Minister Manmohan Singh has thus far resisted jingoism and has made it evident that India would not be stampeded into military action. In the case of Sri Lanka, the policy was to intensify conflict until victory. What is needed is a clear policy that is carried out effectively, not a zig-zag routine that confuses the international community and results in a loss of credibility for India.

Military sales can become an effective instrument of diplomacy, were they deployed by India. Within the region, including in Sri Lanka and Nepal, the military is a significant component of the policy process, often the crucial player. Because of New Delhi's longstanding policy of not permitting foreign military sales save for exceptional situations, China has been provided an opportunity to fill the gap. Had Bangladesh, Nepal and Sri Lanka been more reliant on Indian equipment and training for their armed forces, New Delhi would have been in a much stronger position to influence policy in those places than it is today. Instead, the "weapons gap" isincreasingly being filled by China.

The mantra of "non-alignment" has in most instances become a cover for lack of action. Even during the period of the Cold War, when India suffered many of the consequences of being seen as a Soviet ally, not a single Soviet soldier was ever stationed in India or trained here, nor did any Indian soldier undertake any sort of mission in the USSR. In contrast, there are regular exchanges of U.S. and Indian soldiers and joint training exercises have become routine. The warming of ties is because there is a natural fit between the two sides. India has a significant pool of trained (and trainable) manpower, while the United States has abundant stocks of equipment that could be transferred to New Delhi rather than mothballed or left under-utilized. This is especially the case with naval vessels, where India is now being made to pay $3 billion for a secondhand Russian aircraft carrier that it is finding it difficult to float and move at the same time.

Progress in U.S.-India military to military relatives has been slow and is still far below its potential in substantial part because of the wariness of the Indian establishment over China's reaction. Compare this with Pakistan which has built up close military ties with both China and the United States, its friendship with one not affecting the other. In the military field, the choice is between going with the United States or going alone, because a military alliance with China is not an option. Beijing sees New Delhi as a potential competitor and has repeatedly shown through its actions its commitment to a strategic policy that inhibits the growth of Indian power. Unfortunately, in this case, Indian ambivalence is now being matched by the United

States under the Obama administration, which has downgraded ties with India to a level much below that set under President George W. Bush. It seems inevitable, however, that both countries will, hopefully within the present presidential term, awaken to the need for a partnership that can ensure that Asia does not fall under the sway of any single power.

The persistent Indian ambivalence in policy was visible in Sri Lanka, where India simultaneously called for a cease-fire while backing the unity of the island nation. As a consequence of simultaneously conveying two contradictory messages, neither the Tamil nor the Sinhala zealots have anything other than distaste for India, while the abundant provision of military supplies has led the Sri Lankan military towards becoming as close to Beijing as are their counterparts in Pakistan.

In Nepal, after first helping to get King Gyanendra to abdicate, New Delhi threw its support behind the Maoists, who promptly reacted by threatening to scrap the India-Nepal agreement and replace it with a similar deal with China. After its embrace of the Maoists, which ended only after their tilt to Beijing became manifest (by the end of 2008), no other Nepali party is willing to trust New Delhi and see it as a reliable partner, even the once-friendly Nepali Congress. Meanwhile, in a show of deft footwork, Chinese diplomats have been active in Kathmandu renewing ties with the non-Maoist parties that today run the government (after the departure of the Maoists), so as to accelerate the growth of PRC influence in Nepal.

Today, there are almost as many radical training camps located within Bangladesh as there in Pakistan, camps whose specific purpose is to replenish the stream of jihadis into India. Yet, unlike in the case of Pakistan, the Indian government is not posturing as if was is likely. A hostile Pakistan, an unfriendly Bangladesh, and Nepal and Sri Lanka heading towards the PRC. These are the wages of a diplomacy that refuses to go for the jugular in the pursuit of objectives, but almost invariably crafts a compromise that gives much less geopolitical benefit. India presents an example of how a most important power that avoids a clear policy line or a better deployment of its assets gives way to the other who is ruthless and willing to complete the marathon rather than slow down and stop before the finish line. Such a policy is the delight of politicians and anathema to statesmen, who understand the need for not just vision, but for will and perseverance.

CHINA'S UNPLEASANT IN SOUTHEAST ASIA

Most mornings, activity in Phnom Penh all but stops when the morning heat begins to rise. But on that day, the city resembled a festive papal visit to a devoutly Catholic nation. Nearly a hundred thousand Cambodian children lined the streets, many in threadbare school uniforms and waving tiny Cambòdian and Chinese flags or small photographs of Jiang's face.

The children cheered and screamed for Jiang as his open car toured through the city, chanting as if he were David Beckham or Bono, rather than an elderly politician with thick glasses and an oily, swept-back hairdo. Jiang's route did not take him past one of the city's most important attractions. Only a few blocks from his motorcade, foreign tourists wandered through Tuol Sleng, an old high school that Cambodia's Maoist Khmer Rouge regime had converted into a killing factory in the 1970s. Tens of thousands of Cambodians were brought to Tuol Sleng between 1975 and 1979. Fewer than 10 made it out alive.

During the Khmer Rouge's murderous four-year reign, during which they killed as many as 2 million Cambodians, China served as the regime's most important foreign patron. Beijing sent the Khmer Rouge over 15,000 military advisers and provided the bulk of its external aid. Beijing knew what was going on in Cambodia. Before Jiang's visit, Chinese leaders had actively worked to forestall a special international tribunal for the Khmer Rouge officials still alive.

But standing alongside Jiang that day, Cambodian Prime Minister Hun Sen did not mention the Khmer Rouge era or the tribunal. Instead, he praised Jiang's "historic" visit to Phnom Penh and called China's relatives with Cambodia "a precious gift." A beaming Jiang replied that he was "overwhelmed by friendship and joy" and promised that the relationship would become much closer.

Jiang was right. Within five years, China had become probably the most important foreign influence in Cambodia, and Hun Sen shuttled to and from Beijing constantly. Beijing became Cambodia's most important provider of foreign aid, giving Cambodia one of the largest Chinese aid packages of any nation in the world while also forgiving Cambodia's entire debt to China. Chinese language programs quickly dominated downtown Phnom Penh: one Chinese-language school alone drew over 10,000 students. As a result, although older Cambodians who remember the Khmer Rouge remain suspicious of China, their sons and daughters, who once would have headed to Australia, France, or the United States for higher education, now look to universities in Shanghai and Beijing. Chinese newspapers, films, television, and radio have become increasingly popular. Thousands of Chinese businesspeople have moved into Phnom Penh and northern Cambodia, creating entire villages of recent migrants. Chinese tourists descend en masse on the capital. Today, even when the prime minister has concerns about China's influence, he keeps quiet. Cambodia is hardly unique. Since the late 1990s, perceptions of China in Southeast Asia have shifted significantly, so much so that elites and publics in a most importantity of the 10 members of the Association of Southeast Asian Nations (ASEAN) now see China as a constructive actor—and, potentially the preeminent regional power.

China's image transformation has resulted from a range of factors. China has benefited from missteps by the United States and Japan, ranging from the response to the 1997 Asian financial crisis to Washington's post–9-11 focus on counterterrorism in Southeast Asia. But the transformation also stems from a rise in China's "soft power" in Southeast Asia—that is, China's ability to influence Southeast Asian countries by persuasion, rather than coercion. This growing attractiveness is conveyed through various means, including culture, diplomacy, participation in multinational organizations, businesses' actions abroad, and the gravitational pull of China's economic strength. When Joseph Nye coined the term soft power, he originally used a more limited definition that excluded investment and aid and formal diplomacy—more traditional, harder forms of influence.

But in the context of Asia today, both China and its neighbours enunciate a broader idea of soft power, implying all elements outside of the security realm, including investment and aid. Soft power stems from both governments and nongovernment actors—from businesspeople and pop stars and language teachers. Nongovernment actors do not necessarily operate in concert with the state, and no state can be said to have a completely coherent foreign policy. Still, it is possible to identify broad strategies Beijing has enunciated and policy tools it has used that allow nongovernment actors to more effectively wield soft power. Just as us policies between World War II and the end of the cold war made Washington popular in the region and smoothed the way for American soft power, it is these frameworks that today make it easier for Chinese soft-power actors, from language schools to businesspeople, to have a growing impact on the ground.

The Unpleasant Begins

Nineteen ninety-seven provides a convenient date to mark China's soft-power emergence in Southeast Asia. Whether or not Beijing explicitly recognized that the United States and Japan were fumbling their responses to the Asian financial meltdown that began with the Thai baht's collapse and soon spread across the region, China's own reaction proved savvy. Beijing refused to devalue its currency, which would have exacerbated devaluations in Thailand and Indonesia, and portrayed its decision as standing up for other Asian nations. After the crisis, ASEAN Secretary General Rodolfo Severino announced, "China is really emerging from this smelling good."

Since then, Beijing has begun to employ several strategies to boost its soft power in Southeast Asia. In statements and speeches, Chinese leaders enunciate a doctrine of "win-win" relations, highlighting that Southeast Asians can benefit from their relationship with China even as China benefits from its relationship with them. China will not interfere or meddle: foreign nations benefit because China will not make demands on other nations' sovereignty, economic models, governance, or political culture. "We don't believe that human rights should stand above sovereignty," the head of Beijing's premier state think tank says. China implicitly contrasts its "win-win" philosophy with that of the United States, a non-Asian actor that Beijing portrays as disrespectful of sovereignty, imposing a web of sanctions on Southeast Asia and demanding economic and political concessions.

The Chinese have backstopped this "win-win" rhetoric with real initiatives. Over the past five years, China has ended nearly all of its old border disputes and has signed Southeast Asia's Treaty of Amity and Cooperation, a document that commits the signers to mutual respect for a country's sovereignty and equality. Beijing has committed to creating a code of conduct on the South China Sea. It has enthusiastically signed bilateral cooperative agreements with several Asian states. Beijing seems willing to sign these agreements en masse, leaving details to be hammered out later. (In the lawyerly—and democratic—US political system, this type of sign first, talk later diplomacy would be virtually impossible.)

Beijing also has reversed its previous disdain for multilateral organizations, which older Chinese leaders had seen as constraints on China's power. It has not hurt that, as the United States became less interested in multilateralism between the late 1990s and today, China's participation in multilateral groups has made it look better by comparison. Again, Beijing has backed up its changing strategy with real initiatives. As a dialogue partner with ASEAN, China works closely with the organization, trying to strengthen it and, according to Asian diplomats, initiating far more joint projects than other partners, such as Japan or the United States.

China's strategy also includes focusing on developing nations whose bilateral relationships with the United States or Japan are faltering. After President Gloria Macapagal-Arroyo pulled

Filipino troops out of Iraq in 2004 as part of a deal to win the freedom of a Philippine hostage, the United States cut assistance to Manila. Shortly after, China invited Macapagal-Arroyo for a state visit, and then aggressively wooed Philippine policy makers, offering greater cooperation and aid.

Another most important component of China's appeal to developing nations involves Beijing's portrayal of China as a potential ideal, as a model. China emphasizes top-down control of development and poverty reduction and the sidelining of political improvement for economic improvement. China's model particularly appeals to rulers in authoritarian or semi-authoritarian nations. With the Chinese model, the regime has time to think of ways to co-opt businesspeople and other elites that it needs to keep on its side to remain in power.

Flaking Old Insecurities

Until the past decade, China exerted minimal soft power in Southeast Asia. Following Chinese leader Deng Xiaoping's advice, an insecure Beijing still pursued a defensive foreign policy and focused on rebuilding China's domestic economy from the ravages of the Cultural Revolution. The Chinese public still lacked confidence that Beijing could become a global actor, let alone a regional power. A poll taken by the research organization Horizon Group in 1995 asked Chinese citizens their views of the "most prominent countries in the world": one-third ranked the United States most prominent, with only 13 percent choosing China. The Chinese imperial court's treatment of mainland Southeast Asia as vassal states, and the modern history of Maoist China supporting communists in Thailand, Malaysia, and, most disastrously, Cambodia, left a residue of mistrust in the region. China's limited engagement with Southeast Asia foundered on Beijing's continuing claims to the South China Sea, China's suspicion of ASEAN's multilateral forums, and concern among ASEAN nations that China's continuing economic growth would siphon foreign investment from Southeast Asia. Meanwhile, China's policy tools remained weak. It was not a most important aid donor, its diplomatic corps remained dominated by older envoys, and its public diplomacy was blunt.

In the late 1990s all this began to change. China's breakneck economic growth fostered greater confidence within the Chinese public. By the end of the 1990s, many Chinese urbanites were too young to remember the Cultural Revolution. They no longer shared an inherent distrust of the state's wielding of power and ideology. In 2003, the Horizon Group again polled Chinese citizens. This time, nearly 40 percent picked China as "the most prominent country in the world." America came in a distant second. China's leadership was also becoming more confident. Until the mid-1990s, the generation that had grown up around Mao still dominated China's inner circle. But this generation passed away in the 1980s, or was forcibly retired to make way for younger officials. After the crackdown at Tiananmen Square, the leadership recognized that China could not rely on the United States, but had to develop better relations with its neighbours and become a greater international player.

China recognized, too, that its hard power was still limited. In the mid-1990s, Beijing tried to signal its rising military strength to the world by aggressive moves like sending ships to unoccupied, disputed reefs in the South China Sea. This approach backfired. Provocative military exercises, including missile tests in the Taiwan Strait, frightened neighbouring states and evoked old memories of Chinese military adventurism.

Even as they saw that China's aggressive moves triggered Southeast Asian balancing against Beijing, Chinese leaders could not help but notice another trend. Wang Jisi, director of American studies at the Chinese Academy of Social Sciences in Beijing, one of China's elite think tanks, noted in Chinese publications that America's weakness might be its soft influence, not its unrivaled hard power.

Wang was right. After the finish of the cold war, America had retreated from the world, consumed with its own economic boom, its culture wars, and its political scandals. Significant pluralities of Americans opposed US interventions abroad and called for Washington to slash foreign aid, and the White House listened. Washington cut public diplomacy abroad and merged the United States Information Agency, the main public diplomacy outfit, into the State Department. The Clinton administration sidelined many of the multilateral institutions that America had built after World War II, creating perceptions of the United States as a unilateral actor— a perception that would only increase as the Bush administration eviscerated multilateralism.

Support and Trade Tools

China's economic tools also have become more sophisticated. China's aid has undergone a serious transformation. According to a study by Henry Yep of the National Defence University in Washington, in 2003, China's aid to the Philippines was roughly four times greater than America's, China's aid to Laos was three times greater, its aid to Indonesia was nearly double, and its aid to Cambodia nearly matched US levels.

Beijing has revamped its aid programs to better tie assistance to discrete policy goals, including promoting Chinese companies abroad, cultivating important political actors, and bolstering China's benign regional image. In Thailand, for instance, Chinese aid has been used for the kind of lobbying familiar in Washington: to bring important elected Thai politicians to study trips and conferences in China. Beijing has also used funds to purchase surplus Thai agriculture, mollifying Thai farmers worried about the impact of China's free trade agreement with Southeast Asia.

China's embrace of free trade in the region and its promotion of the idea that it will become a most important source of foreign direct investment also bolster its image. In addition to the ASEAN-China Free Trade Agreement, Beijing is negotiating closer bilateral trade ties and economic partnerships with individual Southeast Asian states. By the end of 2006, Southeast Asia's total trade with China probably will eclipse Southeast Asian trade with the United States or Japan. (China-ASEAN total trade in 2005 was roughly $130 billion; US-ASEAN total trade in 2005 was about $150 billion.) By comparison, the United States struggled to complete a bilateral free trade agreement with Thailand.

On visits to the region Chinese leaders set targets for future Chinese investment into Southeast Asia. These targets, usually for five or even ten years in the future, tend to be enormous, and obscure the fact that, at present, Chinese direct investment still lags far behind investment from the United States and other wealthy countries like Japan.

Finally, over the past decade the Chinese government has not only lifted restrictions on migration within China but has also made it vastly easier for Chinese to leave the country for business and tourism. Partly as a result, Chinese migration, often on overstayed short-term visas, is transforming the demographic makeup of northern mainland Southeast Asia, from northern Burma to northern Vietnam. Because of outmigration from Yunnan and other border provinces, ethnic Chinese now dominate entire towns in places like Luang Namtha, in northern Laos. The recent migrants are much more attuned to trends in China than older generations of ethnic Chinese, and they also have created a kind of renminbi zone in northern mainland Southeast Asia, where the Chinese currency serves as a de facto second currency.

9

China's Impact on India-Nepal Relations

The increasingly loud and belligerent assertion of China's claims in South China has become a matter of strategic concern for many nations for diverse reasons. It comes at a time when nations with diverse interest in the Southeast Asia from the India to Vietnam to Japan and the U.S. are already concerned about China's growing strategic strength. Even other nations of the ASEAN group, who do not vocalise their concerns over this development for reasons of real politick, are equally uncomfortable though China is fully established as a trading partner among them. The recent U.S.-Australian agreement to station U.S. Marines in bases in Australia is directly related to this concern.

For India, it sends clear message of China's sensitivity to India's efforts at upgrading its relations in Southeast Asia. Read in the light of escalating strategic collaboration between China and Pakistan including the involvement of PLA troops in the construction of strategic road links in Pakistan Occupied Kashmir, and build up of PLA force levels in Tibet with better strategic access to Indian borders, the possibility of Chinese belligerence shifting to India's Himalayan frontiers has increased.

India appears to have at last woken up to the gravity of the situation with the Indian Prime Minister and Defence Minister publicly stating their concerns on China in the recent months.

In response to the changing strategic environment along the Northern borders, India is in the process of doubling its force levels in the eastern sector. India has also strengthened its strategic links with Vietnam and Afghanistan. Inevitably, in the coming months Indo-U.S. strategic linkages would also be given more form and substance as indicated in the latest meeting of Prime Minister Manmohan Singh and President Obama on the sidelines of East Asia summit at Bali, Indonesia.

China's biggest strength has been its tremendous ability to formulate and execute timely, objective-oriented, action strategies in diplomatic, economic and military fronts for three decades. China's multifaceted military capability has been demonstrated in the recent years in cyber warfare, space missions and anti-satellite warfare, developing and producing fighter aircraft, building aircraft carrier, and building a modern submarine fleet. India's modest strategic response to these developments had been mostly reactive, lacking long term vision. While its space, missile, naval, air force and electronic warfare capabilities, the process appears to lack dynamism and commitment to produce timely results. Due to lack of goal clarity, even the few successful initiatives have not been translated to strategic advantage.

India also does not appear to be taking full advantage of the tremendous geo-strategic advantage it enjoys by virtue of its location between Central and Southeast Asia. Even in South Asia, only during the last decade or so it has started seriously making efforts to build strategic relations with its neighbours like Bangladesh and Sri Lanka. However, Nepal with which it has a complex relationship seems to be an exception to this for various internal and external considerations in both the countries.

India borders Nepal with India on three sides while its Northern frontier lies with Tibet (China). This confers a natural advantage to India as movement from south to north along Terai plains of Nepal is easier than from Tibet across the Himalayan range and through the Northern mountainous regions. So it is not surprising that hundreds of years of interaction between the populations in both Nepal and India have created tremendous religious, ethnic and cultural affinities. The two countries enjoy a special relationship formalised since British colonial days. Although Tibet also enjoys many cultural, ethnic and religious affinities with Nepal, these have been marginalised by China after its occupation of Tibet.

Since the late 90s Nepal had been undergoing tectonic socio-political changes that culminated in the end of monarchy in 2006 and ushering in of multi party democracy. However, political articulation of democracy continues to be stilted and the country retains the potential for eruption of social conflict once again due to political instability.

The Communist Party of Nepal (Maoists) CPN (M) – now morphed into the Unified Communist Party of Nepal (Maoist) UCPN (M) – spearheaded the "peoples' war" against monarchy and has emerged now as a major political factor in the country. Its impressive performance in the 2008 constituent assembly elections demonstrated its popular support. Its founder Pushpa Kumar Dahal, better known as Prachanda, had shown strong pro-Chinese leanings all along. He has also articulated anti-India sentiments more vigorously than some of the leaders of other political parties. After the end of monarchy, CPN (M) found it difficult to give up its revolutionary idiom and join mainstream multi-party politics. Its difficulty in resolving the ideological contradictions to suit democratic governance had created factionalism within its leadership. These problems of Maoists had held up the process of drafting a democratic constitution and usher in functional democracy so far.

Given this setting, the recent visit of Nepal's Prime Minister Baburam Bhattarai, who belongs to UCPN(M), to New Delhi is significant in many ways. It came a few days before four leading parties – the UCPN(M), the Nepali Congress (NC), the Communist Party of Nepal (Unified Marxist Leninist), and the Madhesi Janaadhikar Forum agreed on a 7-point deal on November 1. The deal settled the vexing issue of the future of 19,602 Maoist combatants; it was agreed to integrate a maximum of 6,500 fighters into the Nepal Army, and assist rehabilitation of the rest. They have also agreed to complete the stalled peace process by preparing the draft constitution by end November 2011.

However, implementing the agreement in full, particularly drafting the constitution, within 30 days appears a tall order. Already, Prime Minister Bhattarai has suggested the extension of the life of Constituent Assembly by six months. Much would depend upon the sincerity and determination of UCPN(M) in working with other parties to successfully conclude the task.

There are encouraging indications that increase the chances of success with the UCPN(M) playing a more constructive political role. If Prime Minister Bhattarai can successfully implement the agreement, the country could expect a period of stability so essential for the young democracy to take roots. This would be a welcome development for strengthening India-Nepal relations. And India has to work on it hard as in the past it had given the impression of taking its relation with Nepal for granted.

Among South Asian nations, India's relations with Nepal are perhaps the most complex, subjected to periodic crests and troughs. Prime Minister Bhattarai, summed up its current state in an article in *The Hindu* on the eve of his recent visit to India: "Nepal and India share a very unique relationship. Nepal is sandwiched between two huge states of India and China. But we are virtually India-locked, as we have an open border on three sides. Most of our socio-economic interactions take place with India. Two-thirds of our annual trade is with India, while only 10 per cent is with China. Given this historic tilt towards India, our bilateral relationship is unique. When you have more interaction, you have more problems and more friction. At times, there are misgivings and misunderstandings on various issues — some are genuine, while others are born out of scepticism."

The pronouncements of Prime Minister Bhattarai on Nepal-India relations should give India hope that Maoists are perhaps softening their attitude to India. This situation could be rudely changed under political compulsions and when China takes the initiative to further widen the scope and content of its strategic options against India.

Such a possibility is neither remote nor far-fetched in the overall context of China's ambitious expansion of its power and influence in this part of Asia. When the uneasy relationship between two Asian giants degenerates into a confrontation, Nepal will find it extremely difficult to balance its relations with them. In such a situation, weaknesses in Indo-Nepal relations would be open to exploitation by unfriendly elements. This is the reason why Nepal remains the soft underbelly of India's strategic security.

Nepal's unique relationship with India was formalised when Nepal and Britain signed an agreement of friendship in 1923. After India became independent, the traditional close and friendly relations between the two countries with open borders have continued. Independent India avowed its friendly relations with Nepal with the signing of the India-Nepal Treaty of

Peace and Friendship (INTPF) in 1950. Under this treaty citizens of both nations are treated on par in matters like business, jobs, and owning property. Nepal also has bilateral trade and transit treaties with India. These treaties opened up opportunities for Nepalese citizens to travel, study, and do business freely in India. The extension of non-reciprocal duty free access for Nepalese goods to Indian markets has huge potential as Nepal develops further.

India has contributed significantly for Nepal's development over the years. Indian development projects include building schools, libraries, campuses, primary health centres, hospitals, micro hydro projects, bridges, drinking water projects, and gift of school buses and ambulances. Major Indian projects include the construction of 200-bed Emergency and Trauma Centre in Kathmandu and assistance to BP Koirala Health Institute in Dharan. Major road construction works include building 1450 Km of feeder roads in the plains next to India, cross border railway links, and integrated check posts at four border crossing points. These links provide strategic access to Nepal from India.

Indian outlay for 411 projects under way in Nepal since 2003 is about Rs 4000 crores. The Mahakali Integrated River Project to generate hydro-electric power to benefit both Nepal and India is yet another on-going project, though it is mired in controversy over power sharing.

Though Nepal largely gained from this arrangement, over dependence upon India has created an anti-India backlash. Under the INTPF, Nepal agreed to depend upon India for security, as well as seek Indian consent to import arms, ammunition and military equipment from other countries. As Nepal gained greater international exposure, these were seen as signs of Indian

domination. As a result Nepal has stopped adhering to such stipulations. Many saw the India-assisted development projects as more beneficial to India than Nepal. On trade and transit issues also there had been the strong differences between the two countries as land-locked Nepal was keen to diversify its trade access to other countries over riding Indian concerns.

As Nepal tried to assert its independent stance on both foreign policy and strategic security issues, inevitably the INTPF has come under criticism particularly since King Bhirendra's rule (1972-2001). As Indian diplomat Rajiv Sikri observed, "Landlocked Nepal's umbilical and all round dependency on India, understandably made anti-Indianism the foundation of Nepali nationalism. Some of the fault for this lies with India. India's perceived priority to projects that served India's security and other needs rather than the development of Nepal aroused animosity and distrust of Nepal in India." Seen as the 'Big Brother', most of the political parties in Nepal find it convenient to flog India for all major problems of the country and Maoists have always focused on this issue. And this situation is unlikely change in multi-party democracy dominated by Maoists. Though India would not like to give up its advantages under the INTPF, it appears to be reconciled to changes in the form and content of INTPF as inevitable. China does not have the socio-political baggage India carries due to its closely networked relations with Nepal. It had been cultivating Nepal particularly after Nepal signed a boundary settlment agreement and a separate treaty of peace and friendship with China in 1960 even as China was increasingly locked in boundary dispute with India.

However, China kept away from getting involved in Nepal's internal affairs even during the height of Maoist civil war. Actually, it had supplied arms to King Gyanendra when India had not come forward to do so. However, it has strengthened its relationship taking advantage of the pro-Chinese leanings of Maoists. Its long term plan appears to be to link Nepal with Tibet's large network of road, rail and air infrastructure. This would give a big boost not only to trade but also neutralise India advantage in having better strategic access to Nepal.

In 2007-08, China began construction of a 770-kilometre railway connecting Lhasa, the Tibetan capital, with the border town of Khasa in Nepal. Nepal had requested the link to be extended to Kathmandu. When China completes the ambitious project, it would significantly improve China's strategic access to India's borders as Chinese are involved in other communication projects underway beyond Kathmandu. China's involvement in a project to build a road link between Kathmandu and Lumbini, an important Buddhist pilgrimage site located very close to Indian border, is one such effort. The Chinese government-backed Asia Pacific Exchange of Cooperation Foundation (APECF) is involved in the project. APECF has already agreed to provide $ 3 billion for the Lumbini Development Project (LDP). (It is interesting to note that Prachanda is the Vice Chairman of the LDP.) APECF was also to begin a survey for construction of a direct fast railway link between Kathmandu and Lumbini as part of the LDP. According to Nepalese media, the $1.5 billion first phase of the project includes construction of an international airport and a fast track railway. The project also includes the construction of five star hotels, convention centres, new highways, Buddhist temples and a Buddhist university. China's trade with Nepal had been growing fast, although it is overwhelmingly weighted in favour of China. In 2010-11 bilateral trade was at Nepal Rs 45.63 billion (Nepal Rs 100=$ 1.2) although Nepal exported goods worth only

NRs 746 million. But as Tibet develops further the two-way trade would flourish further when multiple communication links with Nepal are completed.

Thus as India-China relations get more complex we can expect China's multifaceted involvement in Nepal will also to increase in form and content. And as Chinese land and rail links improve with Nepal, its strategic options against India will also multiply. So India will have to fine tune its relationship with Nepal to be more responsive to changing dynamics of strategic environment, drawing upon the advantages it enjoys and try to overcome the latent anti-Indian sentiment. This is the reality.

During Nepal's period of political instability from 2006 to 2011, despite occasional glitches India had wielded its influence carefully and positively to ensure the peace process is not derailed. In appreciation of this, Prime Minister Bhattarai on the eve of his recent visit wrote "India played a positive role in the peace process in Nepal, and during our transition towards democracy. My visit [to India], at this juncture when we are at the last stage of completing the peace process, assumes special significance." This probably reflects the growing realisation in UCPN(M) how Indian influence could be useful to achieve win-win results in stabilising democracy.

India has also reciprocated this welcome change in the attitude, during the October visit of Prime Minsiter Bhattarai with the signing of two agreements with Nepal. The Bilateral Investment Promotion and Protection Agreement (BIPAA) was a long awaited one; it would smoothen and encourage the flow of Indian investments in Nepal. Bhattarai had apparently chosen to ignore the objection of hard line faction of his party in signing the BIPAA as evident from the black flag wielding party cadres who greeted him on his return to Kathmandu. However, many analysts in Nepal consider this development as success of the country's economic diplomacy. The other agreement relates to extension of $250 million Dollar credit line from EXIM bank of India on highly concessional terms (1.75% interest with repayment in 20 years). This will be used to finance infrastructure projects including highway, bridges, railway, irrigation, hydro-power etc. Bhattarai had called this development as historic and a major step towards removing distrust in the bilateral relations between Nepal and India.

More important from Indian security point of view, both countries have agreed to check cross-border crime including smuggling of fake currency into India which had been a major cause for concern to India.

India has also agreed to facilitate the speedy execution of construction of roads, rail and Integrated Check Posts along the border areas of Nepal and India. Hiccups in trade and transit issues are also scheduled to be discussed at the ministerial level. India has also agreed to the use of Vishakapatnam port to facilitate Nepal's third-country trade. It has also conceded Nepal's demand for importing 200 MW of power from India.

These developments are strategically significant. It would also demonstrate India's abiding interest in ensuring political stability in Nepal and help its neighbour to take the peace process to its logical end. In the current state of India-China relations when both countries are focusing on positive aspects rather than dwell on contentious issues, a stable Nepal should be welcome to China also. However, both countries cannot afford to ignore strategic imperatives in their policy perceptions; this would mean continuation of their efforts to further their influence in Nepal. The

importance of steps now taken by India and Nepal to strengthen their relationship would be taken note of by China. Coming in the wake of two Indian strategic initiatives – signing a strategic partnership agreement with Afghanistan and strengthening strategic security relations with Vietnam – it sends a strong signal that India is taking significant measures to strengthen its strategic relations with Nepal.

INDIA FEARS DEMOCRATIC SYSTEM IN NEPAL

There would have been many considerations behind that decision - Nepal's terrain, the people's passionate opposition to the King, the presence of Nepalis in the Indian Army, India's own problem of Left extremism and India's open borders with Nepal. However, India will have to resist any maneuvering by Western countries with the idea of deputing an international peacekeeping force in the neighbourhood, said a former diplomat and expert on Nepal. "Jaswant Singh's visit must not send wrong signals to the people of Nepal who are ready to shed blood to get taste of real democracy," he added. There is a fear that Singh, who belongs to the erstwhile Sisodia dynasty of Rajasthan, may look too cozy in King Gyanendra's company.

At the moment, the sort of election that King Gyanendra envisages is a farce by which his cronies will come back to power. This has been rejected by the politicians and the Maoists. Experts believe that India must persuade King Gyanendra to restore the Parliament by inviting the Seven Party Alliance. This move will either throw out the monarchy or reduce its power.

At that stage, India could, at the most, play some role to help local parties reach a balance of power to facilitate stability in multi-ethnic Nepal. Nepal's problems have been magnified since October 2002, with King Gyanendra bent upon harming his own cause.

His arrogant ways and insensitivity to people's demands drove him away from political parties. The Maoists, the political parties and the king, backed by Nepal Army, are the three main power blocks in Nepal. When the King and Nepalese politicians were drifting away from each other, India did not use its good offices to maintain a balance. While India was passive and did not think ahead, the Maoists captured the people's imagination.

While Nepalese political leaders lost clout because of their in-fighting and tainted images, the Maoists became more powerful. They killed more than 3,000 security men and hundreds of innocent people. Today, about 70 percent of Nepal's villages are under the direct control of Maoists.

Although its leaders Prachanda and Baburam Bhattarai are now sending positive signals and giving mature interviews, Indian experts, except those who are ultra-Left, agree that in the long run, if Maoists control Nepal, it would be disadvantage

India and advantage China. Nepal experts believe that once in power, the Maoists will change their ways. And what cannot be denied by anyone is the fact that their win will hugely benefit Indian Maoists.

These may just be apprehensions but they cannot be shrugged off because they indicate that India has one more big worry in its neighbourhood. Though India-Nepal relations have a strong economic edge and they share cultural ties, India will have to gear up to face a 'new Nepal', which will be a challenge. In fact, two days before Singh and Saran visited Nepal, the Cabinet Committee on Security, along with Army Chief J J Singh, discussed the issue. According to intelligence sources, India is unlikely to send troops to Nepal but it was admitted that absolute power in the hands of Maoists is more than a distinct possibility in the future.

India's Nepal Dilemma

A large chunk of the blame lies on Nepal's politicians, who are unable to control the fury that's filling the streets. It seems likely that any day now, the underground Maoists will take control of the revolutionary passion of the Nepalis.

If Maoists ultimately emerge victorious, India cannot escape blame either because of its inactivity when the King trampled upon democracy to restore the absolute power of the monarchy under the pretext of countering the Maoists. And the Maoists took advantage of the resulting situation to encourage a people's movement against the present political dispensation in Nepal.

Nepali King Faces Tough Choice

If the King still manages to cling to power it is only because he has the army on his side, which has always looked upon the King and not elected representatives as its source of power. It is clear by now that the Nepalese Army is not well-disposed with democratic norms.

It cannot defeat the Maoists, who are scattered in the hinterlands, but, at the same time, does not want to see them in power. The crucial questions is how will it function if the Maoists win an election and come to power. India's capability and clout will be reflected in whether it convinces the King, the army and the political parties to avoid confrontation. In the meantime, as the King, the Maoists and the political parties bicker, a fourth power bloc has emerged in this Himalayan kingdom, taking the destiny of Nepal by storm. It is the power of the people, out on the streets, for all the world to see.

CHINA INTENSIFIES TUG OF WAR WITH INDIA ON NEPAL

For years, Nepal never bothered too much with policing its northern border with China. The Himalayas seemed a formidable-enough barrier, and Nepal's political and economic attention was oriented south towardIndia. If Nepal was a mouse trapped between elephants, as the local saying went, the elephant that mattered most was India. But last week a Nepalese administration delegation visited Beijing on a trip that underscored, once again, how China's newfound weight in the world is altering old geopolitical equations.

As Nepal's home minister, Bhim Rawal, met with China's top security officials, Chinese state media reported that the two countries had agreed to cooperate on border security, while Nepal restated its commitment to preventing any "anti-China" events on its side of the border. Details of the meetings were not yet known, but the two countries were expected to finalize a program under which China would provide money, training and logistical support to help Nepal expand police checkpoints in isolated regions of its northern border.

The reason for the deal is simple: Tibet. At a time at what time President Obama's decision to meet with the Dalai Lama has infuriated China, Mr. Rawal's meetings in Beijing could have greater practical effect on the lives of Tibetans. Prodded by China, Nepal is now moving to close the Himalayan passages through which Tibetans have long made secret trips in and out of China, often on pilgrimages to visit the Dalai Lama in his exile in India.

If it once regarded Nepal with intermittent interest, China is now exerting itself more broadly toward its small Himalayan neighbor, analysts say — partly because of its concern that Nepal could become a locus of Tibetan agitation, partly as another South Asian stage in its growing soft-power fencing match in the region with India. "Nepal has become a very interesting space where the big players are playing at two levels," said Ashok Gurung, director of the India China Institute at The New School. "One is their relationship with Nepal. And the second is the relationship between India and China."

In the broadest sense, India and China share similar goals in Nepal. Each wants Nepal's political situation to stabilize and is watching closely as the country's Maoists negotiate with other political parties over a new constitution that would fundamentally reshape the government. Each is also worried about security, as India is concerned about political agitation on the Nepalese side of their shared border, as well as the possibility that terrorists trained in Pakistan could transit through Nepal.

But India is also paying close attention to what many India experts consider newfound Chinese activism in South Asia, whether by building ports in Sri Lanka and Pakistan, or signing new agreements with even the tiniest South Asian nations like the Maldives. An expanding Chinese presence in Nepal would be especially alarming to India, given that India and Nepal share a long and deliberately porous border.

"India has always been worried about what access China might have in Nepal," said Sridhar Khatri, executive director of the South Asia Center for Policy Studies in Katmandu. "India has always considered South Asia to be its backyard, like a Monroe Doctrine." From China's perspective, Nepal's geopolitical significance rose after Tibetan protests erupted in March 2008, five months before Beijing hosted the Olympic Games. Those protests began inside China, in Lhasa, the Tibetan capital, and other Tibetan regions, but also spread across the border to Katmandu, where an estimated 12,000 Tibetans live. Even as Chinese officials were able to block international media coverage of the crackdown under way in Tibet, the protests in Nepal attracted global attention as photographs circulated of the Nepalese police subduing Tibetan protesters. In a few cases, media outlets mistakenly identified the photographs as coming from inside Tibet.

"There was a shift after March," Mr. Gurung said. "The Chinese realized that Nepal is going to be an important site where they could potentially be embarrassed on Tibetan issues." V. R. Raghavan, a retired general in the Indian Army, said that China for years had tacitly allowed Tibetans to cross into Nepal, many of whom were making pilgrimages or attending universities in India. But the March protests made China realize that it had a "southern window" that needed to be closed, he said.

"Every movement of important personages and priests and others from Tibet has taken place through Nepal," said General Raghavan, now director of the Delhi Policy Group, a research institute. Chinese officials tightened security on their side of the border in the name of preventing pro-Tibet agitators from slipping into, or out of, the country. They also pushed Nepal to become more vigilant.

Last fall, Mr. Rawal announced that Nepal, for the first time, would station armed police officers in isolated regions like Mustang and Manang on the border with Tibet. Meanwhile, Tibetan advocates say the tightening border security has already sharply slowed movement. Until 2008, roughly 2,500 to 3,000 Tibetans annually slipped across the border, according to the office of the Dalai Lama. By last year, the number dropped to about 600, a change that Tibetan advocates attribute to closer ties between China and Nepal.

"As they get closer," said Tenzin Taklha, secretary for the Dalai Lama, "it is becoming more difficult for Tibetans." In fact, many Nepalese believe that moving closer to China is in the best interests of the country.

For more than a half century, India has been deeply influential in Nepalese affairs and remains Nepal's biggest trading partner and economic benefactor, even as some Nepalese resent India's role in their affairs. Nepal's currency is pegged to the Indian rupee, and citizens of the two countries are allowed to pass freely across the border. More than one million Nepalese work in India, sending back remittances. But trade with China has quadrupled since 2003, according to government statistics, and Nepalese business leaders want to increase economic ties.

In recent years, Chinese airlines have opened routes into Nepal as the number of Chinese tourists has risen steadily, and Nepalese officials also want China to extend rail services to the border so that Nepal can be linked to the same high-altitude line that connects Beijing to Tibet. Kush Kumar Joshi, president of the Federation of Nepalese Chambers of Commerce and Industry, said his group was trying to establish special economic zones to lure Chinese manufacturers to Nepal — and for Indian companies, too.

"We need to have both countries as our development partners," he said. Mr. Khatri, the analyst in Katmandu, said that India would remain Nepal's dominant neighbor, but that China's expanding global reach would inevitably make it more engaged than before. To assume that China would not exert itself more in South Asia and Nepal, he said, "would be to neglect the reality."

CHANGING TRENDS IN INDIA-NEPAL RELATIONS

India-Nepal relations have been shaped and wrought by their geographical contiguity and socio-cultural identities which has influenced their historical past. The historical linkages emanating from the racial, religious and linguistic affinities were possible because of the 1,750-km- long open border which made communication easier and possible. The crossing of the border by the people has not only influenced each other's history, culture and tradition but also had an impact on the political, economic and strategic relations between the two countries.

The geo-strategic site of Nepal between India and China has also shaped its relations with its neighbours. The high peaks and rough terrain towards the north made communication and people's movement and habitation difficult, if not impossible, towards the Tibet region of China. This is not to say that Nepal did not have historical political linkages with its northern neighbour. However, the presence of imperialist China and Russia in the north led British India to consider Nepal has a buffer state and integrate Nepal into British India's security parameters. Independent India also could not ignore the geo-strategic importance of Nepal and considered it as a buffer between itself and Communist China. It was not only the ideological differences with China that alarmed India but also the Chinese efforts to undermine India's security interests by undertaking road construction projects in Terai area which is contiguous to the plains of India. In fact, soon after Communist China's expansion towards Tibet, India entered into the Treaty of Peace and Friendship with Nepal in 1950 which defined the political, economic and strategic relations between the two countries. The Chinese expansion towards Tibet had perturbed Nepal as it not only exposed China's historical claims of maintaining the Himalayan state as its feudatory but also Nepal's vulnerability in containing any armed aggression from the north. Hence, Nepal agreed to enter into treaty arrangements with India. However, too much dependence brings forth to the small state fear of being incorporated or turned into an ally of the dominant state. The open border between India and Nepal had created ideological and political linkages between the two countries much to the chagrin of the monarch. For instance, the Nepali National Congress, a protagonist of democracy and a socialistic society, had links with the Indian National Congress even before the independence of India. Landlocked Nepal utilised its geographical location to its advantage by undertaking strategies of distancing with India, neutrality or non-alignment with its neighbours, to preserve its own interest. Such as Nepal developed diplomatic relations with China in 1960 under King Mahendra's rule and tried to assert its independence and sovereignty.

The internal supporting dynamics in Nepal also influenced the making of its foreign policy with India. There have been frequent changes in the political system in Nepal from the rule of Ranas to the monarchy to the Panchayat democracy and constitutional democracy and in every political change the ruler has looked towards those out of power with suspicion.

Such as when King Mahendra faced opposition from pro-democracy political parties like the Nepali Congress and Communists, he apprehended Indian support to them. To strengthen the monarchy, King Mahendra tried to diversify relations with extra-regional countries and tried to maintain a distance from India. Similarly, King Birendra tried to maintain a distance from India which was alleged by Nepal to be supporting the pro-democracy and anti-monarchy Congress rebels, by proposing to be a Zone of Peace in the region. Despite the Government of India's assurances on various occasions, Nepal remained unconvinced. One reason could be that certain political idealogues in India, like the socialists, supported the cause of the Nepali Congress. Even during the agitation against the monarchy in 1989, the socialists like Chandrashekhar and Communist leaders from India were present in Kathmandu to extend their support to the democrats. However, they have to be differentiated from the official stand taken by the Government of India.

The Cold War politics also exaggerated India-Nepal relations. The impact of Sino-Soviet differences alongwith the growing Sino-US rapprochement in the international politics percolated down to South Asia where the Sino-India differences drew India and the Soviet Union closer. Nepal also made use of the Sino-India differences and followed the policy of distancing from India to reap advantages from the global and regional actors. For example, in 1961, King Mahendra signed an agreement on the road construction from Kathmandu to Kodari with China in 1961. The agreement came at a time when the monarchy had dissolved the Parliamentary democracy, a move not favoured by India, and Nepal needed to allay any fears of outside support to democracy for which nothing could have been better than to use China whose relations with India had fallen to the lowest.

Since then the ground realities have changed. The Cold War has come to an end with the disintegration of the Soviet Union in 1989 and the worldwide resurgence of democratic forces. The Chinese policy makers have done a rethinking on their policies after the disintegration of the Soviet Union. China has tried to create its own "Socialist Market Economy" and has opened its doors to foreign investors in order to globalise its economy. In this task it will not be favourable for it to have any irritant impeding its growth. Hence, China responded favourably to the Indian desire to improve their relationship. Indian Prime Minister Rajiv Gandhi visited China in 1989, the first ever visit by an Indian Prime Minister. Three agreements were signed, on cultural exchange, air service between the two countries, and on science and technology. This opened up diplomatic visits between the two countries. During his visit to India in November 1996, the Chinese President, Ziang Zemin, said that "though we still have some outstanding problems left over from history, I can say for sure that our common interests far outweigh our differences, as neither of us poses a threat to the other." Emphasis has been laid on economic cooperation though a Joint Working Group has been set up to resolve the border issue. In the latest round of border talks on August 5, 1997, both the sides agreed to identify an interim border and accelerate the pace of demilitarisation of the eastern border. There has been an attitudinal change in India and China commensurating with the global trend where all the countries cooperate with one another keeping aside their differences and disputes.

In the meantime, Nepal was also undergoing rapid political changes. Invigorated by the worldwide movements for democracy, the democratic forces in Nepal worked with added vigour to overthrow the Panchayat regime. In 1990, King Birendra accepted the popular demand for greater participation of the people's representation and multi-party democracy was established in Nepal. A democratic government of Prime Minister K.P. Bhattarai consisting of the Nepali Congress and the Communist Party of Nepal-United Marxist Leninist [CPN(UML)] took control of power. The democratic government had the responsibility to steer the country towards the radically changed world polity devoid of clear-cut Cold War politics and define foreign policy in the region where the security situation is threatened from within.

The Rising Ties

The multi-party democracy in Nepal infused new hopes of normalising relations between the two countries who had become aware of the post-Cold War world order where emphasis was laid on economic relations. The first requirement to forge closer ties was by normalising trade relations which had nosedived following the expiry of the treaty of trade and transit in 1989 and the subsequent closure of the border except for two points at Raxaul and Jogbani.

The interim government of K.P. Bhattarai declared it would improve trade relations with India on a priority basis. The Nepalese perspective was favourably responded to by India. In fact, the then Foreign Minister of India, I.K. Gujral, declared India's readiness to "accommodate the economic aspirations of the Nepalese people."

During K.P. Bhattarai's visit to India in 1989, the trade relations with India were resumed. The trade embargo was removed and the bilateral relations were restored to the situation prevailing on April 1, 1987. The date was significant because it annulled the "work permit system" restricting Indians from seeking employment in Nepal. Emphasis was given on developing economic relations between the two countries with areas identified for joint cooperation. The Joint Communique signed on the occasion declared that the countries would cooperate on "industrial and human resource development, for harnessing of waters of the common rivers for the benefit of the two peoples and for the protection and management of the environment." However, instead of creating an environment of trust and confidence, the media and the Opposition parties criticised the term "common rivers" considering it as the surrender and compromise of Nepal's sovereign rights over water resources.

The two Prime Ministers gave assurances to each other that all the bilateral disputes would be settled peacefully and pledged "territorial integrity, non-use of force and non-interference in each other's internal affairs." They agreed to be sensitive to each other's security and agreed not to allow activities in their territory inimical to the interest of each other. They agreed to "have prior consultations with a view to reaching mutual agreement on such defence related matters which, in the view of either country, could pose a threat to its security." These assurances were not something novel and are contained in the Treaty of Peace and Friendship (1950). Article V of the treaty allows Nepal to import arms, equipment or war-like material from or through the Indian territory for its security provided the imports are done with the prior consultation of the latter. The letter exchanged along with the treaty substantiated the security provision contained in the treaty and said that "neither government shall tolerate any threat to the security of the other by a foreign aggressor. To deal with any such threat the two governments shall consult with each other and devise effective counter-measures." However, reiteration by both the countries was important in the background of Nepal granting road construction deals to China in the Terai or importing arms from China, for instance, in 1989, which was against the spirit of the 1950 Treaty. In fact, the last consignment of arms coming from China was deferred by Nepal as a goodwill gesture towards India. The interim government showed its sincerity to develop friendly, unique and brotherly relations with India and even dropped the Zone of Peace proposal from the Constitution as was propounded by King Birendra in 1974.

The welcoming gestures made by the interim government were significant as it consisted of the Nepali Congress and the CPN (UML), the two forces committed to the cause of democracy who also had historical linkage with India. Also the relations developed between Nepal and India acted as a guideline for the future governments. The Nepalese Prime Minister's visit was shared by the Indian Prime Minister, Chandrashekhar, on February 13-15, 1991. Chandrashekhar had been in close association with the Nepali Congress and had extended his vocal support to the pro-democracy movement in Nepal. He had attended the meeting organised by the Nepali Congress on January 18, 1990, to chart a future course of action to restore democracy in Nepal. Hence, Chandrashekhar's visit raised lots of expectations from Nepal. He accepted the Joint Communique signed in 1990 as the basis for India's relations with Nepal. It was decided that India would restore the Jayanagar-Janakpuri-Bizalur railway line.

Under its aid programme India agree to open three more entry points at Nepalganj, Gauriphaula and Banbasa for third country nationals on the Indo-Nepal border. Discussions were held on harnessing of water resources, restoration of registration facilities for vehicles owned by Indian residents, removal of impediments to ensure free movement of Indian currency from Nepal to India and removal of discriminations against the Indian teachers working in Nepal. Both the countries agreed to set up a High Level Task Force to identify areas of economic cooperation and propose its recommendations to the two Prime Ministers. Accordingly, the High Level Task Force was set up in 1991.

Nepal had its first universal election in 1991 in accordance with the new Constitution formulated by the interim government. People voted the Nepali Congress to power which had a long history of fighting for people's rights and multi-party democracy. Girija Prasad Koirala became the Prime Minister of Nepal. He gave primacy to developing relations with the neighbouring countries.

His visit to India, his first ever visit abroad as Prime Minister, from December 5 to 10, 1991, was not only fruitful in defining relations with India but was also successful in concluding two separate treaties on trade and transit for five and seven years respectively. India also reduced the domestic content and labour requirement on Nepalese goods from 65 per cent to 50 per cent to provide duty free access to India. The agreement to control unauthorised trade was also extended for five years. The signatories committed themselves to ensure the interests of each other by not allowing illegal trade, narcotic and psychotropic substances and agreed to exchange information on such related matters.

A memo of Understanding was signed for cooperation in developing agricultural yield through cooperation in science and technology, research, processing and agro-based industries. As a measure towards closer trust and confidence, the B.P. Koirala Foundation was set up to promote exchange of views on education, culture, science and technology.

In fact, India agreed to improve and simplify the rules for export of goods from Nepal during Prime Minister P.V. Narasimha Rao's visit to Nepal in October 1992. India agreed to extend stand by credit facility to Nepal from (IC) Rs.35 crore to Rs.50 crore. The term of the agreement was extended from one to three years during which period the interest rate of 7 per cent per annum was levied. Nepal's private vehicles were allowed to move from its border to Calcutta and Haldia ports and back provided the vehicles were authorised by the Nepal Transit and Warehousing Company Ltd or Nepal Transport Corporation. This was agreed to facilitate Nepal's exports to India. Movement of vehicles from Nepal to Nepal via Indian territory was allowed without any bond or cash deposit. Nepal was also allowed to import goods from India in convertible currency.

Taking the discussion further on cooperation in harnessing of water resources, both the sides agreed on a time-frame for investigations, preparation of project reports on Karnali, Pancheshwar, Sapta-Kosi, Budhi Gandaki, Kamala and Bagmati projects. Priority was given to work on the Pancheshwar and Budhi Gandaki projects. On the Tanakpur Barrage, it was accepted that the area remains under the sovereign control of Nepal. However, the barrage project does not make any consumptive use of water. India agreed to supply 150 cusecs of water to irrigate 4,000 to 5,000 hectares of land and would supply 20 million units of power, free of cost to Nepal. It was also agreed to either renovate or replace the missing boundary pillars at Tanakpur Barrage by May 1993.

India showed keen interest to accelerate the pace of economic development in Nepal which was necessary to consolidate the democratic aspirations of the people who had expected overnight change in their status quo. Lack of employment opportunities could create frustration and disappointment amongst the people who expected miracles from their representatives.

The improvement in the relations resulted in the increased industrial production which increased by 19.26 per cent for the year 1990-91 whereas the rate of growth in the last fiscal year was estimated to 4.4 per cent. The first volume of trade between the two countries increased from NRs 5,273.6 million in 1988-89 to NRs 9,473.6 million in 1990-91.

Another matter of anxiety which needed special attention of the two countries was the use of the open border by subversive elements against Indian security interests. Prime Minister Koirala has assured India of Nepal's total cooperation in curbing terrorism from its soil against India, it being a threat to Nepal's security also. The Nepalese Prime Minister was keen to include Indian participation in any negotiations with Bhutan on the issue of refugees which was turned down by India as it considered the issue to be affecting the relations between Nepal and Bhutan which had to be resolved by both the parties bilaterally.

The significant change in the political relationship between India and Nepal was the frankness in negotiations and discussions which was virtually absent during the monarchy which looked towards democratic India with suspicion. However, the change of the political system from monarchy to multi-party democracy in Nepal did not bring forth changes in its political culture. For instance, the erstwhile monarchy and the Panchayat regime had used anti-India slogans to counter any opposition at home and stabilise their power by heightening the passions of the people. After the change of the political system, those not in power used similar tactics to criticise the government in power. The Nepali Congress is considered to be pro-India and the Opposition utilised this label to criticise the government and involved India's name to give authenticity to their charges. The perfect case was of Tanakpur. The Opposition considered Tanakpur as a sellout to India. They claimed that India had constructed the 577 metres of the bund in the Nepali territory without the government's approval. Koirala blamed the Opposition for instigating anti-India feeling in Nepal straining the upward movement in their relations. He said, "We have not compromised our sovereignty with India."

The Tanakpur subject brought into prominence the fears and apprehensions of Nepal of not being given "mutual benefit" on earlier agreements on the Kosi and Gandak. Since the matter was of national importance, they expected it to be discussed at home before taking it for bilateral discussion with India. Also recognising the sensitivity of the issue which could be related to the sovereignty of the country, the Tanakpur agreement was politicised by the political parties in Nepal for their own political gains. However, its impact on India-Nepal relations cannot be ignored. The politicisation of any project slows down the progress in the development of the project as happened in the Tanakpur Barrage where the work had come to a standstill. Much time was consumed in taking the matter to the Supreme Court of Nepal and the Parliament. However, Nepal did learn a lesson of taking a consensual approach before taking the issue on water resource or any matter of national importance with India as was done in the Mahakali Agreement in 1995.

Domestic compulsions pressurised Koirala to resign and mid-term elections were held in November 1994. Man Mohan Adhikari heading the CPN (UML) formed the government. Adhikari also opened his diplomatic initiatives by visiting India in April 1995. In a Press conference he said, "I would like to review all aspects of relations as well as changes in the trade and transit agreements with India. This is in view of the changes taking place in international relations as well as in South Asia." He had reservations on the 1950 Treaty and wanted some changes in it, specifically on clauses related to security issues. However, in the same vein, he said, "Nepal was totally in support of India's security concerns." He reassured India that the Nepalese territory would not be used for anti-India activities.

To keep a vigil on the cross-border movement, a technical committee was set up to discuss the issue. The Adhikari government was eager for Indian investment in the hydro-power sector. However, its tenure was shortlived. The government was ousted from power through a no-confidence motion and the Nepali Congress with the support of the Rashtriya Prajatantra Party and Nepal Sadbhavana Party came to power under the leadership of Sher Bahadur Deuba.

The major attainment of the Deuba government lies in taking a consensus approach in signing a Treaty on Integrated Development of the Mahakali Basin in February 1997 in New Delhi. The treaty envisages construction of the 2,000 MW Pancheshwar power project within eight years. Both governments agreed to workout an umbrella for the sale of power to each other and encourage Indian investment in the hydro-power sector in Nepal as a part of an action plan to further strengthen bilateral economic cooperation. The treaty had put to rest the controversy which had been raised after the signing of the Tanakpur agreement. Nepal's share of water was increased from 150 cusecs and 20 million units of power to 300 cusecs of water in the dry season and 1,000 cusecs of water in the monsoons besides 70 million units of power. Another agreement was signed on the construction of 22 bridges on the Kohalpur-Mahakali sector of the east-west highway.

At home Deuba received an unexpected reaction from the left parties towards the treaty which had otherwise received public support. The CPN (UML), which was initially satisfied with the treaty, along with other left parties expressed dissatisfaction over it. It blamed Deuba for tampering with the treaty which was initiated in Nepal and for signing a new version in New Delhi. Defending the treaty, Deuba called the allegation "baseless and fictitious and is an excellent attempt to mislead people." Despite the furore and criticism, the parties ratified it in the Parliament on September 11, 1996, with certain modifications.

Nepal had learnt sure lessons from the earlier agreement on Tanakpur Barrage. Not to repeat the furore at home, the government had taken a national consensus with all the parties on the subject. Thus, at the time of ratification in the Parliament, the Opposition had no moral right to reject it. More so because it was the CPN(UML) which had initially proposed the Mahakali Treaty during Prime Minister Adhikari's visit to India in April 1995.

Prime Minister Deuba also spoke about modification of the Treaty of Peace and Friendship, especially, the clauses related to the security concerns and said that his government will pursue the same policy on security related matters as was followed by the previous government. Expressing Nepal's concern towards India's security issues, Deuba said that "Nepal will never pose a security threat to India." In fact, both the countries were determined to fight terrorism and reiterated their commitment not to allow any activities on their territory prejudicial to the security interests of the other. Subsequently, a Joint Working Group was set up in August 1996 during the visit of P.C. Lohani, the Foreign Minister of Nepal, to India. The Group is expected to give suggestions on the ways and means to monitor the open border in order to check the movement of undesirable subversive elements inimical to the security of both states.

A major turning point in the relationship was felt when I.K. Gujral became the Prime Minister of India. He gave a thrust on maintaining bilateral relations with the neighbouring countries in the spirit of non-reciprocity and non-interference in the internal affairs. India being dominant in size had to show magnanimity towards its smaller neighbours. One magnanimous gesture shown by India was to allow Nepal to use Phulbari as a transit point to get access to Bangladesh. India had been denying the transit point to Nepal because of its proximity to the Siliguri corridor which is sensitive to India's security concerns. However, Gujral showed trust and confidence in the country's neighbour by allowing it to use the Phulbari-Banglabandh transit route.

During Gujral's appointment to Nepal in June 1997, a power agreement was signed to encourage private and semi-government investment in Nepal. After the Mahakali Agreement this was a significant development because the countries could meet any shortage in power from Pancheshwar. Also, both the countries had freedom to enter into an agreement with a third party to generate resources for exploiting power. India is aware that the excess power can be utilised by its power deficient areas. Letters were exchanged on developing the Raxaul-Sirsiya rail link and supply of medical equipment to a hospital in Kathmandu from India. A Memorandum of Understanding was signed on civil aviation which allows private airlines to operate between the two countries in the light of growing business and tourism; Bangalore and Lucknow airports are open for the flights arriving from Nepal.

There has been an element of "mutual benefit" and "non-reciprocity" in India's relations with Nepal as envisaged in the Mahakali Treaty. India and Nepal relations hitherto defined in terms of geo-politics had to accord primacy to economic cooperation in the light of the changing global economic environment. The main thrust of the economic cooperation has been on four areas: trade and transit relations, sharing of water resources, Indian aided projects and joint ventures. In fact, the countries have moved ahead from bilateralism and are looking towards multilateralism. In December 1996, Nepal submitted an approach paper on sub-regional cooperation within the South Asian Association for Regional Cooperation (SAARC) parameters which suggests creation of growth polygons between Nepal, Bhutan, Bangladesh and India in the fields of transit, multimodal transport, irrigation, energy, environment, tourism, trade and investment.

GEO-STRATEGIC COMPULSIONS MOVING INDIA-NEPAL RELATIONS

The border between India and Nepal is open and the flow of people is allowed without any restriction. The main advantage of an open border is felt by the people living on both sides of the border who can enter each other's territory for daily basic needs. In fact, it is said that there are houses situated on the border where one door opens towards Nepal and the other towards India. Citizens of both the countries enjoy unrestricted freedom of movement through the open border in accordance with the Treaty of Peace and Friendship. Though there is no separate treaty on defining the status of the border, considering the traditional ties between the two countries and taking the geographical reality of the border into consideration which runs through plains, jungles and mountains, the border remains opened. Article VI of the Treaty of Peace and Friendship allows the citizens of both the countries to receive "national treatment with regard to participation in industrial and economic development of such territory and to the grant of concessions and contracts relating to such development." In fact, according to Article VII of the treaty, the citizens of both the countries can move, reside and own property and participate in trade and commerce in each other's territory. However, it is alleged that citizens of other countries also enter Nepal to avail the opportunities under the guise of Indians. Since the border is open it becomes difficult to check the flow of movement of population and to ascertain whether they are from India or some other South Asian country. Similarly, the open border has helped the Nepalese to move and reside not only in India but also in Bhutan from India which has brought its own problems associated with the movement of population like demographic and economic displacement of the locals.

The geo-strategic position of Nepal is such that its Terai opens to the Indian heartland (the plains of UP, Bihar and West Bengal), thus, exposing the country to subversive elements. Nepal is also closer to the Himalayan ranges of western Uttar Pradesh which are demanding separate statehood and the hills of the north-east are active with extremists and militants of Nagaland and Mizoram. Through the mountainous passes of Nepal it is easy to enter the plains and hills of India and exploit the already existing problems.

The open border has been misused by the criminals, smugglers and terrorists who take refuge in Nepal after committing crimes in India or vice-versa. Arms and drugs have also been moving from Nepal to India. The open border is used by the Inter-Services Intelligence (ISI) of Pakistan to facilitate movement of the Kashmiri terrorists to carry out anti-India activities. There are various Muslim organisations in Nepal engaged in imparting education to the religious minorities with the help of financial aid coming from Pakistan or the Gulf. A few organisations are alleged to be involved with the terrorist organisations to carry out anti-Nepal activities. Documents have been received showing that Islamic Yuva Sangh of Nepal is working to establish "Islam in Nepal and Nizame Mustafa in the country...The Sangh is also doing its best, with the help of Islamic countries, to increase the gap between the Hindus and the Buddhists so that they become disunited and Islam emerges as the strongest religion of Nepal." Though it is not possible to turn a Hindu majority state into a Muslim state, the possibility of creating social tension with external interference cannot be ruled out. The fundamentalists or misguided youth can also be engaged in anti-India activities considering their concentration is in the Terai region of Nepal which is adjacent to the densely populated Muslim areas of UP and Bihar known for nefarious activities of smuggling, movement of arms and drugs. Thus, India and Nepal cannot ignore the geo-political realities. They are cautious of the emerging threat of trans-border movement of criminals and subversive elements. The Government of Nepal has time and again emphasised on its total support to India in not to allowing activities adverse to the interests of India from its soil. Geo-strategy still dictates India-Nepal relations.

India-Nepal relations have been responding to the changes taking place in the international arena in the post-Cold War era. The simultaneous political changes taking place in both the countries are also instrumental in shaping their relations. One of the major changes in India is the emergence of pluralism in politics with the decline in the power of the Congress Party which had ruled the country as a major party since 1947. Since 1990, India has had three coalition governments. The governments in India have realised the basic thrust in the changing global environment where it has to develop relations with its neighbours based on trust and confidence and non-reciprocity which is an essential element in defining relations between asymmetrical nations. The change in the Indian policy from the Indira Doctrine to the Gujral Doctrine has been positively received by Nepal which has also been making changes in its foreign policy postulates. Emphasis has been given on developing relations with the neighbouring countries, strengthening the institutional capability of the Foreign Ministry, and resolving the domestic issues affecting the security and stability of the country. The foreign policy of Nepal has come a long way from its policy of special relations with India to the policy of equi-distance with its neighbours to a search of an independent foreign policy. The often played strategy to use one neighbour against the other is no longer effective in the post-Cold War era. As discussed earlier, the growing Sino-India relations have decreased the manoeuvring capabilities of Nepal to play one neighbour against another. Instead, there is a shift from exploiting the differences of the neighbours to its advantage to develop relations with the neighbours on the basis of mutual benefit. However, the changing global and regional political scenario does not undermine the geo-strategic realities. Nepal's buffer status between India and China still exists.

In keeping with the worldwide economic activism, both India and Nepal have emphasised on developing trade relations. Nepal's proposal to develop an economic quadrangle consisting of Nepal, Bhutan, Bangladesh and India is a successful attempt towards promoting economic diplomacy. Commenting on the challenges faced by Nepal in the globalisation of world economies, Kamal Thapa, the Foreign Minister of Nepal, said, "Today the aid era seems to be replaced by a foreign investment era. Hence, the need to use the country's resources as an effective diplomatic tool—in other words, diversification of the investment regime just like trade and aid regimes were done. For the moment, water might be the only potential for the country to become the regional hub for energy not least water itself." India and Nepal have been successful in agreeing on sharing of hydro-power.

However, consistency in foreign policy is synonymous with domestic stability. The weakness in the coalition government of Gujral has created apprehensions in Nepal on the longevity and stability of the Gujral Doctrine. As discussed earlier, Nepal is in the early stages of democracy. It has had five coalition governments since 1991. An unstable government deters investments in a country. The normalisation of Sino-India relations has removed the external output affecting the India-Nepal relations but the domestic issues affecting the relations remain. Unless the domestic issues are addressed in the country, it will weaken the capabilities of the country to cope with the post-Cold War transformations. It would be in the interest of India to consolidate the socio-economic development of Nepal and have continuous dialogue marking areas of cooperation and resolving areas of disagreement.

PROSPECTS AND CHALLENGES OF NEPAL-CHINA EMPLOYMENT

Nepal-China trade relations have grown amicably in recent years. One of the greatest achievements in this regard is tariff free treatment to 391 Nepali goods in the Chinese market announced in May this year to be effective from July 01. China has provided Nepal with "financial and technical assistance" in areas such as infrastructure, industry and human resource development. Being very close neighbours, Nepal and China have economic relations from the time immemorial. Formalisation of this trade relation took place after the enforcement of Nepal-China Peace Treaty in 1792. Following that treaty, Nepal government started sending a delegation every five years to Beijing with goods from Nepal and India and the delegation would come back with Chinese goods. This practice came to an end in 1908. Earlier in 1856, another treaty was signed between Nepal and Tibet (called Thapathali Treaty) which made Tibet pay tribute to Nepal, a practice that continued till 1953. The 1856 Treaty provided for special rights to Nepali traders and pilgrims in Tibet. These privileges were curtailed after the Nepal-China relations were soured following 1908.

The organization of diplomatic relations in 1965 between the two countries marked the beginning of a new era in the history of Nepal-China relations. Trade and economic cooperation expanded after this event. Subsequently, there were a number of industrial units set up (Bansbari Leather and Shoe and Harisiddhi Bricks) and some roads constructed (Prithvi Highway and Arniko Highway) in Nepal with Chinese assistance. According to the Ministry of Foreign Affairs, Chinese financial support to Nepal in the recent years is to the tune of 80 million Yuan every year. However, the recent years have witnessed a sea change in Nepal-China economic relations. Nowadays, it is more in the business to business level than in the government to government level. Nepal, geographically located at the strategic position of economically sound and leading economies of Asia, China and India, has high prospect to reap the benefit from these nations. It is high time that we rethink and redefine our policy and erase from our mind that we can earn more by selling our products in the international market and we are not landlocked but land linked. For decades, Nepal has had trade deficit with its neighbouring countries. These deficits can be minimised either by increasing exports or by decreasing imports. But we should emphasise on producing goods of comparative advantage rather than looking at decreasing imports. It seems that even with zero duty, our products are not competitive in price and quality with the Chinese products. We do not have the capacity to produce qualitative products to satisfy the needs of the Chinese market. However, we can focus our trade with Tibet and certain cities of China.

Agriculture at the moment does not have export potential because of our own internal demands. But tourism could be one possibility between Nepal and China. Each year, 46 million Chinese go abroad. Despite cultural and social similarities, we have been unable to attract Chinese tourists in Nepal. We should reap the benefit of being in between two giant economies and make the best use of this opportunity of our prime geographical location by developing plans and policies to form a hub between South Asia and China and beyond to the central Asia such as Kyrgyzstan and Uzbekistan. This could bring economic growth in the future for Nepal. The Chinese government has attached high priority for the overall development of Tibet Autonomous Region (TAR) and has expressed deep concern to set up factories and other indispensable installations in Nepal as they are cost effective. There are prospects for investment from the Chinese side on hydropower projects as well as in construction, pharmaceuticals, minerals, cement, banking and education.

Despite the geographical constraints, infrastructure and institutional bottlenecks, Nepal has comparative advantage in terms of labour intensive manufacturing and agricultural products. Nepal as a least developed country can acquire facilities while exporting goods to the EU and the USA. Comparatively, it is much cheaper for Tibet to import goods from Nepal than bring them from mainland China. In view of this high level two-sided talks are being held at the regular intervals for cooperation in building a Special Economic Zone (SEZ) with the assistance of the Chinese government. A SEZ on the Nepali border side could attract Chinese businessmen to invest in Nepal and produce goods for re-export to China as well as the rest of the world, which ultimately assists in luring investors.

China's economic growth is close to double digit. The standard of their living is also growing at a rapid pace. China as a WTO member has liberalized its economy and its market is open to all. Being an immediate neighbor, we must look at the means and ways to garner profit from it.

Research on the import pattern and consumer behaviour is necessary to promote exports to China. There is no doubt that while extending the trade and economic relationship, different aspects need to be endorsed side by side such as policy, infrastructure, bank, insurance, warehouse and the like. Infrastructure is what is hampering our trade. We are still using the existing old route, which is narrow for trade and transportation. China has conducted studies for the construction of an Inland Container Depot (ICD) and other infrastructural projects. An ICD with well equipped customs could make our trade competitive and smooth. Direct bus service between Lhasa and Kathmandu has become a 'once upon a time' tale which was initiated to promote tourism. The service was disrupted because of China's restrictive visa policy. This has had a negative effect on sustainable tourism development. The service must resume right away. Nepali authorities must, therefore, be notified of such unpredictable and unexpected decisions by the Chinese government. Similar unpredictable decisions have taken place in Nepal-China trade as well, as was the case with the export of Nepali handicrafts to China, according to entrepreneurs. Nepal's quality and standard certificate is not accepted by the Chinese authorities hindering exporters. Our standard certification centre should be improved with greater resources and should negotiate with the Chinese counterpart for mutual reorganisation and acceptance of certificates. This will certainly enhance the export of agro- products to China.

CHINA WANTS PRACHANDA TO STAY IN NEPAL

In a televised address to the nation on May 4, the Maoist Prime Minister of Nepal, Pushpa Kamal Dahal, popularly known as Prachanda, dramatically announced his resignation. The move comes in the wake of opposition to his decision the previous day to sack the 61-year-old Army Chief Gen Rukmangad Katawal following the General's opposition to the demand of Prachanda for the integration of members of the People's Liberation Army (PLA) raised by the Maoists during their days in the insurgency into the Army.

Gen. Kul Bahadur Khadka, the No.2 in the Army, was asked by Prachanda to act as the Chief of the Army Staff (COAS) until further orders. Before announcing his decision, Prachanda met with Katawal and Khadka separately first, then jointly, before seeking the approval of the Cabinet for sacking the COAS. His decision was opposed by the Communist Party of Nepal (United Marxist-Leninist) with 108 members in the Constituent Assembly, which decided to quit the ruling coalition Government.

"We decided to withdraw our support to protest the Prime Minister's unilateral decision," CPN-UML General Secretary Ishwar Pokhrel said. While the Nepali Congress and the Madhesi Peoples Party joined 17 other parties in opposing the sacking of the General, the Madhesi People's Rights Forum (MPRF) with

51 members in the Assembly and some other smaller parties maintained an ambivalent attitude. The MPRF reportedly submitted a note of dissent disagreeing with Prachanda's decision, but did not leave the coalition. The CPN-Maoist with 229 seats in the Constituent Assembly needed the crucial support from MPRF and other small parties to continue to enjoy a majority in the 601-member Assembly tasked to frame a new constitution for the country after it abolished its unpopular 240-year-old monarchy last year. Prachanda's action in unilaterally sacking the Army Chief despite strong opposition in the coalition Cabinet was nullified by the President Ram Baran Yadav, who faxed a special instruction to the Chief of the Army Staff "asking him to continue in his office in the capacity of COAS as per the Interim Constitution, 2007, and the existing law". The spokesman of the Maoists, Krishna Bahadur Mahara, who is the Minister for Information and Communication, told the media that the President's order to the COAS to continue in office was tantamount to a "constitutional coup" and said that the Maoists would fight back with street protests.

He said: "The President is violating constitutional norms. The President's move has put the peace process in peril. Our party has taken the President's step as a constitutional coup and we will fight against it. The executive power to sack and appoint an acting army chief lies with the government and not the President. We will stick to our decision. We don't have any plans to quit the Government." Prachanda called the Attorney General Raghav Lal Baidya and senior Cabinet colleagues early on May 4 to discuss the constitutionality and consequences of the President's intervention. There was speculation that the Maoists might move for the impeachment of the President. After finding that they would not have the required support for such a move in the Constituent Assembly, he decided to resign.

It remains to be seen whether his resignation is a purely tactical move to confront the other members of the ruling coalition with the danger of serious political instability if they did not support his sacking of the Army chief or was forced by his realizing that there was no way he could have his way against the Army chief. Both the Army chief and Prajwal, the Commander of the seventh division of the PLA, were reported to have ordered the two forces under their respective command to remain in a state of alert to prevent any disturbance of law and order. The peace accord reached by various political parties before last year's election to the Constituent Assembly had provided for the rehabilitation and integration of the members of the PLA and other Maoist cadres, including members of the people's courts set up by the Maoists during their days in the insurgency.

After Prachanda assumed office in August last year as the Prime Minister, differences surfaced over the interpretation of this principle. The Maoists treated rehabilitation and integration as synonymous and insisted that the only of rehabilitating the 19,000 members of the PLA was by integrating them into the Army, barring those physically unfit or unwilling to serve in the Army. The Army and other political parties were strongly opposed to this. They held that rehabilitation and integration were two different processes. According to them, rehabilitation meant enabling the Maoist cadres to be gainfully employed, but not necessarily in the Army. While they were prepared to consider the integration of small numbers of the PLA into the Army if they were found to be professionally suitable, they were not prepared to agree to the wholesale merger of the PLA into the Army. Such an action would have resulted in about one-fourth of the Army consisting of indoctrinated Maoists, with their number steadily increasing with fresh recruitment.

Prachanda also wanted that the Maoists, who held officer-equivalent ranks in the PLA, should be given appropriate ranks in the Army. Thus, he reportedly wanted PLA commander Nanda Kishor Pun "Pasang" to be made a Major General and many others to get the rank of Brigadiers. He also reportedly wanted that there should be no new recruitment to the Army for some years.

Neil Horning, an American expert on the Maoist movement of Nepal, who is himself believed to be sympathetic to the Maoists, wrote: "The mainstream parties, as well as the elite in the army, view army integration in an apocalyptic light. While integrating the PLA into the NA was agreed upon time and again in the course of peace negotiations, the Non-Maoist parties made their agreements under the assumption that the Maoists could not possibly win electoral victory, and would not be in charge of implementing the integration. They counted on returning to the long standing Nepali political habit of agreeing to a demand in negotiation and then reneging on it later when the opponent is not in a position to make a challenge. They are trying to do the same now by continually insisting that Maoists combatants be "rehabilitated" rather than integrated, but it is they who have lost their bargaining position. Yet, why can't they let it happen in the first place? The Maoists don't have more than 20,000 troops to integrate into the more than 90,000 currently in the Army. This would hardly make the army into a force at the Maoists' beck and call. It's not that the army would become the private force of the Maoists, but that it would cease to be a check on them. With at least 25 per cent of troops and officers being former Maoist partisans, the possibility of a reactionary coup becomes impossible. The troops needed to suppress the public would simply turn their weapons on the command. Therefore, the army would cease to be a check and social change would continue unabated."

According to Kanak Mani Dixit, the Nepali political analyst, "At their large National Council conclave in the Kharipati outskirts of Kathmandu in late November 2008, the Maoists came to the conclusion that they were in government but did not control the state, for which the Nepal Army and the independent judiciary were found to be prime obstacles. It decided that the (Maoist) cantonments should not be disbanded until the new constitution is written." When the Maoists found that whenever they had a dispute with the Army over issues such as the ban on new recruitment which was disregarded by the COAS the judiciary was taking up a position, which was unfavourable to the Maoists, they also started talking of integrating the members of the former Maoists' people's courts into the judiciary.

The COAS went ahead with the new recruitment recruiting nearly 2800 persons to fill up existing vacancies in the Army and the PLA retaliated by making fresh recruitment to the PLA in violation of the Comprehensive Peace Agreement. Thus, Nepal under Prachanda as the Prime Minister saw the spectre of two parallel armies—— the state Army and the non-State PLA—strengthening and preparing themselves for a future confrontation should the Maoists' demand for total integration be turned down.

While the Chinese closely monitored the situation by interacting intensely with various political formations, India and the US reportedly cautioned Prachanda against a confrontation on this issue. Prachanda increasingly became unresponsive to the advice for moderation from India and the US and insisted on having his way.

It is not clear why Prachanda decided to force a confrontation with the COAS at this stage instead of waiting till September, when Gen.Katawal is due to superannuate. One possible reason for his hasty action is that Gen.Khadka, who is believed to be not opposed to the integration of the PLA into the Army, is due to superannuate in June. It is suspected that Prachanda wanted to make him the chief before his superannuation and give him a two-year tenure so that the integration of the PLA into the Army could be brought about without any further opposition from the Army. His plans were thwarted by the President.

What could happen now? The following are the possible scenarios:

- A serious political crisis with violent demonstrations by the Maoists which results in one more compromise. The Chinese will try their best to see that the Maoist-led Government, which has effectively put down Tibetan activity in Nepali territory, remains in power.
- A violent confrontation between the PLA and the Army leading to an army coup.
- A new coalition without the Maoists, which will be unstable.

The holding of the elections to the Constituent Assembly before the ground rules for integration were agreed upon and the victory of the Maoists in the elections——significant, but not spectacular as projected by sections of the media— have led to a situation where the Maoists will be at the head of a Government which will take crucial decisions on the post-facto legitimisation of the terrorist infrastructure raised by the Maoists and on the ground rules for the integration of their ideologically motivated and well-trained cadres. The moment the Maoists assume leadership in the seats of power and decision-making, will it be possible to resist their demands? If the integration of over 3000 ideologically indoctrinated cadres of the insurgent army into the Nepal Army comes about, we will have to the west of us an army ideologically motivated by jihadi doctrines and to the east of us an army ideologically motivated by Marxism, Leninism and Mao's Thoughts. There are two possible scenarios— these fears turn out to be baseless and Prachanda turns out to be a genuine democrat and a genuine friend of India or Prachanda after the elections turns out to be different from Prachanda before the elections and takes Nepal on a road, which would be detrimental to our national interests. While hoping for the first scenario, we must be prepared for the second. "

As we try to move Eastwards to cultivate the countries of South-East Asia, it is trying to move southwards to outflank us. China is not a South Asian power, but it already has a growing South Asian strategic presence — in Pakistan, Sri Lanka and Bangladesh. It is hoping to acquire a similar presence in Nepal with the co-operation of a Maoist-dominated Government." China would try its best to see that the Maoists stay in power. Their continuance in power in Kathmandu is important for stability in Tibet. In the past, we supported Maoists thinking that Prachanda would take a neutral line between India and China. These hopes are elusive. Should we facilitate the Chinese designs in Nepal by bringing about a political compromise which would enable the Maoists to continue in power or has the time come to work for a non-Maoist alternative? This requires serious examination in our policy-making circles.

Bibliography

Amitabh Sikdar: *India and China : Strategic Energy Management and Security*, Manas, Delhi, 2009.

Ashok K. : *The Royal Nepal Army : Meeting the Maoist Challenge*, Rupa, Delhi, 2005.

Bottomore, Tom: *A Dictionary of Marxist Thought,* New Delhi, Maya Blackwell, 2000.

Campbell, Ivan: *China and Conflict –affected states: Between Principle and Pragmatism*, London, Saferworld, 2012.

Cox, Robert W.: *Production, Power and World Order: Social Forces in the Making of History*, New York: Columbia University Press, 2012.

Debray, Regis. *Revolution in the Revolution*. New York: Grove Press, Inc., 1993.

Dhanalaxmi, Ravuri. *British Attitude to Nepal's Relations with Tibet and China, 1814-1914*. Chandigarh, India: Bahri, 1981.

Dietmar Rothermund. *A History of India*. Totowa, New Jersey: Barnes and Noble, 1986.

Ellis, F. 2000. *Rural Livelihoods and Diversity in Developing Countries*. New York: Oxford University Press.

Evelyn Goh, *Meeting the China Challenge: The U.S. in Southeast Asian Regional Security Strategies*, DC: East-West Center, 2005.

Gao, Mobo: *The Battle for China's Past: Mao and the Cultural Revolution,* London, Pluto Press, 2008.

Jagannath P. Panda: *China's Path to Power : Party, Military and the Politics of State Transition*, Pentagon, Delhi, 2010.

Kansakar, V. B. S.: *"International Migration and Citizenship in Nepal"*. Kathmandu: Central Bureau of Statistics/UNFPA, 2003.

Kant, Adhikari, Krishna. *Nepal under Jang Bahadur, 1846-1877*. Kathmandu: Buku, 1984.

Keane J.: *Democracy and Civil Liberty*, London, Verso, 1988.

Kumar, Satish. *Rana Polity in Nepal: Origin and Growth*. New York: Asia, 1967.

Leo E. *Nepal: Strategy for Survival*. Berkeley:University of California Press, 1971.

Marie Lecomte : *Hindu Kingship, Ethnic Revival, and Maoist Rebellion in Nepal*, Oxford University Press, Delhi, 2009.

Parmanand. *The Nepali Congress since Its Inception: A Critical Assessment*. Delhi: B.R. Publishing, 1982.

Schurmann, Franz: *Ideology and Organization in Communist Nepal*. Berkeley: University of California Press, 1971.

Sharma, P. 1989. *Urbanization in Nepal*. Hawaii: East-West Population Institute.

Shaun Narine, *Explaining ASEAN: Regionalism in Southeast Asia*, Boulder, CO: Lynne Rienner Publishers, 2002.

Sijapati, Li, : *A Kingdom Under Siege : Nepal's Maoist Insurgency, 1996 to 2003*, The Printhouse, Delhi, 2003.

Stuart R. Schram: *The Political Thought of Mao Tse-Tung*. New York: Praeger, 1969.

Thapa, Deepak : *Understanding the Maoist Movement of Nepal*, Centre for Social Research and Development, Delhi, 2003.

Tse-tung Mao: *Mao and the Nepali Revolution*. London: Oxford University Press, 1965.

Tyagi, Sushila. *Indo-Nepalese Relations, 1858-1914*. Delhi: D.K. Publishing, 1974.

Uddhab P : *Maoist Movement in Nepal: A Sociological Perspective*, Adroit, Delhi, 2007.

Upreti, B C : *Maoists in Nepal : From Insurgency to Political Mainstream*, Kalpaz Pub, Delhi, 2008.

Index

R

S

T

❑❑❑